Dirty Dancing?

CRIME ETHNOGRAPHY SERIES

Series editors: Dick Hobbs and Geoffrey Pearson

Published titles

Holding Your Square: Masculinities, streetlife and violence,
by Christopher W. Mullins

Narratives of Neglect: Community, regeneration and the governance of security,
by Jacqui Karn

Families Shamed: The consequences of crime for relatives of serious offenders,
by Rachel Condry

Northern Soul: Music, drugs and subcultural identity, by Andrew Wilson

Flashback: Drugs and dealing in the golden age of the London rave scene,
by Jennifer R. Ward

Dirty Dancing? An ethnography of lap-dancing, by Rachela Colosi

Dirty Dancing?
An ethnography of lap-dancing

Rachela Colosi

 Routledge
Taylor & Francis Group

LONDON AND NEW YORK

First published by Willan Publishing 2010
This edition published by Routledge 2012
2 Park Square, Milton Park, Abingdon, Oxon OX14 4RN
711 Third Avenue, New York, NY 10017

Routledge is an imprint of the Taylor & Francis Group, an informa business

ISBN   978-1-84392-817-1 hardback
ISBN   978-0-415-62764-1 paperback

British Library Cataloguing-in-Publication Data

A catalogue record for this book is available from the British Library

Project managed by Deer Park Productions, Tavistock, Devon
Typeset by GCS, Leighton Buzzard, Beds

For my mother

Contents

Acknowledgements

I would like to thank all the dancers at 'Starlets' who were participants and friends during my fieldwork – without you all, this book would not have been possible. Although I cannot name the actual individual as this would breach confidentiality, I would like to especially thank Karen for letting me tell her story. As well as the dancers, I would like to thank the other staff at Starlets, including waitresses, bar people, receptionists, bouncers and managers for playing a role in this ethnography.

I am grateful to my colleagues and friends, especially Kayleigh Garthwaite, Andrew Dunn and Mary Whowell, for reading through and commenting on drafts of this book. My thanks also go to my PhD supervisors Robert Hollands and Elaine Campbell at Newcastle University who encouraged me to craft this ethnography in my own way. I also want to thank the Economic Research Council for their financial support during the course of my PhD. Finally thanks to Peter for being patient over the last year.

Chapter 1

Introducing the ethnography: working and researching in a 'deviant' occupation

I walked off stage clutching my dress, which I held tightly against my bare chest in an attempt to shield myself from the cold air as I approached the back corridor of the club. I looked at the managers' PA who guided me to the changing room, and said: 'That was awful. I think I messed up?' She smiled and gave a rather patronizing response: 'Aww, really, you'll be fine.' I was not feeling very confident about the performance I gave, it was unrhythmic and clumsy; I had been used to stripping in pubs and working men's clubs where coordination and elegance were irrelevant for those displays of nudity. Starlets was a new club, it had only been open two weeks when I auditioned; you could smell the freshly painted walls and still feel the tack of the newly glossed doors. This club seemed to exude professionalism: it felt more like a business than a 'strip joint': the managers wore smart suits and the dancers were immaculately presented, with both groups appearing to take their roles seriously; the decor and layout of the club were far removed from some of the hostile and fractured environments I was used to working in. There were CCTV cameras everywhere, door staff, and even house rules to guide dancer and customer conduct; I felt safe, protected and excited at the prospect at being employed here. The PA followed me into the changing room and chatted to me as I put my clothes back on; I was not really listening. Instead I kept replaying my poorly performed audition in my head. After I had finished getting dressed she led me to the manager's office, where Jane, the house mother of the club at the time, was sitting alone. She smiled at me and asked: 'Can you come in to work tonight?' In a stunned manner I quickly said 'Yes!'

The ethnography presented in this book is about the relationships between lap-dancers and the occupational culture with which these women engaged at a lap-dancing club named 'Starlets',[1] based in a large city in the North of England. The setting of this club and the different occupational roles identified are presented early on in this book as a way of setting the scene for this ethnography. Furthermore, the role and position of lap-dancing clubs in the night-time economy is given focus in order to highlight the economic, political and cultural significance of the lap-dancing industry in the UK. Significantly, before embarking on the fieldwork for this study, I had already worked as a 'lap-dancer' and 'agency stripper'; the distinction between these two roles is discussed later in this chapter. The opening extract describes my personal recollection of becoming a lap-dancer at Starlets a few years before starting this project. It did not occur to me when I first started working in the sex industry that I would one day both research and write about this occupation. I started stripping as a Sociology undergraduate and continued to work in this capacity after completing my degree, both as an agency stripper and later lap-dancer. As I explain later in this chapter my motives for becoming a lap-dancer did not match the popular discourse that suggests women are primarily guided in their decision to strip by limited (often financial) choice (see Bindel 2004). In this ethnography I argue that the entry routes of women into lap-dancing are in fact quite complex and based on a number of different motives. The continued participation of women in the lap-dancing industry, based on observations made in Starlets, is not simply financially motivated but driven by a number of different factors including having fun and the camaraderie experienced between dancers. Continuing the theme of dancer motivation the different exit routes taken by lap-dancers leaving this occupation are also discussed. Superficially these exit routes relate to practical explanations such as relocation and change of career; however, like the entry routes, this process is complex and tied in with the impact of the emotional strain of dancing and relationship pressures.

As a university student, when I first started dancing I did not have any academic ambitions. I was happy getting naked for a living and even thought I would remain, in one way or another, working in the commercial sex industry. Being an erotic dancer, for some time, was central to my life, something which is also reflected in the stories of the dancers presented throughout this book. For the most part I enjoyed going to work, doing my job and socializing with the other dancers. Although I no longer work as a lap-dancer or stripper, it still forms part of my identity: I will always be an erotic dancer in my head. In relation to this, the sense of membership and engagement with the occupational culture of lap-dancing is a significant theme which threads throughout this book. I argue that the lap-dancers at Starlets were part of a hierarchical occupational subculture (also see Colosi 2010a), comprising 'new girl', 'transition' and 'old-school' status roles. The different experiences associated with these three positions, which are given considerable attention in this ethnography, reflect the contradictory and complex nature of lap-dancing.

My positionality is central to this ethnography and has been significant in the process of both analysing and writing about lap-dancing after my fieldwork ceased and I withdrew from dancing altogether. Being able to empathize, throughout the research process, is what has enabled me to narrate the dancers' stories so effectively. This does not mean, however, that I did not confront any challenges and difficulties during the research process. This is something I address later in this chapter. As a participant observer already immersed in the occupational culture and chosen research setting, my story, as a dancer, will firstly be introduced as a way of positioning myself in the study as 'dancer-researcher'. In addition, this chapter explores my motivation for conducting this piece of research along with my methodological approach. Furthermore, the conceptual and theoretical underpinnings of this ethnography are discussed before this chapter draws to a close by outlining the content and structure of this book.

My story

Prior to working as a lap-dancer at Starlets I worked as a stripper in social clubs, pubs, bars and nightclubs across the North East of England; a 'hidden' area of the sex industry that has barely been discussed[2] in any academic context. There have, for example, been few academic accounts of 'stripteasers', other than in a historical context (see, for example, Jarrett 1997; Glasscock 2003). In the UK working as a 'stripper'[3] can be quite different from being a 'lap-dancer'; for those already based in the industry 'stripper' usually refers to a woman who works freelance or for an agency. These workers are hired out as stripagrams – as entertainment for private birthday and stag parties – or paid to remove their clothing in front of the crowds of social clubs and pubs. 'Lap-dancers' are often based in clubs specifically designed for this purpose and, in addition, as well as performing stage shows similar to agency and freelance strippers, lap-dancers offer private dances (also known as lap-dances) to customers.

My entry into 'stripping' was initiated by a few of my friends who dared me to do it. I had a reputation for streaking at student parties and generally being a bit of an exhibitionist, so after some encouragement I thought: why not! Of course it is more complex than this. I liked the idea of arousing sexual attention (and approval) and being paid was a bonus. I did not really *need* the money; I had a full student grant, loans and a part-time job working in a mortgage office. I guess I felt like a bit of a rebel, working in a role that people disapproved of; I always liked to shock people. The fact that, in many ways, this was a 'forbidden' occupation simply fuelled my desire to do it even more. I spent almost two years stripping, for 'Glitter Girls',[4] before I became a lap-dancer. It was one of the strippers I had worked with at the agency who, after starting work in Starlets, convinced me to audition for a job there. My former colleague was very positive about 'lap-dancing', describing it as safe, with a 'better class' of customer and overall a more financially rewarding alternative to agency stripping. After a successful audition I started working the very same day. I was instantly impressed with the facilities available to the dancers. The changing room, for instance, was spacious with a shower and toilet, lockers, a built-in dressing table and impressive mirrors which stretched round the walls (the setting of Starlets is discussed in Chapter 4). I had been used to getting changed in small 'make-do' 'dressing rooms', often toilet cubicles, kitchens, corridors and store cupboards. All the girls (dancers) at Starlets seemed to take pride in their appearance and had what I thought at the time was an air of sophistication; of course I was initially comparing it to the stripping work I had previously done. Lap-dancing at Starlets was so far removed from what I had experienced as an agency stripper. One of my first thoughts was 'Why didn't I come here sooner!' I found lap-dancing at Starlets (sexually) tamer than the agency stripping I had previously done. Unlike working at 'Glitter Girls' I was only expected to perform topless and strip down to a g-string. As a stripper, performances were often fully nude with the exposure of the stripper's bodily parts often graphic; in contrast the stage performances and private dances at Starlets seemed more sensual and far more restrained. Former 'strippers', including myself, during my fieldwork, would often talk about the differences between these two forms of erotic dance. It was once suggested by another dancer: 'If you compared them [lap-dancing and stripping] to [styles of] porno magazines, stripping would be like *Hustler*,[5] and lap-dancing would be like *Playboy*.'[6]

I preferred lap-dancing, it felt safer as I had bouncers to protect me, and I could, on a good night, make £500 or £600. But of course, this income is not guaranteed; it was not unknown for dancers to finish a shift having not made any money all. In addition, lap-dancers at Starlets, and similar clubs, must pay a house fee, also known as commission, to work; in Starlets this ranged from between £30 and £80 per shift. However, generally, stripping, as a freelance or agency worker, rarely has the financial potential offered by lap-dancing as a result of there being fewer stripping jobs. However, because of limited data about stripping, comparisons between these two jobs have not been discussed. It is perhaps the commercialisation of erotic dancing and the expansion of the lap-dancing industry which has led to the reduction in stripping gigs in pubs, social and night clubs. Further to this, another problem with stripping as a freelance or agency worker is that sometimes it is physically dangerous. Although some stripping gigs are held in safe environments, where the workers feel protected and unthreatened, there are always places in which the stripper's safety is compromised. For instance, I worked in several venues where I was pulled at, groped, had objects thrown at me and sensed the threat of serious sexual violence. Being a stripper meant learning to manage my own safety; there were no bouncers to protect me, so I became skilled at using my body, eyes and facial expressions, as well as my general wit, to limit danger. However, in some situations, the only way of ensuring safety is avoidance. On a few occasions I kept myself away from the crowd and was quick to locate an escape route.

Lap-dancing enabled me to pay for my first Master's degree as well as maintain a comfortable lifestyle. This is something I would not have afforded had I continued to work as an agency stripper. It was perhaps, when I needed it more, that the money became more significant. Having graduated, I could no longer rely on grants and loans as a source of income. However, money was still not my *only* motivation for continuing to dance at Starlets. I was still driven by the sexual attention and sense of rebellion which initially attracted me to agency stripping. The money alone could not have kept me or anyone else in this line of work; there has to be something else fuelling the desire to strip off. This does not mean, however, that women are not attracted to this occupation because of the financial rewards, or that they do not enjoy making money; as I argue in Chapter 5, the reasons for entering and continuing to dance in this occupation are more complex than this. I did enjoy my work, but of course it was not all good. Some days I hated it and could not muster the energy to talk to customers or socialize with the dancers; the managers would frequently infuriate me and I sometimes considered leaving. But overall, despite bouts of discontent, I had a good time. At its best, to quote a fellow dancer, Nelly, it could be: 'Like being on a night out but getting fuck loads of money'. Also I made some good friends; it felt like we were part of a family unit. I am glad I did it, and in many ways it has made me who I am. However, after completing my fieldwork I decided it was time to retire from lap-dancing. I guess I had grown out of it; I was not really the same person I had been when I first started out. I did not get the same 'buzz' from my work, from the attention or the lifestyle. Nonetheless, leaving was still difficult to take in: I just felt sad. I remember Davina, another dancer, saying to me 'You'll be back Rachela'. But I knew I would not; I suppose I had different ideas about my future now. Although I had not previously considered pursuing a career in academia, I now felt this was something I would like to do. Retiring from lap-dancing gave me a chance to focus on a new career.

On the 'outside', people generally appear not to see beyond the sexual exploitation or immorality they connect with the sex industry. As a lap-dancer you become aware of how 'outsiders' perceive you: as victim or villain, lost in a dark, shameful and dangerous world. I would often read newspaper articles, watch films and documentaries which have helped socially construct lap-dancing as 'exploitative', 'dangerous', 'immoral' or 'over sexualized'. On this basis the free choice to engage in this occupation is rarely considered by the media, politicians and feminist action groups. As Nagle (1997) suggests, 'public discussions about sex work fail to distinguish between voluntary and coerced sexual exchange, a distinction every bit as salient (and problematic) as that between consensual sex and rape' (p. 2). The prospect that one might derive pleasure, as well as experience discontentment, from this form of work rarely seems to be acknowledged. This is no more evident than in a recent campaign fronted by Object and the Fawcett Group to pressure politicians to tighten up the regulation of lap-dancing clubs in the UK. This campaign has been instrumental in the relicensing of lap-dancing clubs under section 26 of the recently passed Policing and Crime Act 2009. A more detailed discussion of the licensing of lap-dancing clubs is provided in Chapter 2. The potential impact of the licensing of lap-dancing clubs as 'sexual entertainment venues' is discussed in Chapter 10.

Research motivation, significance and approach

The original impetus for this ethnography initially stemmed from the aforementioned negative portrayal of the lap-dancing industry. It was my experience of working as a dancer that alerted me to the lack of understanding of and the many myths surrounding the industry. It was apparent that those attempting to tell *my story* and the stories of all my fellow dancers were outsiders, albeit strangers to *our* world. On a personal level then, I wanted to dispel some of these myths deeply ingrained in people's understanding of lap-dancers.

Furthermore, it became apparent that, despite the public debate lap-dancing had brought about, there was an absence of UK-based research about the industry; much of this focus has been from various media sources rather than academic ones. Related studies have been conducted predominantly in the US and Canada. Research has, for example, focused on areas concerned with: the impact of dancing on the dancers' lives (Barton 2006; Deshotels and Forsythe 2005; Wesely 2002) dancer identities (Rambo-Ronai 1992; Reid *et al.* 1994; Wesely 2003); 'counterfeit intimacy' (Boles and Garbin 1974c; Enck and Preston 1988; Pasko 2002); dancer interaction strategies (Rambo-Ronai and Ellis, 1989; Pasko 2002); customer and dancer relations (Bell *et al.* 1998; Brewster 2003; Egan 2006a; Erickson and Tewksbury 2000; Frank 2002a, 2002b); working conditions (Holsopple 1999; Lewis *et al.* 2005; Maticka-Tyndale *et al.* 1999, 2000); the emotional labour of dancing (Barton 2007; Frank 1998); gender-power relations (Bott 2006; Murphy 2003; Wesely 2002; Wood 2000); customer and dancer typologies[7] (Brewster 2003; Enck and Preston 1988; Lewis 1998; Montemurro *et al.* 2003; Sweet and Tewksbury 2000) and stigma management strategies (Thompson and Harred 1992, 2003; Bradley 2007). Although there has been a broad range of themes addressed, there is still little that specifically focuses on the relationships between the actual dancers, and although the culture with which dancers engage features in many of the studies produced, none have had a UK focus.

The focus of this ethnography, Starlets, was a club in which I had already worked for approximately two years prior to conducting this project. It was therefore my knowledge of and relationship with the dancers who worked there which provided both motive and opportunity. It made sense to conduct my research in this very environment rather than seek out a new setting which would not provide me with the same advantages. As an 'insider' and dancer I was already immersed in the world of lap-dancing; understanding the native language, so to speak, and having unlimited access, I had an opportunity to generate what I believed to be meaningful data. It is this insider role that has also contributed methodologically to the body of research available. Although some researchers in this field have generated data by working as dancers, most, with the exception of Holsopple (1999) and Rambo-Ronai (1992), have entered the lap-dancing club setting having never previously lap-danced or worked in the industry. This inevitably means these researchers must spend time learning the culture and gaining membership as 'dancers' and researchers, something that is not guaranteed. As Goffman (1959) points out 'no one is in quite as good an observational position to see through the act as the person who puts it on' (p. 17).

The decision to use an ethnographic approach was based on two main reasons. Firstly, as an insider already situated as a dancer in Starlets, I had the opportunity to conduct a very intensive, in-depth ethnographic study by observing and participating for some 2,000 hours.[8] Secondly, the use of extensive participant observation would enable me to generate data that other methods alone would not, helping me make sense of the complex symbolic meanings dancers attach to lap-dancing and the culture associated with it. As a participant observer I was able to gather information about an informal dancer hierarchy, something that would not have been possible to identify outside of this environment or from just interviewing participants. Observing dancers also enabled me to make sense of the space in which they worked and the role the different areas in the club played in their occupational culture. It was also possible to make sense of the various 'social rituals' dancers in Starlets partake in, which might have included drinking alcohol and taking illicit drugs (see Chapter 7). In-depth interviews were used to supplement the core findings generated from the observations I made; they proved a useful way of understanding the dancers' individual stories. These interviews were by no means the basis for this study, as the main body of data was generated from participant observation, but helped reinforce and emphasize some of the findings which had emerged from my observations.

Ethnographic research provokes debates about ethical conduct (Norris 1993), particularly with regard to the use of participant observation. Ethical concerns around informed consent, in particular, bring the validity of this particular methodology into question (Hammersley and Atkinson 2004). This ethical issue is traditionally associated with covert ethnographic research. However, despite opting to conduct overt participant observation in this study I was still confronted with some problems around the issue of informing participants. It had always been my intention to inform all of the main participants (dancers), as far as possible, about my research; however, I quickly realized that it would be difficult if not impossible to inform many of the customers. Informing dancers and other staff members was always going to be easier as I had regular access to these participants. However, with the exception of 'regulars', customers frequently changed, I therefore only had limited access to Starlets' clientele and as a result was not able to inform every customer entering the club. In order to overcome this, the identities of all participants have been protected by changing names and, where appropriate, their appearance. Furthermore, as well as changing names of participants, the names of lap-dancing clubs, stripping agencies and any other organizations discussed in this book have been changed.

The dancing-ethnographer

> ... It's a strange experience dancing and observing. In many ways it's as though nothing has changed, I'm still 'Rachela the dancer' doing what I always do, having a laugh with the girls, dancing for the customers, doing the stage shows, complaining to Deano [DJ], feeling tired ... Although now I've got to stay switched on and tuned in to what's going on around me. Everything I do, say, hear and feel has suddenly been magnified and what was once just 'stuff', now has some kind of meaning attached to it ...[9]

Entering Starlets as a researcher meant there was a whole new agenda I needed to take into account. Before now I was not expected to think about my surroundings, the interactions I made, the daily routine of coming to work, paying my house fee, getting ready in the changing room, chatting to dancers, dancing on stage, chatting to customers, dancing for customers, getting ready to go home. Working as a dancer, like in any other job, you become robotic in your routines, everything starts to be taken for granted, the smallest details of what you do go unnoticed. It was difficult, initially, to think like a 'researcher', and I would often revert back to just being a 'dancer', something I wrote about in my fieldnotes:

... I found myself slipping back into 'dancer mode' and ended up having a couple, too many, glasses of wine this afternoon. A customer offered me the drinks, I was feeling pretty low after a stage show; I'm not sure if it was paranoia but I thought a group of stags[10] were being critical of my performance. I guess this is what led me to accept an offer of alcohol. Thinking back I should have acted as a researcher and NOT a dancer, but I'm starting to find it increasingly hard not to. I'm starting to feel more like a dancer than a researcher and forgetting why I'm here! I need to take a few steps back and take a bit more control over the situation ...

This of course not only reflects problems with having this dual identity of dancer/researcher, but also suggests the problems associated with being an established 'native' in the field of study. It is often the dangers of going 'native' in the field (Junker 1960; Pearson 1993) rather than the dangers of already being 'native' which are debated (Becker and Faulkner 2008). Although I was able and willing to enter my social environment with new motives and concerns as a researcher, it would be impossible to have erased my past and my identity as a dancer: I would always be a 'native'. In a similar way, after spending time as a dancer and then researching the industry, Rambo-Ronai (1992) articulates the difficulty of identifying the researcher from the dancer while involved in participant observation; she even goes as far as to argue that her identity was 'fracturing' during her fieldwork, suggesting that there is something almost schizophrenic about being in this position. In relation to this, it was important for me to be able to use the roles of researcher and dancer alongside each other. It was about learning to modify the dancer rather than suppressing her, therefore still ensuring natural interaction but having the ability to carefully observe and analyse my surroundings. It was necessary to be introspective about the experience, through self-analysis and discussions with others outside of the lap-dancing club. A similar approach was used by Rambo-Ronai (1992). As part of this process she found it useful to question the way in which she was conducting observations throughout her research and to take critical feedback from fellow academics not directly involved with her work. In relation to my own research, a significant revelation was made when visiting the research setting with one of my peers, following which we discussed my research in length. This discussion helped me think about my research setting differently, leading me to recognize phenomena I had taken for granted as a dancer. It was useful to get somebody else's perspective on the setting I was observing. After becoming comfortable with my role as researcher in the field I moved on from being overly selective to recording and internalizing as much as possible, however insignificant it might have appeared to be at the time.

Conducting participant observation has been an emotional roller coaster. Even in the early stages of the research process it became apparent that emotions are a powerful force in the field; this is something acknowledged by other researchers (see Blackman 2007). I was not only aware of my own feelings but those of the participants. Throughout my fieldwork I experienced a mixture of negative and positive emotions ranging from anger to excitement; inevitably it was my negative feelings that caused problems and that I struggled to resolve. As a dancer, my empathy was mostly with the dancers. Customers and managers in particular were not considered part of the dancer circle and the dancers, including myself, rarely empathized with them to the same extent dancers would with each other. Working as a dancer prior to becoming the researcher I had been caught up in the 'them and us' dancer motto. This specifically relates to the dancers' feelings towards management, and is something emphasized by Alicia, one of the dancers who participated in my research: 'They [managers] don't understand what we have to go through coz they don't have to do what we do, so why should they expect us to give a shit about them.' The relationships between dancers and managers, while not being the main focus of the book, are nonetheless a significant theme discussed throughout. However, there were also dancers with whom I had never truly bonded due to personal differences, and as a result caused me some level of frustration. To my advantage, as a dancer I had rarely been confrontational, often dealing with difficult situations by avoiding the source of my frustration. However, this posed another problem: as a researcher I could no longer avoid difficult situations, it would have been unproductive. Instead it was important to engage with and make sense of these situations. Other difficulties arose during informal conversations with participants, when I became aware of my internal dialogue. For example, I would sometimes find myself thinking: 'No, you're wrong, I don't agree with what you said' or 'I'm not sure if I really like you' or 'I'm not enjoying this, I want to go home'. I discovered that these feelings would change and fluctuate as they would during any other conversation I might have outside of the research environment. I sometimes found that my internal dialogue would direct my conversations with participants and instead of allowing participants to freely express themselves, at times

I felt that I might have influenced the outcome of our conversations without even being aware of it. In response I initially attempted to control my internal dialogue as I felt the interests of my research would be compromised, but I soon realized that instead of restricting it, I could in fact use it. There were a number of ways in which I found my internal dialogue useful. It has made me more aware of the limitations of research and by questioning what motivated my feelings, I was aided in the analysis process, leading me to ask further questions about the environment I was studying. However, I could not guarantee I would not continue to make mistakes during the research process and inevitably there were occasions when I reverted back to being judgemental. This emphasizes how difficult it is to be an objective researcher and that our opinions will always interfere with data; however, an awareness of this can help *limit* the problems encountered.

Conceptualizing lap-dancing

Early accounts of stripping were discussed and theorized within a deviant framework (see Boles and Garbin 1974a, 1974b, 1974c; Carey *et al.* 1974; Skipper and McCaghy 1970) in which dancers were portrayed more negatively and, according to Jarvinen (1993), fall in line with some of the earlier 'functionalist' thinking around sex work. Since the 1970s stripping[11] has been conceptualized within an interactionist (see for example Enck and Preston 1988; Pasko 2002; Wood 2000) and various feminist frameworks (see, for example Barton 2006; Frank 2002; Holsopple 1999; Price 2008; Wesley 2002). However, more widely, although the majority of feminist discussions concerned with 'sex work' have concentrated on prostitution and/or pornography, the increasing interest in erotic dance, particularly in the US, has drawn feminists to broaden their focus. As a result there has been a shift away from the 'deviant' and even 'interactionist' frames of understanding, with contemporary work now largely being feminist. Within a feminist framework, 'liberal' (see, for example, Bell *et al.* 1998) and 'radical' accounts (see, for example, Bindel 2004; Holsopple 1999; Jeffreys 2008) have become popular in discussions about erotic dance.

To put these frameworks into context it is necessary to outline the different feminist approaches to 'sex work'. According to Chapkis (1997) this is not straightforward: 'Feminist thinking on the subject of sex defies simple division into coherent positions. Not only have many feminists argued in favour of a third camp beyond the two polarized ones, but important differences of perspective exist within the two identified camps' (p. 12). Chapkis refers to what have come to be known as 'radical feminism' and 'sex-radical feminism'. In an attempt to make sense of the complexity feminism presents Chapkis (1997) argues that each of these perspectives can further be divided. 'Radical' feminism, it is suggested, comprises 'pro-"positive" sex feminism', in which 'sex can be divided between its "positive" expression in passionate love and its violent articulation in pornographic objectification' (p. 13); and 'anti-sex feminism', where all forms of 'sex' are a manifestation of male domination. In contrast, within 'sex-radical feminist' thought 'a distinction can be drawn between those most closely aligned with the extreme individualism of libertarian ethics and politics, and those who explicitly situate sex (and the individuals enacting it) within structures of power and privilege' (Chapkis 1997: 21). The more 'libertarian' position understands sex, including pornography and prostitution, to be a site in which women are empowered. In contrast other sex-radical feminists are argued to acknowledge that sex, and the sex industry, are produced through and a consequence of social inequalities (patriarchy), but are simultaneously 'sites of ingenious resistance and cultural subversion' (Chapkis 1997: 29). It is this latter inclination that is increasingly apparent in the body of literature concerned with the stripping industry (Barton 2006; Egan 2006a; Frank 2002; Liepe-Levinson 2002; Price 2008; Rambo-Ronai 1992; Wood 2000). What has been welcoming about this particular 'sex-radical' approach evident in these discussions is that as well as acknowledging women's subordinate position in society, it recognises that women can find ways of both resisting and manipulating their position. Further to this, 'sex-radical' feminists are less interested in doing away with the sex industry ... and instead advocate better work environments for sex workers and safety from police harassment ... To attend to women's various experiences is not to deny that exploitation and violence can occur, rather it acknowledges that sex work is not a flat or unitary experience' (Egan 2006a: 80). This approach has welcomed the voices of sex workers themselves (see Rambo-Ronai 1992), where prior to this 'the voices of feminist sex workers themselves have been glaringly absent in such discussions' (Nagle 1997: 1). Not only has this been addressed, but researchers have also, themselves, since taken on and played sex-worker roles to generate richer data and better place their understanding of the sex industry. Successful and meaningful examples are apparent in the work of Egan (2006a) and

Frank (2003). Both have focused on the relationship between lap-dancer and customer and made sense of their data through a 'sex-radical' framework, thus acknowledging 'sex work' as a complex site. For instance, Egan, in utilizing a 'sex-radical' perspective describes 'sex work' as a liminal site:

> Liminality is a dynamic model, which highlights the boundaries of static representations and codification. Making visible the ambiguity of experience ... liminality exposes how people's understandings of their lives reside between ... categories. Theorizing liminal experience elucidates how women sex workers are agents and located in the intersections of multiple vectors of sociocultural power differentials. (2006a: 81)

It is the liminality of lap-dancing that is echoed in this book, drawing on the 'good' and 'bad nights', as Egan (2006a) puts it, and moving away from the public discourse which portrays lap-dancers as 'victims' or 'villains'.

As well as an implicit sex-radical approach underlying the discussions and arguments constructed throughout this book, other theoretical frameworks outside of feminism are also utilized. For instance, alongside the use of ethnographic methods, an interactionist approach is also evident through the use of Goffman (1959, 1963). The works of Goffman support and conceptualize some of the key themes which emerged from the study, including stigma (see Goffman 1959) and 'cynical performances' of dancers during their interaction with customers (see Goffman 1963). Other themes to emerge, such as 'risk-taking', are discussed with reference to Lyng's (1990, 2005a) concept of 'edgework', drawing attention to the dancers' deliberate engagement with high-risk activities and behaviour for the sensory experience of pleasure. This is discussed, for example, in relation to dancers' entry routes, personal relationships and the 'social rituals' they regularly partake in. There has been a tendency for lap-dancing literature to pay attention to the dangers faced by the dancers, as opposed to the active pursuit of 'risk' as a source of pleasure. The role of power, which continues to be central to other discussions about 'sex workers' (see Frank 2007), is relevant here to the self-regulation of dancers and in particular the 'tacit rules' and the hierarchical relationships between dancers. A Foucauldian (1977, 1980) approach is taken to help illustrate the complex and fluid nature of power between social actors within the lap-dancing club setting. Further to the hierarchy suggested through the different career stages identified in Starlets is how lap-dancing, underpinned by the engagement of various 'social' and 'emotional' rituals and a unique 'code of conduct' evident through the 'tacit rules', is subcultural. Drawing on the work of Cressey (1932) it is argued that the lap-dancers at Starlets were part of their own unique 'social world' (also see Colosi 2010a). Furthermore, what is significant in each of these discussions is the role of emotions. The work of Hochschild (1983) is used in order to highlight the emotional labour involved in lap-dancing, as others have previously done (see, for example, Barton 2006 and Wood 2000). However, as a way of building on the sociology of emotion further, attention is paid to the emotional bonds between dancers, evident through the 'emotional rituals', and the various pleasures and strains experienced by these women working in lap-dancing clubs.

Chapter outline

Chapter 2 looks at the commercial growth of lap-dancing and its role and position in the night-time economy, considering how much this industry is economically valued in the UK and its contribution to economic growth. Furthermore, the regulation of lap-dancing venues in the UK through the current licensing laws is also discussed.

As indicated in this chapter, in the UK, lap-dancing is a unique form of erotic dance in comparison to stripping, for example. The purpose of Chapter 3 is to outline what lap-dancing actually *is* and what lap-dancers actually *do* to make money in this occupation. Further to this, the different occupational roles of those who worked at Starlets is also introduced, as a way of opening the setting of Starlets discussed in Chapter 4.

Chapter 4 is the first empirical chapter which explores the research setting of Starlets. This primarily involves exploring the club's location in the city as well as the various key areas situated *inside* the club, including the changing room, the main floor, the dance reception and the manager's office. Each of these social spaces, in different ways, plays an important role for the lap-dancers.

The motives for entering a career in lap-dancing are complex and not just financial, despite the assertions of previous accounts. In light of this, the reasons identified for entering a career in lap-dancing and the processes women experience when entering this occupation, from enquiring about becoming a lap-dancer to actually auditioning for this position, are explored in Chapter 5.

Three main hierarchical phases experienced by women while working as lap-dancers have been identified in this study, including 'new girls', 'transition dancers', and 'old-school dancers'. Chapter 6 focuses on the position of the 'new girl', as applied to a new dancer starting out in her career. Further to this, this is a period in which she learns to *do* the job, make sense of her surroundings and adapt to becoming a lap-dancer, all of which is the focus of discussion.

Following on from being a 'new girl', lap-dancers enter a 'transition' phase in which they not only learn to become more accomplished at their job, but also, and more significantly, establish themselves as part of a lap-dancing (sub)culture. In addition, this phase is very much a time in which dancers begin to fully *experience* lap-dancing and the stigma of working in a 'deviant' occupation. Further to this, it is a period in which lap-dancers are more likely to *experience* the emotional and psychological strains of dancing and yet develop various coping strategies. Chapter 7, in a similar way to the previous chapter, explores some of the key features associated with being a 'transition dancer'.

The ultimate achievable status is that of an 'old-school dancer'; this is a position in which the lap-dancer in question is *fully* immersed in the culture of lap-dancing, and is an established member of this occupational (sub)culture. As a much respected position in the lap-dancing club, the 'old-school' dancer is able to exercise some level of control over the conduct of other lower-status dancers in the club, often going unchallenged. Chapter 8 reflects on what it means to carry 'old-school' status in the lap-dancing club setting for those women, but also for other lower-status dancers.

Different motives have been identified for women exiting lap-dancing; further to this, there is evidence to suggest that lap-dancers often return after an initial retirement. In a similar way to those entering a career in lap-dancing, the exit routes are often complex. Chapter 9 examines some of the key reasons for retiring from lap-dancing and explores the motivation for re-entering a career in lap-dancing, outlining the complexities of these patterns of behaviour.

Finally, as well as drawing on some of the main themes which are threaded throughout the book, Chapter 10 considers the future of the lap-dancing industry in the UK, reflecting upon how changes via policy, in relation to licensing for example, might impact on the careers and futures of women working in this branch of the sex industry.

Notes

1 The name of the club has been changed to preserve anonymity.
2 For photographic depiction of London 'strippers' see Clifton (2005).
3 In the US and Canada 'stripper' is used generically to refer to erotic dancers who work in lap-dancing clubs; regular 'strip' clubs; freelance etc. This is evident in the academic literature, where the term 'stripper' rather than 'lap-dancer' is used.
4 The name of this agency has been changed to preserve anonymity.
5 An American 'semi-hard' pornographic magazine founded by Larry Flynt.
6 A 'soft' pornographic magazine founded by Hugh Hefner.
7 This only gives examples of the most common sub-themes to emerge from the general body of literature.
8 This includes observations of dancers inside and outside of the lap-dancing club environment, made as a researcher.
9 All observational data presented was recorded in a field diary between November 2003 and February 2006.
10 Members of a stag party.
11 Stripping is the favoured terminology used to refer to lap-dancers as well as other erotic dancers.

Chapter 2

Lap-dancing and the night-time economy

The historical trajectory of erotic dance, and the subsequent existence of the contemporary lap-dancing industry in the late twentieth and early twenty-first century, is complex and discussed comprehensively elsewhere (see, for example, Jarrett 1997 and Frank 2002a). Lap-dancing-style venues originate from the USA and Canada where the industry became a commercial sensation in the late 1980s and early 1990s (Egan 2006a), although other styles of strip clubs opened as early as the 1970s (Beninger 2004). The 'strip club boom' during the 1980s/1990s has been linked to the rapid growth of the pornography industry, which led to pornography entrepreneurs such as Larry Flynt, owner of the Hustler chain, making enough profit to open strip chains (Jeffreys 2008). The lap-dancing-style venues discussed in this chapter differ from earlier 'strip' clubs in which women were traditionally paid to work; alternatively, in these new clubs, it is custom for the dancers to pay a fee to managers or owners to work on the premises. This has, it is argued, 'enabled the venue owners to increase their profits considerably' (Jeffreys 2008: 152) and therefore attracted corporate investment, helping to make lap-dancing a global multimillion pound industry. In the UK where lap-dancing-style venues did not appear until the mid to late 1990s (Jones *et al.*, 2003) this term is used rather generically to refer to commercial 'stripping' outlets, often represented by chains such as 'Spearmint Rhino' and 'For Your Eyes Only (FYEO)'.[1] In the UK, prior to the 1990s, with the exception of Burlesque theatre and the Soho peepshows, striptease had been confined to private parties, pubs and clubs, where strippers performed on stage for a fee and were not expected to offer private dances[2] (Glasscock 2003; Jarrett 1997). The term 'lap-dancing', in the UK, does not refer to 'contact-clubs' in which dancers and customers physically interact; unlike in the USA, where both contact and non-contact clubs are featured (Egan 2006a), laws in the UK prohibit contact. In relation to this, in Chapter 3, the typical work activities of the dancers, as observed in Starlets, are discussed.

As will be discussed in this chapter, the commercialization of erotic (also referred to as 'exotic') dancing has been marked by the 'gentrification' of nightlife (Hollands and Chatterton 2003; Egan 2006a) in which lap-dancing clubs have increasingly become marketed as 'entertainment' venues and 'gentleman's clubs' rather than 'sex' establishments. The commercialization of lap-dancing reflects the normalization and mainstreaming of 'sex' (McNair 2002) and 'sex work' (Attwood 2009; Hollands and Chatterton 2003). Bradley (2008: 504) argues that:

> The sex industry is undergoing legitimization, with increasing representation in popular culture. Those in the exotic dance industry have been at the forefront of these changes. Exotic dancing, stripping, and strip club culture is increasingly present in movies, music and other media.

Some lap-dancing clubs now offer entertainment for women by offering pole-dancing lessons (Holland and Attwood 2009) to hen parties and by hosting 'women only' nights with male erotic dancers. This process of legitimization is further argued to be evident in the UK by the corporate association of investors such as the SFI Group plc (Surrey Free Inns) with lap-dancing club chains such as For Your Eyes Only (FYEO), previously known for their investment in popular pubs and night-clubs (Chatterton and Hollands 2003). It has been suggested by a number of sources, that lap-dancing clubs in the UK are part of one of the fastest-growing leisure industries (Aitkenhead and Sheffield 2001; Horton 2006; Jones *et al.* 2003). Although there is some contention regarding the exact figures offered, various sources suggest that there were estimated to be around 200 lap-dancing clubs in 2002 (Jones *et al.* 2003) and over 300 clubs in the UK in 2008 (Object 2009; Ford 2010). However, these figures are regularly disputed by the Lap Dancing Association (LDA) who contend that there are only currently 150 lap-dancing clubs operating in the UK (2008). As these contradictory figures suggest, it is not possible to accurately predict the exact numbers of lap-dancing establishments as clubs can both open and close from month to month (Tyke 2008). Nonetheless these figures are still indicative of an expanding industry. The proliferation of the lap-dancing industry is not only suggestive of a wider mainstreaming of sex, but is also part of a process in which sex industries have been subjected to a kind of 'McDonaldization' (Hausbeck and Brents 2002). What is certain, as indicated by the multi-million pound annual turnover (Adult Entertainment Working Group 2006), is that through the expansion of chains such as Spearmint Rhino, FYEO, Wildcats and Secrets, lap-dancing clubs are becoming a successful commercial feature of the night-time economy as well as a global industry. It is important to point out that, although there has been a commercially motivated 'mainstreaming' of sex, significant in the proliferation of lap-dancing clubs, this is, however, still at odds with dominant public and political discourses about 'sex' and 'sex work'. There is, for instance, a contradiction at play, in which 'sex' is commercially legitimized and yet still highly stigmatized (see Chapters 1 and 7). This is clearly reflected in the recent relicensing of lap-dancing clubs, discussed later in this chapter.

This chapter discusses the way in which lap-dancing clubs have become an important part of the night-time leisure economy in the UK. This includes examining how chain-operated gentlemen's clubs, such as For Your Eyes Only and Spearmint Rhino for example, are at the forefront of the proliferation of the lap-dancing industry. In addition, the regulation of lap-dancing clubs within the UK is discussed. This focuses on the recent changes from the licensing of lap-dancing clubs under the Licensing Act 2003 to 'sexual entertainment venues' as outlined in the Policing and Crime Act 2009.

Understanding the role and regulation of lap-dancing clubs within the night-time leisure economy highlights the economic, cultural and political significance of this branch of the commercial sex industry within the UK. Furthermore, it specifically sets the scene for Starlets as a chain-operated lap-dancing club. Highlighting the economic, cultural and political factors which relate to this club is important as each influences the nature of the business and the rules which govern the conduct of dancers.

Commercializing lap-dancing

As a result of the decline in traditional employment roles, which were once a feature of the 'industrial' city, the leisure sector has become a significant component of the urban economy, replacing manufacturing in this role (Worpole 1992). This transition from an industrial to post-industrial economy has therefore impacted on the city and has been vital in the development of the night-time (leisure) economies. It is suggested that the city, at night, has been transformed into a thriving economy, where night-time leisure facilitates economic growth in the UK (Chatterton and Hollands 2002). For instance, in the last decade, the pub, club and bar industry had an annual turnover of £23 billion, which amounts to 3 per cent of the UK gross domestic product (Home Office 2000). It is therefore inevitable that the night-time leisure economy has increasingly been a prominent source of employment as well as entertainment (Chatterton and Hollands 2003; Hannigan 1998; Hobbs et al. 2000). It has been estimated that in England and Wales the licensed trade (pubs, clubs and bars) employs around 1 million people and has created around one in five of all new jobs (Home Office 2000), although, like other markets, the impact of the recent economic depression and smoking ban has had some effect on the financial turnover of the leisure industry (Mintel Report 2008). The British Beer and Pub Association estimated that due to a combination of the smoking ban imposed in 2006 and the economic depression in 2000s it was expected a high number of pubs would close (cited in Hickman 2008). Nonetheless, the night-time economy still continues to be significant in urban growth and development.

Corporately owned and operated night-time entertainment has led to the 'gentrification' of the night-time economy (Hollands and Chatterton 2003) in which nightlife has been 'upgraded'. This term 'gentrification' was originally applied to housing and the transformation of neighbourhoods, including schools, shops and leisure outlets, to describe a process whereby they became 'middle-class' spaces (Glass 1964). 'Gentrification' is now being applied to entertainment and night-life as the markets have become dominated by mainstream spaces (Chatterton and Hollands 2002) as a result of an injection of corporate money into the heart of the night-time leisure industry. In relation to this, Chatterton and Hollands (2002) contend that there are three distinct markets which are part of the night-time economy, including 'mainstream', 'residual' and 'alternative' spaces. It is the 'mainstream' spaces which are particularly significant in this discussion as they apply to those dominated by commercially recognised pubs, clubs, bars and restaurants which are corporately owned and often concentrated in large city centres. This inevitably means that the city has become a place for the cash-rich and the middle classes with high disposable incomes and who are therefore more likely to access the new urban economy (Hannigan 1998). The encouragement of upmarket and exclusive leisure spaces in the city is motivated by profit generation (Harvey 2000). Examples of 'mainstream' spaces include popular branded chain pubs such as JD Wetherspoons, Slug and Lettuce and Scream pubs among others. Through the saturation of corporate investment since the 1990s, the 'mainstream' market has flourished, forcing 'residual' and 'alternative' spaces to the periphery of the night-time economy and entertainment city. It was reported, for example, in 2008 that JD Wetherspoons accounted for 40 per cent of the pub and bar high-street market (Mintel Report 2008). Similarly, corporately owned 'chain' lap-dancing, as a global industry, generates high profits. For example, in the USA this industry is estimated to be worth in the region of $15 billion, making up around one-fifth of the US$75 billion world market (Montgomery 2005, cited in Jeffreys 2008). In the UK the adult entertainment industry estimated value is around £300 million (Adult Entertainment Working Group 2006; Jones *et al.* 2003). This is not only a reflection of the success of chain operated lap-dancing venues such as Spearmint Rhino and For Your Eyes Only, but also indicative of how they are part of the 'mainstream' spaces identified by Chatterton and Hollands (2002) and signify the 'gentrification' of the night-time economy (Bradley 2008). In relation to this, it is suggested that 'sex-related businesses are now widely regarded as integral to urban economies' (Hubbard *et al.* 2008: 396), with the adult entertainment (AE) industry bringing positive benefits to the local area by diversifying its economy (Jones *et al.* 2003).[3]

Although there are a number of independently owned lap-dancing clubs which target working-class groups and do not ascribe to the polished 'gentlemen's club' image, increasingly more 'regular' clubs are being replaced by the more luxurious chain clubs. 'Regular' clubs are often not as centrally located in cities as many of the chain operated 'gentlemen's' clubs now tend to be. There is also a sense that these lap-dancing clubs are not as strictly controlled as the corporately regulated venues. For instance, dancers based at Starlets who worked in different independent clubs made this observation. Becks, a dancer, recalls her experience at a 'regular' venue called 'Sapphires:[4] 'The bouncers didn't care if the customers were being dickheads. They just ignore everything. I didn't feel safe at all.' Although Becks expressed a strong dislike of working in 'regular' clubs, this was not unanimous, as other dancers suggested a preference for the 'down-to-earth' working-class clientele independent venues more readily attracted. However, because of the limited research available in the UK about lap-dancing clubs, there is no data to compare 'regular' and 'chain' venues.

Regardless of the dancers' views on these clubs, the shape of the lap-dancing industry is changing as venues are increasingly corporately owned and branded as 'gentlemen's clubs', a theme apparent in major UK chains such as Spearmint Rhino, FYEO, and Secrets. These venues, in some cases, have become lap-dancing clubs which offer 'fine dining' and 'business lunches' (Egan 2006a: 11). The sophisticated image reflected in the brand promotes these venues as ' "high-class" enterprises, business oriented, and expensive' (Bradley 2008: 507), as suggested in the lap-dancing club customer charges. For example, although entry fee prices vary, they can be as much as £20. In addition, the cost of both alcoholic and non-alcoholic drinks can sometimes be almost double the price of those served in other 'mainstream' pubs, clubs and bars; this was certainly reflected in the prices charged at Starlets. Furthermore, the cost of purchasing a lap-dance can be between £5 and £20, depending on the venue and type of private dance (whether semi or fully nude). The careful branding of lap-dancing clubs as 'gentlemen's' clubs', beyond serving to attract a particular cash-rich clientele which has made them increasingly profitable (Egan 2006a), also helps maintain the clubs' 'high'-status image and legitimize the 'sex industry' as part of the leisure industry. Further to this, the lap-dancing clubs have increasingly become associated with 'celebrity', reflected in the endorsement by those such as Madonna, Kate Moss, Jude Law and Sadie Frost, along with premiership footballers who are frequently linked with clubs such as Stringfellows and Spearmint Rhino. Stringfellows, in particular, has well documented celebrity interest and support; the Stringfellow website has a celebrity blog, which allows celebrities to comment on their time spent at the club (Stringfellows Website). The owner, Peter Stringfellow, has even gained 'celebrity' status, appearing on 'celebrity entertainment television' in programmes such as *Come Dine With Me* broadcast on Channel 4. This is perhaps suggestive of how 'sex' businesses increasingly attempt to normalize their existence through a process of commercial mainstreaming. The image of the Stringfellows club has been significant in its attempts to legitimize the industry, by providing with it 'celebrity' and 'glamour' associations; these have now become important features of the lap-dancing 'brand'. Such branding is indicative of a particular lifestyle experience (Klein 2000) that people want to buy into (Miles 1998). With the 'lap-dancing' brand epitomizing 'wealth', 'glamour' and 'celebrity', it not only becomes an important lifestyle choice for those already part of the economic elite, but significantly is attractive to those who aspire to the lifestyle image it promotes. Therefore, rather than just attracting businessmen, the lap-dancing image is increasingly attractive to young male adults with disposable incomes. This follows Hollands' (2002) assertion that gentrified spaces have become successful as they specifically target young professionals and service employees. Weekends become a prime time to attract these groups, along with large numbers of stag and birthday parties. This is supported by figures produced in the Mintel Report (2003) *Stag and Hen Holidays* which suggest that most visitors (46 per cent) of adult entertainment venues cited stag or hen parties as their main motivation for attending. It is further evident that the industry has become an important part of tourism, increasingly attracting visiting stag parties in particular (se AEWG 2006) as well as those from the local population.

The commercializion of erotic dance through the introduction of chain operated lap-dancing clubs has inevitably brought this 'hidden' form of adult entertainment into the mainstream night-time economy; specifically through the club chains such as FYEO, Spearmint Rhino, and more recently Secrets. As this chapter has indicated, lap-dancing clubs have become a predominant feature of the erotic dance industry across the West, namely in the US, Australia and the UK. As independently owned lap-dancing clubs decrease, it is the chain-operated venues which have become significantly visible features of the night-time economy. In the UK, the two most successful lap-dancing chains have been FYEO and Spearmint Rhino. This is reflected in their continuing expansion and excessive profits (Doward 2001). FYEO opened the first lap-dancing club in the UK (Grandy 2005) and currently leads the market with nine across the UK. Following behind are Spearmint Rhino with five and Secrets owning six. These figures are, however, subject to change as lap-dancing clubs frequently open and close. FYEO, until 2004, was under the ownership of the SFI Group plc, which, at the time, was one of the fastest-growing operators of drinking and eating establishments in the UK; by 2002 the company boasted nearly 186 outlets (however, SFI have since gone into administration). In 2001 SFI decided to sell the FYEO chain; it was predicted that the South East clubs would be bought for around £8 million (Griffin 2001). In 2003 the Ladhar Group purchased a large number of the FYEO lap-dancing club outlets (Grandy 2005); this group currently own bars, clubs, pubs and nursing homes, and claims to be the biggest pub and club operator in the North East of England, as well as owning a number of other leisure outlets across the UK (Pearce 2007).

Spearmint Rhino, although in the UK it is the second largest lap-dancing club operator, still remains the most successful lap-dancing club chain in the world, with over 30 clubs in the US and an expanding club scene in Australia. To emphasize its dominance in this market, Spearmint Rhino is described as a multinational four-star gentlemen's club, with as many 6,000 dancers working across the US, UK, Europe and Australia (Egan 2006a). John Gray, who founded the successful chain, has an estimated wealth of over £38 million derived from his Spearmint Rhino brand (Morris 2002). The turnover of the most prosperous of the Spearmint Rhino clubs, on London's Tottenham Court Road, was estimated at £300,000 per week (Doward 2001). Despite this, in 2004 Spearmint Rhino reported a dramatic reduction in economic turnover, signalling that the company might be in trouble (Armitage and Prynn 2004). Despite this, the Spearmint Rhino chain have continued to develop their brand by expanding into television, with their UK clubs being made the central theme of a TV series aired on Bravo.[5] *Inside Spearmint Rhino* follows the pursuits of the UK business and the dancers' lives who work in these clubs. This is not only indicative of this brand's success in the UK adult entertainment market but inevitably acts as a great advertisement for Spearmint Rhino.

Legislating on and regulating lap-dancing

As a result of the recently passed Policing and Crime Act 2009, lap-dancing clubs will now be licensed as 'sexual entertainment venues/establishments'. This change of policy came into effect from April 2010. Prior to this lap-dancing clubs were regulated in a similar way to other entertainment venues such as pubs, bars, night clubs and restaurants under the Licensing Act 2003. Under this licensing regime, lap-dancing club regulation additionally involved a number of special conditions. Firstly, each lap-dancing establishment had to provide licensed door supervision; secondly, a strict age-related admissions policy was required; thirdly, the use of CCTV surveillance was insisted upon, and finally the club had to provide a clear statement regarding the nature of the entertainment it provided, for example, partial or full nudity. Furthermore, the Licensing Act 2003 offered residents the right to oppose a licence application on the grounds that the four obligations stated would not be fulfilled. This right was put into practice in 2008 when a lap-dancing club in Durham was refused licensing as a result of sustained public protest, thus indicating the power of the citizen in the future of lap-dancing club regulation (LDA 2008). The licensing of Scottish lap-dancing clubs is somewhat more complex than the situation in England and Wales, with local authorities having less power to control these premises. Adult entertainment in Scotland, which includes lap-dancing clubs, is governed under a number of different provisions, including the Civic Government (Scotland) Act 1982, the Licensing (Scotland) Act 1976, the 1976 Scottish Licensing Act and the Licensing (Scotland) Act 2005. In Scotland, in most cases an entertainment licence will be granted; however, where there is no sale of alcohol, a licence in these venues is not necessary if the public entertainment is not clearly specified under section 9 of the Civic Government (Scotland) Act 1982. Further to this, local authorities' powers are inhibited by the 1976 Scottish Licensing Act as it only allows licensing boards to refuse an entertainment license on the basis that the establishment in question is unsuitable for the sale of alcohol (for a thorough account of the licensing of Scottish lap-dancing clubs see the Adult Entertainment Working Group Report 2006).

Chain-operated lap-dancing clubs attempt to remain strictly controlled and regulated, often by officially contracting dancers to work on their premises and by producing strict 'house rules' (discussed further in Chapter 3), which intend to guide the conduct of customers and workers. In addition, as stipulated by the Licensing Act 2003, these clubs continue to have CCTV in operation as well as security operating the venue doors and main floors of the club where customers and dancers interact. This is in tune with the way in which many of the 'mainstream' spaces are now governed, with increased usage made of private policing from CCTV and security (Chatterton and Hollands 2002; Hobbs et al. 2000). Inside these clubs, customers are often strictly controlled, an example of which was identified in Starlets, as a chain operated venue. During the time of the research, customers were permitted to remain seated at all times, unless going to the gentleman's washroom, going to the dance area for a lap-dance, going to the bar or leaving the club. Customers who did not adhere to this rule were often corrected and in some cases removed from the club by security.

Prior to the recent change in the licensing of lap-dancing clubs, attention was drawn to the regulation of these venues by women's groups such as Object and the Fawcett Society. In 2008 these action groups led a campaign which challenged the regulation of lap-dancing clubs under the Licensing Act 2003. The Fawcett Society (2009) argues that 'Lap-dance clubs are a form of commercial sexual exploitation and promote the sexist view that women are sex objects'. Likewise Object (2009) who have worked in partnership with the Fawcett Society in their anti-lap-dancing campaign, suggest that the industry strives to 'promote the sexist view that it is acceptable to treat women as sex objects, not people'. The joint campaign was intended to encourage the government to address the regulation of lap-dancing clubs and to classify them 'sex encounter establishments' (or venues). According to the campaign the licensing regime, as outlined by the Licensing Act 2003, was an insufficient and inappropriate method by which to regulate these clubs. This is on the basis that lap-dancing clubs are part of the commercial sex industry and where they are said to offer, whether through physical contact or not, some form of sexual stimulation. This has been disputed by the Lap Dancing Association (LDA) which, as a way of detaching lap-dancing clubs from the sex industry, contends that instead lap-dancing is part of a 'sexy industry' (LDA 2008). The LDA's attempt to dissociate lap-dancing clubs from the commercial sex industry is a tactical move and one which it is perhaps believed will help ensure the continued growth of the lap-dancing industry in the UK.

As was proposed, relicensing lap-dancing clubs as 'sex establishments' or 'sex venues' under Schedule 3 of the Local Government (Miscellaneous Provisions) Act 1982 positions them with sex cinemas and sex shops, recognised as part of a commercial sex industry, and not as part of the leisure industry. A change in licensing found political support from the former Home Secretary Jacquie Smith, who proposed these changes in the Policing and Crime Bill which was successfully passed in November 2009. The Policing and Crime Act 2009 which 'contains measures to protect the public, increase police accountability and effectiveness, and tackle crime and disorder' (Home Office 2008), directly addresses the proliferation of lap-dancing clubs and the alleged problems this expansion has instigated according to groups such as the Fawcett Society and Object. More specifically, under section 27 of this Act, local authorities must now license lap-dancing clubs as 'sexual entertainment venues' and have up to 12 months to do this if clubs are still licensed under the Licensing Act 2003. Local authorities may set a cap on the number of 'sex venues' it thinks appropriate and can refuse a licence application on this basis: if 'the number of sex establishments, or of sex establishments of a particular kind, in the relevant locality at the time the application is determined is equal to or exceeds the number which the authority consider is appropriate for that locality' (section 27, paragraph 12). This is perhaps similar to the 'zoning laws' introduced in the US, which prevent adult entertainment businesses, such as erotic dance clubs, operating in residential and family areas of various cities (Ryder 2004). Under section 27, paragraph 12 of the Policing and Crime Act 2009, local communities will be given an opportunity to consult with local authorities about the licensing of particular 'sex venues'. Further to this, where a local authority does not adopt new provisions after one year of the Bill being in place, they must consult with the local community. In contrast, under the Licensing Act 2003, public consideration is taken into account; however, it can still be overruled by the licensing boards that have the power to make the final decision. Further discussion of the impact the change in licensing will have upon the industry and dancers will be discussed in Chapter 10.

Despite much opposition to the proliferation of lap-dancing clubs, the expansion of this industry has been beneficial for the women who have been working in this industry as agency strippers. For many of these women it has not only given them an opportunity to increase their earning power, but importantly, as will be discussed further in Chapter 10, has offered a safer and more regulated space to work in. Further to this, it is clear that lap-dancing clubs have become, along with other 'leisure'-based night-time entertainment, viable employment for a number of other roles outside of 'dancer', including bar staff, managers, waitresses and security, the positions of which, along with how the lap-dancers at Starlets do their job, will be the focus of Chapter 3.

Notes

1 'Lap-dancing' is also interchangeably referred to as 'pole-dancing', 'table-dancing' and 'stripping'.
2 Refers to a personal lap-dance performed by a dancer; this is discussed further in Chapter 3.
3 However, conversely, according to the Department of City Planning in the USA, it is argued that AE venues are more likely to decrease the market value of property within 500 feet of these establishments (Department of City Planning, 1994).
4 The name of this club has been changed to preserve anonymity.
5 A cable and satellite channel available to UK viewers.

Chapter 3

Rules, contracts and players

As discussed in Chapter 2, erotic dance has been commercialized in the form of 'lap-dancing', and is now, both in the UK and globally, becoming a significant feature of the night-time economy. As well as understanding the position of lap-dancing within the British night-time (leisure) economy and as part of a much wider global industry, it is important to understand what work dancers perform in these clubs, in order to effectively set up this ethnography. Although inevitably some variation exists between clubs, there is still significant overlap with the regulation of dancers and the work they perform. The purpose of this chapter is to outline how lap-dancers do their job, based on observations made in Starlets. Furthermore, some of the 'main players' who make up this 'social world', which includes dancers, managers, security, bar staff and customers, will be introduced.

Rules, rotas and 'contracts'

Part of the contractual process of becoming a lap-dancer at Starlets, following a successful audition, involves dancers signing an 'employment' (also known as a 'dancer') contract,[1] which is drawn up by the club; this is standardized across the chain of which Starlets is part. Like in other lap-dancing clubs across the UK, dancers at Starlets are contracted as self-employed workers. The contract dancers commit to requests that the dancer provides personal information, including her full name, date of birth and home contact details, as many employment contracts do. In addition, a list of the 'house rules', 'house' or 'club' fee details (also known as commission) and a description of the potential penalties dancers should expect for breaking house rules are provided on the contract. This is reflective of other lap-dancer contracts provided by employers of chain establishments in the UK (AEWG 2006). The dancer contract at Starlets did not prevent these workers from dancing in other lap-dancing establishments. Nonetheless, dancers are still obligated to abide by the house rules and pay a 'house fee' to conduct their 'business' on the premises of the lap-dancing club or face dismissal. These contracts are extremely biased and drawn up in the club/ industry's favour, providing few, if any, owner/manager obligations (AEWG 2006). Further to this, because of the ad hoc contractual process, dancers were rarely given copies of their contracts; in most cases these would be retained by managers. The admission process on my initial entry as a dancer, and early fieldwork, was quite informal and required nothing more than the dancer's signature on the contract. However, the contractual process became increasingly formal, as dancers were eventually expected to provide photographic evidence of their identity in the form of a passport or driving licence. This formal and more thorough procedure of verifying a dancer's personal identity is a measure that came into effect after a number of underage dancers were reported in the media to have worked in various lap-dancing establishments, with managers and club owners fearful of prosecution and public ridicule. A notable example involved a case where a 15-year-old girl claimed that she managed to secure a job as a lap-dancer in Birmingham's 'Spearmint Rhino Extreme' lap-dancing club. It is alleged that the managers of the club in question did not verify her claim to be 18 years old and did not request any identification from her (Cartledge 2004).

To clarify some of the terminology referred to in the dancer contracts used at Starlets: the 'business' of the dancers refers to the generation of their income through private (lap) dances and sit-downs. The 'house fee', which is the fee paid by the dancer to the club to conduct their 'business', is not a fixed amount. The fee is set by the management of the club and varies from day to day, month to month, and year to year; this is reflected in the rapid increase in commission witnessed during the time the fieldwork for this ethnography was conducted. For instance, on the start of this project the minimum commission was fixed at £20, with the maximum fee never exceeding £60; by the end of my time spent in the field, house fees were fixed at a minimum of £40 and a maximum of £80. House fees are a common feature of both independent, more 'regular' lap-dancing clubs, as well as chain-operated clubs marketed as 'gentlemen's clubs' (AEWG 2006). At Starlets, during Saturday evening shifts, towards the end of my fieldwork, dancers were expected to pay £80, regardless of customer intake or income generation during that shift. The management of Starlets justified this unfair charge by claiming Saturdays were the club's busiest day and therefore dancers should be able to pay the set house fee of £80 without complaint. Gerard (one of the club's managers), for example, commented in relation to this: 'you dancers are rolling in it, so £80 is nothing to you'. It was clearly apparent, as it is further suggested later in this book, that as workers, dancers at Starlets experienced some exploitation, primarily evident in the fluctuating and unreasonable house fees, fines and contractual obligations. The exploitation of dancers in this way is something discussed elsewhere (AEWG 2006; Barton 2006; Wesely 2003), but is an area that requires closer scrutiny than it has been given in a UK context. In Starlets, dancers did, however, attempt to resist management control by generating their own rules and regulations evident through the 'tacit rules' (see Colosi 2010b forthcoming). In addition, dancers would also directly challenge management by arguing and even threatening to strike, as demonstrated in the following field diary extract:

> Lisa [dancer] had managed to gather most of the dancers in the changing room; she was standing on a stool with all the girls waiting for her to speak. 'We need to stop taking their [managers'] shit; they're letting girls get away with dirty dancing ... if we all stop working, what are they gonna do? Sack us? We should stand our ground.' Some of the dancers agreed but the majority objected claiming that the managers would indeed just sack them ...

The managers did not respond favourably to the dancers' actions and the dancers were clearly told by Gerard 'get back onto the main floor otherwise I'll sack you all! There are plenty of other girls who I can get to work here instead of you.' This scare tactic was frequently used by the managers and was one that proved effective; in this instance the dancers quickly abandoned their 'revolt' and returned to the main floor to work. Suggestions of unionization often circulated the changing room and were discussed seriously by a number of dancers. However, many of the workers at Starlets felt it would never be an effective solution to their often unfair treatment. For instance, Lynda (a dancer) explained to me 'It'll [unionization of dancers] never work. Do you think they'd [managers] stand for it? They'll just find some way of getting rid of us.'

In addition to house fees, dancers were contracted to adhere to a number of house rules. House rules were created in order to guide a dancer's conduct in the lap-dancing club. These rules serve to ensure that dancers work effectively and that there is a sense of order in the club. The house rules were not fixed and frequently changed, with new updated versions being put forward by the managers. These rules were initially available to all the dancers, with one copy pinned up on the wall of the changing room; this, however, disappeared and was never replaced early on in my fieldwork. Other than from the dancer's contract, access to the club's house rules could only be found on customer menus, though often circulated via word of mouth. Dancers, however, often resorted to their own 'tacit rules', which often took priority over the house rules (see Chapters 6, 7 and 8).

Like lap-dancers at other clubs across the UK, dancers had some autonomy in choosing their work shifts as a result of being self-employed (AEWG 2006). At Starlets, during the time fieldwork was conducted, dancers had the option to work between Monday and Saturday, during which time the club was open. Dancers completed a shift rota on a monthly basis which they would return to the managers. The number of shifts each dancer worked inevitably varied and was dependent upon a number of factors, including lifestyle and/or family and other work commitments. Only on rare occasions would a dancer opt to work the full six shifts available per week. Although initially dancers were given absolute autonomy to select their own shifts, this gradually changed towards the end of my fieldwork. For instance, it became necessary on the managers' insistence that each dancer work at least two Saturday night shifts and two shifts early to mid week in each month for which they had submitted a rota. This was claimed to be necessary in order to meet the needs of the club, as on Saturdays a high intake of customers was anticipated, and it was therefore necessary for there to be enough dancers working to meet the demands of the customers. However, the dancers' cynicism led many to believe this was motivated by the managers' greed, as each dancer would be charged £80 to work during this shift. Although this rule was officially implemented by the managers, dancers found ways to exploit this regulation (see Chapter 8).

Dancers' earnings

There are two ways in which dancers at Starlets generated their income, through private dances (also known as lap-dances) or sit-downs, conducted on the main floor of Starlets. The setting and the way in which it is utilized is discussed further in Chapter 4. Providing an exact weekly, monthly or annual figure for a dancer's income is difficult as there was inevitably some variation between the incomes generated among the dancers. High earners on average would make anything from £100 to £300 per shift between Monday and Thursday, but during Friday and Saturday shifts could generate anything between £300 and £600. This does not mean, however, that high earners were not likely to experience 'bad nights' (Egan 2006a) in which they made very little or indeed no money at all. Average to lower income dancers could generate anything in the region of £0 to £100 per shift between Monday and Thursday. During Friday and Saturday shifts these dancers still made smaller amounts of money than 'high earners', which could range from £0 to £300. Again as likely as these dancers were to experience 'bad nights',[2] they could of course have 'good nights'[3] (Egan 2006a) in which their income was significantly higher than usual. Being a high or low earner in Starlets did not appear to be dependent on anything other than the effort a dancer was willing to go to in order to make money. For example, this might include the extent to which they would invest in personal appearance and their persistence with customers and willingness to put on an 'act' to entice customers (this is something discussed further in Chapter 7). Tilly, one of the club's highest earners, was described by her colleagues as 'hard working' and rarely seemed to complain of having 'bad nights'. In contrast Sandy, who was an average to low income dancer, regularly talked about 'having no money' and 'getting another job with a guaranteed income'. Dancers, however, experienced fluctuations in earnings which were sometimes outside of their personal control and relate to time of year, day of the week and the numbers of dancers working per shift. For instance, January to April were less profitable than May to December, a period which brought with it stag parties, followed by the Christmas 'party season'. During weekdays, Monday to Wednesday often attracted fewer customers than Thursday to Friday. These patterns were often reflected in the dancers' earnings.

The lap-dance

The lap-dance, also referred to as the private dance, is one of the primary ways in which dancers earned money in Starlets. Unlike in many American lap-dancing clubs (also referred to as strip clubs) where dancers can earn money by being tipped during stage performances, in UK chain-operated lap-dancing clubs stage tipping is often prohibited and perhaps a reflection of the no-contact regulations imposed on clubs by local authority licensing committees. Starlets, for example, was licensed as a topless only, strictly no-contact club, although, as it will be made apparent, this regulation was not always adhered to by individual dancers. In the US there is more variation in the levels of contact allowed in clubs, based on the differing state laws, but again, the dancers' and managers' interpretation of or adherence to such regulations varies somewhat (Barton 2006; Egan 2006a).

A lap-dance, as observed in Starlets, involved a dancer performing a sensual dance routine stripping down to her g-string in front of the customer while he/she remained seated. At the time of this fieldwork a dancer was only permitted to perform topless during a private dance and stage show. In preparation for the private dance, the dancer would often ask the customer to sit with his hands on the sides of the chair away from his lap and place his legs apart in preparation for her dance. The dancer would then perform between the customer's legs in close proximity to his body but not necessarily making contact with him. Interestingly Starlets, on opening, was licensed under the premise that dancers remain three feet away from the customer during private dances, referred to as the 'three foot rule'. Initially dancers adhered to this, but over time this rule seemed to be overlooked by managers and club owners. Dancing closely to a customer helps create the illusion of intimacy; both dancers and managers were aware of this and therefore disregarded the original rule. At the time this ethnography was conducted a private dance would last for the duration of one song (or three minutes) and would cost a customer £10. Special offers were available at different times and on different days of the week which would enable the customer to purchase either two dances for £10 or one dance for £5. Neither dancers nor customers were able to select the music danced to as it was dependent on what songs were played by the DJ at the time the private dance was performed.

The sit-down

Other than earning money from lap-dances, dancers also generated income from 'sit-downs'. Sit-downs involved a customer paying for the company of a dancer for an allotted period of time; anything from 30 minutes up to the entire duration of a dancer's shift which could be as long as six hours. The customer paid by the hour for the dancer's company and although there is variation between clubs, at Starlets sit-down fees were: £50 for 30 minutes and £100 per hour thereon. During a sit-down a dancer was not expected to offer the customer private dances unless requested to; some customers were happy to spend this time drinking and talking to the dancer. The majority of the dancers at Starlets held sit-downs in high regard as they could generously boost their income; generating an income solely from lap-dances alone inevitably means harder physical and emotional work (see Chapter 7). Unfortunately, for many dancers at Starlets, sit-downs rarely proved to be a regular source of income. Only a few dancers regularly had sit-downs with customers, with the majority relying on private dances to make money.

The stage show

At Starlets stage shows would take place throughout a dancer's shift when the customers were present in the club; each dancer would take it in turn to perform a six-minute routine, approximately the length of two songs, on the stage in the area of the club where the customers were present. For example, during the Monday to Saturday night shifts customers would be seated on the main floor upstairs in Starlets, therefore the main stage in that area would be used for such performances. During Saturday day shifts when the customers were located in the dance reception area, stage shows would take place downstairs. Each dancer would be expected to add her name to the stage show rota made available by a manager or the DJ at the start of a working shift; the order would usually reflect the time and order in which dancers arrived for their shift. In relation to this, it was not uncommon for some dancers to deliberately arrive late, in the hope that their name would not be included on the list, or that they would at least not be expected to be the first one to perform on stage. Although some dancers enjoyed stage performances, a number did not and saw them as unnecessary extra work or time wasted, which could instead be spent making money via private dances on the floor.

Once or twice during an evening shift, as part of their contractual obligations, dancers were expected to take part in 'the parade' on stage. This involved all of the dancers taking it in turn to walk around the stage once before exiting onto the main floor. Following the brief parade, the next two songs played onto the main floor by the DJ would be offered to the customers at the cost of one dance (£10) which was usually indicated by one song.

Starlets' main players

Within the setting of Starlets there were a number of social actors, including different staff and customers. These included managers, bouncers (security), waitresses, bar staff, receptionists, hosts and DJs, all of whom played a significant role in this ethnography, as they form part of the rich tapestry of the research setting. This section will briefly outline the different roles within the club setting in order to make sense of the general occupational structure of Starlets, as well as the various interactions in which dancers are involved, to further help set the scene of the club.

The dancers

It makes sense to begin with the main social actors for which this ethnography was the focus: the dancers. Over the period in which fieldwork was conducted, Starlets hosted many different dancers. Although most of these dancers were incorporated into my original fieldnotes, not all have been included in the discussions within this book for various practical reasons. It was inevitable that only a proportion of my findings could be discussed, therefore some of the participants who featured in my fieldnotes could not always be included. Those who have been included are represented in Table 3.1 as a way of offering an initial introduction. The dancers are presented in relation to the three status roles including: 'new girl', 'transition' or 'old school'[4] as this represents their position in the dancer hierarchy, an identification that will be discussed further in Chapters 6, 7 and 8, and is a central feature of this ethnography.

Table 3.1 Starlets dancers by status

Name of dancer*	Status role**	Name of dancer*	Status role**
Annie	New girl	Candy	Old school
Carmen	New girl	Charley	Old school
Emerald	New girl	Cindy	Old school
Eva	New girl	Davina	Old school
Kate	New girl	Dina	Old school
Katrina	New girl	Eliza	Old school
Kristy	New girl	Hally	Old school
Maisie	New girl	Hazel	Old school
Mel	New girl	Jan	Old school
Melissa	New girl	Janey	Old school
Paula	New girl	Janine	Old school
Sam	New girl	Jenna	Old school
Simone	New girl	Joe	Old school
Alicia	Transition	Karen	Old school
Bella	Transition	Kelly	Old school
Beth	Transition	Kitten	Old school
Crystal	Transition	Leanne	Old school
Dana	Transition	Linda	Old school
Elle	Transition	Lisa	Old school
Jen	Transition	Lucy	Old school
Leila	Transition	Mandy	Old school
Lotti	Transition	Nelly	Old school
Kat	Transition	Paris	Old school
Kerry	Transition	Phoenix	Old school
Sasha	Transition	Princess	Old school
Sandy	Transition	Ruby	Old school
Terri	Transition	Sally	Old school
Tiger	Transition	Stacey	Old school
Adele	Old school	Stella	Old school
Amy	Old school	Tilly	Old school
Becks	Old school	Vienna	Old school

*The pseudonyms given to the dancers in the table reflect a mixture of stage and non-stage names. For example, 'Jan' was usually referred to by her everyday name, not her stage name. In contrast, 'Paris' was always referred to by her stage name, not her everyday name. The psuedonyms have been selected for each dancer to reflect this.

**This refers to the status roles of dancers discussed in this book. It does not, however, suggest that during the time in which the fieldwork was conducted their status did not change.

Managers

> ... It was one of the club's monthly meetings which all the dancers who worked at Starlets were expected to attend. As usual this particular meeting was held on a Saturday afternoon, between 6 pm and 7 pm, after which dancers would start to get ready for the night shift. Gerard was the only manager present as Ken was away on holiday. There were a few absences but most of the dancers were present. I could tell from the expression on Gerard's face that he was not in a good mood. This became more apparent as he launched into an attack on the dancers: 'Listen up, you're all starting to get a little shabby in your appearance. Some of you have been wearing the same outfits since the club opened. You need to put the work in to get money. I'm sick of girls complaining about not making any money when they look a mess!' This barrage of complaints went on for some time, but most of the dancers were not listening to Gerard. This was not unusual, Gerard or Ken would be talking and the dancers would quietly mock, it had become a routine ...[5]

Although there were some changes in the managerial team over the period in which the research was conducted, those who are predominantly discussed in this ethnography are Ken and Gerard; the two assistant managers who worked alongside them were Darren and Amy. The role of management in this club was to coordinate and regulate the general running of the club and all the staff. Darren and Amy were employed to help Ken and Gerard fulfil this role more effectively, Amy in particular was introduced to manage the dancers and make decisions concerning their shifts.

The bouncers

> ... Tonight Bobby and Simon were taking it in turns to work on the main floor. As it was a Tuesday night and not expected to become particularly busy, one member of security was considered to be enough to keep an eye on events on the main floor ... Simon was standing next to the dance area looking bored, he was chewing gum and kept looking at his phone. Then, all of a sudden, one of the customers jumped up, clambered on to the stage and attempted to swing round one of the poles. Simon quickly alerted Bobby on his CB radio (security and managers use these to contact one another) as he raced across the floor to stop the very drunk customer. From the back entrance, Gerard

and Bobby then appeared, all three of them were now trying to pry the man off the front pole. Everybody on the main floor stopped what they were doing to watch, I could see some dancers laughing and others shaking their heads in disbelief. It looked like a fiasco, and I was not sure if the dancers were reacting to the customer or the overzealous actions of the bouncers and Gerard ...[6]

There were a number of bouncers employed to work at Starlets. However, the regulars included Gordon (head bouncer), Bobby, Chris, Simon and Phil. The role of this security team was to protect all staff members, particularly dancers, and to ensure customers conducted themselves appropriately without breaking club regulations (for further discussion about bouncers see Hobbs *et al.* 2003). This is echoed by DeMichele and Tewksbury (2005) who argue that the role of the bouncer in the strip club is 'to provide a safe environment for alcohol consumption and socializing ... to enforce rules and maintain order' (p. 539).

Waitresses and bar staff

... Most of the waitresses did not like the outfits they were expected to wear; Yvette had been complaining that it made her thighs look big. The outfit is not the more usual white shirt/blouse and plain black trousers/skirt, worn by waitresses in many other establishments, instead it is more in tune with the sexually provocative nature of lap-dancing; in fact they resemble majorettes rather than waitresses. A black legless Lycra leotard is worn over shiny flesh coloured tights, over which a dark blue, majorette style jacket is worn. All that is missing is the hat and baton ...[7]

Before the bar was constructed on the main floor of Starlets, customers were solely reliant on a waitress service to purchase beverages. As customers were seated, each table would be allocated a waitress who would be responsible for taking and serving customers' orders. The use of waitresses in the lap-dancing club environment is a common phenomenon (Boles and Garbin 1974a). There were several waitresses based at Starlets, with a high staff turnover. Bar staff operate both bars on the main floor and reception dance area downstairs; the bar on the main floor was the only one in use between Monday and Thursday.

Receptionist

> ... I was talking to Bobby in the reception area downstairs while Emma
> was seated behind her desk. It was a quiet night and she looked bored
> and miserable ... we never really saw Emma, but Liz, who sometimes
> worked on a Saturday afternoon, would pop in the dance reception to
> talk to some of the dancers ...[8]

There were two receptionists, Emma and Liz, who were employed
to tend the main reception situated in the entrance of Starlets.
The nature of this job meant that neither Emma nor Liz regularly
interacted with the dancers. The receptionists, however, had regular
contact with managers and bouncers. In many ways their role in
Starlets was quite an isolated one.

Host

> ... Daniel would stand in the same place every Saturday and Friday
> night, somewhere between the two customer entrances. He looked like
> a member of the management team in his smart black suit. Daniel
> stood against the wall attentively, waiting for customers. Tonight he
> did not have to wait long, and I could see him on his CB radio, every
> couple of minutes, being informed of another customer about to enter,
> soon after which the door would open and in would trot a group,
> whom he would escort to their seats ...[9]

This role was introduced towards the end of my fieldwork at
Starlets, and was employed only during Friday and Saturday night
shifts when the customer turnover was expected to be high. Daniel,
who also worked as a bar man in the club, acted as host during
weekends; in this role he would escort customers to their table and
indicate their presence to a waitress.

DJs

> ... Trev was bopping up and down to the music he was playing in
> the DJ booth with a fixed grin. He always turned the volume up
> high, so it was difficult to communicate with anyone on the main
> floor when he was working. His choice of music was always fast and
> furious, non-stop thumping remixes of various songs. Trev would
> often make the dancers laugh when he spoke over the microphone, but
> unfortunately they would be laughing at him not with him. Tonight
> he was particularly lively, and, according to Stella, he'd taken loads of

ephedrine[10] tablets. She explained: 'He's taken about eight! You only need one!' Trev, kept interrupting songs to talk over the microphone, and on this particular occasion he had most of the dancers rolling around laughing as he injected the word 'shabba!' into the songs he played. By imitating Shabba Ranks[11] Trev was not, however, trying to be ironic, he is very serious about his role as DJ, and fancies himself as a bit of an MC ...[12]

There were two DJs employed at Starlets, originally Deano and Trev; however, Trev was eventually replaced by Manny. The DJs were responsible for all the music played in the club, when dancers were on and off the stage. Deano worked between Monday and Thursday, whereas as Trev, then Manny, were allocated to DJ on Friday and Saturday.

Customers

... I was sitting with Jose, a Spanish customer in the UK on business; this was his third consecutive night in Starlets. He was friendly, softly spoken, articulate and very polite, but reluctant to buy dances; instead he wanted to buy me drinks and talk. Jose was an intriguing man, who appeared to use the setting of Starlets to enact his fantasies; the club became a place in which he could transform his identity and act out roles unacceptable in the outside 'world'. For Jose, on entering Starlets he was no longer merely a software engineer, but took on a more adventurous role. After a few (too many) alcoholic drinks he would start to make suggestions that he was in fact an undercover assassin, on assignment in the UK, comparing his life to that of Leon, the main character from the film of the same name. The more alcohol Jose consumed the more elaborate his stories became. It was not uncommon for some customers to use Starlets as a place in which they could transform their identities and live out their fantasies; as a dancer you learn to accept these stories and play along. After all there might be a dance or two in it ...[13]

There were a variety of customer types who entered Starlets, each of them with an equally varied set of motivations; for this reason it is impossible to homogenize the clientele. A variation in customer types based on motive, along with their relationships with lap-dancers, has been addressed elsewhere (see Egan 2006a; Frank 2002). Customers would visit Starlets as part of stag and birthday parties, predominantly on a Thursday to Saturday night, whereas Monday to Wednesday would attract different customers, including 'regulars' and smaller groups visiting in twos and threes.

The different players along with the nature of the work lap-dancers undertake, like the content of Chapter 2, help further set the scene for this ethnography. Whereas Chapter 2 provided the wider economic, cultural and political context in which Starlets is positioned, this chapter demonstrates how these factors shape the business. Chapter 4 continues to set the scene for this ethnography by drawing attention to the actual setting of Starlets, describing the different areas in which dancers interact with one another and the other main players discussed in this chapter. Discussing the physical setting of Starlets enables a better understanding to be developed of the environment in which these women work. Furthermore, offering detailed descriptions of the main spaces of the club which hold significance to the dancers helps place the different interactions between the main players into context.

Notes

1 More formally the 'contracts signed by dancers are known as codes of conduct', however, informally it is referred to as a 'contract'.
2 A night in which a dancer makes a small amount of money.
3 A night in which a dancer makes a large amount of money.
4 These three stages are defined and explored in Chapter 6, 7 and 8.
5 Field diary extract.
6 Field diary extract.
7 Field diary extract.
8 Field diary extract.
9 Field diary extract.
10 A drug used clinically for asthma, it is, however, taken recreationally for its stimulant effects. Recreational use of ephedrine is currently illegal in the UK.
11 A Jamaican DJ and recording artist who was famous for UK hit 'Loverman'.
12 Field diary extract.
13 Field diary extract.

Chapter 4

Introducing Starlets: a lap-dancing club setting

... I went into Starlets with Sarah, a friend of mine who had never been in a lap-dancing club before. She was surprised by how it looked inside, having expected somewhere seedy, full of naked women being mauled by customers. Sarah explained to me: 'It's really different. It just seems so sexy ...' This reaction is not unique, other customers and personal friends who visited Starlets for the first time had made similar remarks. Graham, for example, a customer, who came to Starlets as part of a stag party, described how it had exceeded his expectations: '[I] thought it was going to be pretty rough in here. But I'm pleasantly surprised.' ...[1]

There were certainly preconceptions about Starlets, as suggested in the opening extract, with most of these ideas being based on conjecture from various public sources.[2] It is not uncommon for environments, like lap-dancing clubs, which are surrounded by secrecy and mystery, to be assessed largely on the grounds of speculation (see Sanders 2005). As expected, the 'true' knowledge of Starlets, as with other lap-dancing clubs, is limited to its staff and clientele. Understanding their intimate knowledge of this space is therefore an important aspect of this ethnography and something this chapter will develop, setting the scene of the club by exploring the various spaces used by the dancers and other social actors. Understanding the spaces in which the dancers work and sometimes socialise helps convey a more located picture of lap-dancing club culture by placing the dancers' interactions into the context of the setting. The significant role of space in a cultural and social analysis is something already emphasized by other authors (Cressey 1932; Massey 1995, 1998; Nayak 2003). Part of setting the scene for this ethnography involves describing some of the central areas in Starlets that were meaningful to the dancers and other social actors, such as the changing room, manager's office, main floor, dance reception and main stage; these areas are represented pictorially by the diagrams I sketched during my fieldwork in Figure 4.1 and Figure 4.2. In relation to the interior areas, these played host to a number of interactions between those who were, in one way or another, part of the lap-dancing club setting. The way in which these social actors interacted within these areas denotes the different meanings attached to the spaces. As will be discussed in Chapter 7, specific spaces, such as the changing room and main floor in particular, were host to 'emotional' and 'social rituals' which were fundamental to the occupational culture of dancers working at Starlets. In addition to the cultural significance of the actual spaces, the decor also played an important role: for instance in the creation of an ambience most likely to make an impact on those who use these spaces – on the main floor, for example, where the decor was used to help arouse and maintain feelings of sensuality. Ironically, other research in this area has often neglected to discuss the physical setting of the lap-dancing club in any detail despite its significance for social interaction, with the exception of Liepe-Levinson (2002) who includes discussions about location and use of decor in US lap-dancing clubs. This chapter firstly describes the location of Starlets and considers some of the public responses to this lap-dancing club. Furthermore, the interior setting of Starlets is explored, including the changing room, managers' office, main floor and dance reception.

The heart of the action: Starlets

Starlets was situated just outside of the city centre, hidden amid the tall buildings that frame the city, remaining inconspicuous and a mystery for those who have not intentionally sought out its location. Positioned some distance away from pubs, other clubs and bars, Starlets seemed out of place here on the edge of the city core; it is almost as though it was not meant to be part of the city's thriving night-time economy, despite the commercialization of this industry and all the efforts to make it part of the entertainment city (Chatterton and Hollands 2003). Outside the club, instead of the sounds of people engaged in the city's nightlife, all that could be heard was the drone of traffic from the nearby roads which carry vehicles in and out of the city. At night it was even quieter with only the occasional rumble of a passing lorry and the hoot of taxi horns.

Its locality is also reflective of how it has been negatively received by the local community,[3] though its location is nonetheless in contradiction to reports of lap-dancing clubs being a main feature of the high street (Object 2009). Starlets, however, was one of the first major chain clubs introduced to this city. Since then more lap-dancing clubs, which are part of the same chain, have opened, and although they are positioned closer to the core of the city, they are by no means distinct features of the high street. There continues to be unease about lap-dancing in this city, and dancers were aware of this, as Princess, a dancer at Starlets, conveyed to me: 'I don't tell people what I do. I say I work in a bar, otherwise they just judge you.' Some of the other dancers at Starlets, who were all perhaps reacting to the negative reception to which the club had been subjected since it opened, echoed this understanding of a need for secrecy about their occupation. Other research also acknowledges dancers' cognizance of the stigma associated with their job (Barton 2006; Bell et al. 1998; Bradley 2007; Forsyth and Deshotels 1998a; Grandy 2008; Lewis 1998; Maticka-Tyndale et al. 2000; Thompson and Harred 1992, 2003). Dancers' denial of their occupation, as reflected by Princess, is something that has been accounted for by Thompson and Harred (1992, 2003), who argue that this behaviour is a common response among erotic dancers as a way of managing the prejudice they confront. Stella, a dancer from Starlets, talked to me about the protesters who objected to the opening of the club. Rather than appearing distressed or angry, Stella seemed amused by the actions of the protesters: 'They were all outside with their banners screaming "SLUTS OUT" while we were inside in the warm, drinking champagne.' Bobby, one of the bouncers, explained to me how some of the protesters had tried to gain entry with cameras and tape recorders: 'Don't know what they thought they'd be getting. But we hoicked them out.'

However, not all reactions to Starlets have been negative; there were for example people outside of the industry who seemed to celebrate its uniqueness and sexually liberal ethos, imagining it to be a glamorous world filled with celebrities and businessmen making dancers wealthy. Jack, a taxi driver who occasionally drove me to Starlets, seemed fascinated by the nature of the job: 'I bet the girls are rolling in it. I think it's great. I bet you're drinking champagne with footballers every night.' Jen, a dancer from Starlets, found encouragement from her mother: 'She thinks it's great, she tells all her friends what I do, they're all jealous!' Both the negative and positive reactions described are an indication of the interest Starlets aroused among 'outsiders'. However, their understanding of the club holds quite different meanings from those who participated in this enclosed world on a daily basis during the time of my fieldwork.

Starlets was once a social club, where locals and members drank, played bingo and may have watched strippers on a Sunday afternoon.[4] The building was old, unattractive and clumsy from the outside; head-on it looked as if it was built from mismatched Lego, carelessly slotted together. There were several windows around the building which were blacked out by thick shutters. Above the main entrance there was a large fixed sign upon which the name Starlets was written in bold silver lettering. Two large glass doors marked the entrance, through which the reception desk was just visible. During opening hours a member of the security team would usually stand guard inside, directly behind the glass doors. The reception was a small area (see Figure 4.2), where some of the bouncers congregated when they were not on the main floor policing the customers. Scott, a taxi driver, who regularly drove some of the dancers, would, during a quiet period in his shift, often stand talking to the head bouncer Gordon, while waiting for potential clients. A receptionist sat behind the desk in the reception area collecting the entrance fees from customers as they came into the club and answering the telephone for 'busy' managers. When Emma was working in this role she often seemed serious and unfriendly, perhaps a reaction to the incessant teasing she encountered from the bouncers. Gordon in particular would often play practical jokes on Emma, which seemed to provide entertainment for him and his security team on the quieter nights. However, the jovial atmosphere was curiously halted with the arrival of customers.

As soon as a customer entered the reception area it was no longer a playful space; the security team's demeanour changed, they became watchful, their faces sullen. The behaviour and strictly scripted 'welcome' by the bouncers was repeated verbatim as customers entered. For example, before leaving the reception the customer was clearly told the abridged version of the house rules, 'No propositioning the girls. No touching the girls'. The protection of the dancers, as indicated by DeMichele and Tewksbury (2005), is one of the main priorities of the bouncers in the lap-dancing club setting. Propositioning the dancers for any romantic or sexual liaison and making unnecessary physical contact was strictly prohibited in Starlets. As far as the bouncers and dancers were concerned, these were the most important rules to which customers must adhere.[5] A 'look', which signalled an unspoken understanding between customer and bouncer, would follow the verbal warning. Between the lines it read: 'Don't mess with our girls; don't mess with our club and we won't mess with you'. The physical presence of the bouncer alone is an important way of 'notifying customers that boundaries exist regarding permitted sexual contact' (DeMichele and Tewksbury 2005: 549).[6] Gordon disliked the customers at Starlets and it was not something he ever attempted to hide or deny, referring to them as 'perverts' and 'weirdos', scowling at them as they walked past him in the club. This contempt seemed to reinforce the bouncers' power in the lap-dancing club setting, encouraging customers to abide by the rules given to them as they entered.

The changing room

> ... It's a Tuesday night and despite it not being the busiest shift of the week the changing room is almost full; there is the loud chatter of voices and an incessant hissing spray of canned deodorant as the girls prepare themselves for the main floor. There is an underlying mustiness in the air, soon masked by the aroma of burning hair product from those straightening their hair. Some dancers are sitting in their underwear applying their makeup, some are putting on their costumes, while others just stand around and talk. There is a general ambience of merriment in the changing room, a buzz of excited anticipation reminiscent of that generated by a group of girls preparing themselves for a night out ...[7]

When first entering the changing room (see Figure 4.1) it seemed spacious. The white walls were tiled with large square mirrors bordered with bright lights, the reflections from which provided the illusion of a wide space. Around the walls and beneath the mirrors there was a built in dressing-bench that stretched around most of the room. To the left of the entrance there was a toilet cubicle and separate shower. In the opposite corner of the changing room stood two four-storey cage lockers; most were locked and contained the dancers' personal belongings while others remain open and filled with lost property. Despite the sophisticated West End theatre design of the changing room, its physical appearance was rather worn and chaotic. The once brilliant white walls had, over time, become discoloured by makeup and fake tan; many of the lights around the

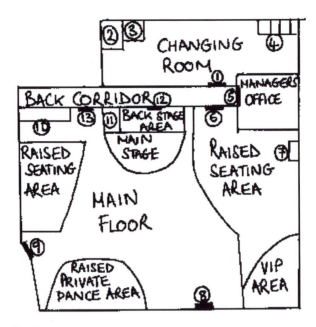

Figure 4.1 Starlets upstairs

Key:

1 = changing room entrance
2 = shower cubicle
3 = toilet cubicle
4 = lockers
5 = entrance to managers' office
6 = staff entrance to main floor
7 = DJ booth

8 = customer entrance to main floor
9 = customer entrance to main floor
10 = bar
11 = walk-in cupboard
12 = backstage entrance
13 = staff entrance to main floor

impressive mirrors no longer worked and there was a musty smell of cosmetics, fake tan and sweat that permeated the room. The toilet did not flush properly and as a result was often blocked, and the once pristine white plastic toilet seat was speckled with cigarette burns. Dancers' bags were scattered across the changing room floor while their costumes draped the randomly placed stools. Originally from the club's main floor, the stools themselves were a mismatch of leopard print and crimson and crudely contrasted with the worn dark-grey carpet, sticky from the mix of spilt alcohol and crushed bronzing powder.

The changing room was the 'home' quarters for the dancers, in the sense that it was a place in which they could relax, away from the customers and managers. It was not just an area in which dancers

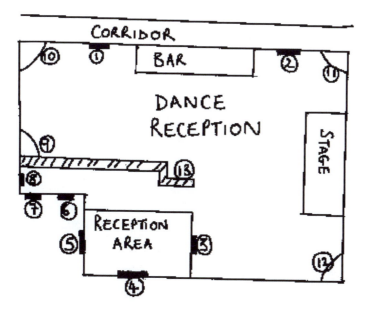

Figure 4.2 Starlets downstairs

Key:
1 = staff entrance
2 = staff entrance
3 = customer entrance to dance reception
4 = main entrance to club
5 = customer staircase leading to main floor

6 = ladies' washroom
7 = gents' washroom
8 = staircase to main floor
9, 10, 11, 12 = small dance platforms
13 = wall

prepared themselves physically for their work on the main floor and dance reception, but in a more symbolic way they were able to shed their everyday selves and begin the process of metamorphosing into their dancer persona ready for the customers. As the only area in the club intended for the dancers, they were automatically given ownership of this space. Most staff members and customers were not permitted into the changing room. Although managers did have access to this space, they rarely entered without good reason. Dancers took advantage of this, finding refuge in the changing room when attempting to avoid management. For example, at the beginning of a shift, some dancers would sneak past the managers' office and into the changing room to postpone paying the club start-up fee (initial house fee).

Price emphasizes the importance of this space for dancers and argues 'dressing rooms promote and sustain stripper solidarity' (2000: 14). Further to this, as suggested by Barton (2006), it is in the changing room that dancers can develop close and supportive relationships and where they discuss issues concerning managers and customers with one another. For example, following a disagreement with a manager or customer, dancers would use the changing room as a place to freely voice their frustrations. In this way then, the changing room was an area in which dancers felt they could express themselves without restriction, as they were away from the surveillance or interruption of customers or managers. In this way then it also offered an escape from the realities of the club. Further to this, the relaxed nature of the changing room, compounded by its 'lived in' appearance, created an ambience in which dancers were encouraged to talk intimately with one another about themselves, where comfort and reassurance was provided, making this a place in which dancers regularly engaged in 'emotional rituals' (see Chapter 7). For example, when dancers were unhappy or distressed, they would often retire to the changing room to seek comfort from their peers. The sense of ease dancers felt with one another was also manifested in this space in other ways, apparent from the liberal and open conversations that took place:

Charley: *Have you seen my top (pointing to a stain)?*
Phoenix: *What's that?*
Charley: *Spunk[8] (laughs). I was giving Gav a blowjob before I came out and forgot to change my top!*
Phoenix: *You dirty bitch (laughs)![9]*

This conversation took place at the beginning of a shift in the changing room where, at the time, most of the dancers were getting dressed to work. Despite the way in which Charley and Phoenix publicly aired their conversation, it did not seem to cause embarrassment or disgust among those present; instead many of the other dancers seemed amused. It was perhaps a combination of all these factors, which, as Barton (2006) suggests, made the changing room an environment in which strong bonds between dancers could be developed and strengthened.

The managers' office

... Gerard[10] was swinging around in his chair in the office, waiting to collect the dancer's start-up fees before they entered the changing room. I was standing behind Becks and Davina when he suddenly shifted sideways in his seat and spotted some of the other dancers sneaking

into the changing room. Clearly thinking they were deliberately trying to avoid paying, he called out: 'Ladies, are you not forgetting something?' The two dancers reluctantly joined the short queue behind me. As each dancer parted with her money, he'd write the amount paid next to their name that was printed on the sheet attached to the black clipboard next to the moneybox. Gerard always seemed particularly happy when collecting money from the dancers, especially when it was handed over without any fuss[11] ...

With the managers' office situated next to the changing room (see Figure 4.1), dancers would sometimes press their ears against the dividing wall listening in on any arguments or heated discussions taking place in the office. The door of the managers' office was often open at the beginning of a shift, with one of the managers eagerly awaiting receipt of the dancers' club start-up fees. The office was small, just over half of it fitted with built-in work units, above which were several shelves stacked with paper, files and miscellaneous items. The coffee stained workbench in a similar way was littered with piles of paper, files, odd coffee cups, glasses and car magazines. A desktop computer sat in the corner of the room with a chair in front of it; although it was intended for official club administration, Gerard and Ken (managers) would often be seen surfing the Internet. A strong smell of stale tobacco smoke[12] pervaded the office, impregnating the nicotine stained walls and the grey carpet which was discoloured and slightly sticky from spilled alcohol and other beverages brought in by managers and dancers. There were no windows in the room which was illuminated with a bright fluorescent strip light. The office floor was cluttered with various objects scattered about, such as promotion posters, boxes filled with fliers and other miscellanies. Across from the workbench and neatly positioned in one of the corners of the room were two filing cabinets and a safe on which sat a CCTV monitor.

The use of this space is complex in this sense as it shifted between workplace and 'playground'. For example, the managers' office was primarily a place in which business was conducted, including various administrative duties, and where dancers and customers were monitored from CCTV screens linked to the CCTV cameras that were strategically placed around the club, including dance areas, reception and outside the building surveying the car park and grounds around Starlets. This was an effective way for the managers to observe the behaviour of dancers and customers without being seen (Egan 2004). Dancers would sometimes speculate about the purpose of CCTV in the club. Charley once joked: 'I bet he [Gerard] sits in there [the office] watching the girls and wanks[13] off!' In an official capacity the managers' office, as already mentioned, was where dancers visited at the beginning of their shift to pay the club start-up fee, and at the end of their shift to pay any additional commission, known as a top-up fee. In a secondary context, when the office would sometimes take on a less formal role, it transformed into a more public, communal area, where dancers smoked,[14] drank alcohol and chatted with managers. Again, in a similar way to the changing room, the disorganized and cluttered appearance of the office helped create a relaxed atmosphere. It was, perhaps in part this ambience that enabled dancers to sometimes feel comfortable socializing with managers and other dancers in this space. The informal use of this area, behind a closed door, became a more private space. This is something which dancers at Starlets were aware of and frequently discussed. Leanne, for example, explained: 'I've seen so much stuff going on in there [manager's office]. Princess [a dancer] used to have sex with Gerard in there you know!' Another example was provided by Linda (a dancer), who explained how she had seen one of the managers taking drugs in this space: 'I walked into the office and saw the manager taking a line of coke'. The managers, who ultimately controlled this space, dictated the shift between private and public, workplace and 'playground'. In a similar role to that played by the changing room for the dancers, the office provided an escape for the managers away from stresses of the club.

The main floor

... Some of the dancers went to the office to see Gerard about the temperature in the building. At the start of every evening, dancers would sit on the main floor shivering. However, by the end of the night, after the heating had been on for some time, dancers would complain that it was too hot ... I was sitting with Becks and Candy; we were three of five people sitting on the main floor. None of the customers had arrived yet; it was, after all, a Monday night, so it wasn't unusual, especially in January when Starlets was quieter, for customers to arrive later. Deano [the DJ] was late again, and I had seen Gerard marching around looking frustrated, perhaps he was thinking of asking Adrian, the bar man, to step in for Deano again. This had not gone well with some of the dancers last time, as they did not appreciate the soft rock he insisted on playing all night. This time, however, the dancers were spared as Deano managed to turn up just before any customers arrived ...[15]

The main floor was situated upstairs in Starlets, directly above the dance reception (see Figure 4.1), which was on the ground floor. There were four entrances to this space, two of which led from the back corridor. Staff members, including dancers, were the only ones permitted to use these entrances; customers were prohibited from using these doors as they led to the managers' office and changing room. The other two entrances, both of which were intended for customers, were at the opposite side of the main floor, one leading to the dance reception downstairs and the other to the main entrance. The DJ booth was in the far corner near one of the staff entrances. A small lamp hanging over the booth illuminated this area; above the booth the DJ's face could be seen peeping out. The brightness of this area was in sharp contrast to the rest of the dimly lit floor.

The walls of the main floor were papered in a deep crimson and dark blue on which several large mirrors and monochrome pictures were fixed. Both the mirrors and pictures were bordered with elaborate gold or silver frames. The carpets were patterned in blue, crimson and gold, which complemented the colours running across the walls. Small round tables were carefully positioned around the room, surrounded by stools upholstered with leopard print, crimson or blue fabric.

There were three raised seating areas set around the edges of the main floor. Each of these raised areas had its own set of steps for access and was surrounded by bold brass rails; one of these areas was predominantly used for private dances and referred to as the 'dance area'. Framing the large open entrance to this 'dance area' were two large blue velvet curtains, which were draped to either side. The VIP section was situated on one of the other raised areas and faced the side of the DJ booth. Separating the VIP area from the other seating was a brass rail. The surveillance cameras were positioned around the main floor, watching the dancers and customers. The air was redolent of perfume and tobacco smoke[16], which became even stronger as the club filled with customers, dancers and other staff.

The main floor was the chief area in which dancers conducted their business with customers, offering private dances and sit-downs for a fee. It was also a space in which dancers advertised their performances on stage and interacted with the customers through conversation. The dim lights, the deep crimson and blues, and the general decor of the main floor begat an almost palpable aura of sensuality and sexual desire. The lighting in particular helped create silhouettes of semi-naked slow moving bodies, adding to the sense of mystery about the dancers working the floor. The decor and lighting in Starlets was reminiscent of other lap-dancing clubs nationally and internationally and was intended to create a sensual atmosphere (Liepe-Levinson 2002). It is suggested that 'three-dimensional landscapes of desire' (Liepe-Levinson 2002: 51) are created through the use of interior decoration, seating and table arrangement. This sense of eroticism thus created was used to encourage customers and dancers to interact in a flirtatious manner.

The main floor, dance reception and the public washrooms were the only places to which customers were allowed access. As well as the dancers and customers, other staff members, including waitresses, bar staff, managers, DJs and security all had access to the main floor. As a result of this, and the persistent play of music, warm dancing bodies and the steady flow of alcohol, it was one of the liveliest spaces in the club. The energy felt throughout the main floor helped transform it into a social arena. It became a place in which dancers not only conducted their business but also socialised both inside and outside of working hours. As discussed in Chapter 7, this was an important space in which the dancers both engaged in and experienced different 'social rituals'.

The main stage

... Not all of the dancers are equal in their ability to dance on the stage. Phoenix, however, never fails to impress both customers and other dancers. Watching her from the main floor, it is impossible not to be impressed with her skills on the pole and her floor work. She struts onto the stage to Christina Aguilera's 'Dirty' thumping out of the speakers, her eyes fixed on the crowd. Phoenix makes use of the whole stage during her performance, it is possible to recognise that she has had professional training as a dancer. It looks as though she has spent time carefully choreographing her moves, but this is not the case; dancing is something that comes naturally to her. Phoenix falls into a handstand against the pole at the front of the stage and elegantly glides her legs down into the splits; across the floors she contorts her body around into the box splits, remaining coordinated and in time with the music[17] ...

Along the back corridor almost opposite the changing room there was a white door with a glass panel which led backstage (see Figure 4.1). The paint on the door had become worn over time and was covered with black scuff marks left by the dancers kicking it open while passing through carrying their drinks, cigarettes and various personal items. Inside the confined, oblong backstage area, it was large enough to fit only five or six people comfortably. At one end there was a full-length mirror and at the other a large walk-in cupboard filled with wires leading to a large fuse box. There were two stools from the main floor next to the entrance of the stage. Dancers sat there, resting their feet against the opposite wall; there was evidence of this from the numerous scrapes, marks and holes left in the wall from the dancers' stiletto heels. The once white walls were, like those of the changing room and managers' office, nicotine stained, and there was makeup smeared around the full-length mirror. Dividing the backstage area from the main stage (see Figure 4.1) was a thick, black curtain woven with silver threads which glistened in the light from the stage.

Walking out onto the main stage, which was elevated off the main floor, it was possible to see all the customers and dancers scattered around the club. The stage was spacious with a single pole at each separate corner and an open space in the middle for dancers wishing to perform floor work. The floor was hard, cold, dusty and covered in marks from the dancers' shoes. The poles were brass, covered in hand and finger marks from the dancers using them during stage shows. The stage lighting, set above and around the ceiling, had been positioned to best highlight the sexual and sensual nature of the dancers' movements on the stage, in the same way that the decor and lighting on the main floor was intended to arouse eroticism. From the stage floor, smoke was occasionally pumped from the dry ice machine, controlled by the DJ and again designed to make the atmosphere seem enigmatic and sensual, although this did not always suit the dancers, who often remarked that Trevor (DJ), who had a tendency to make the most of this equipment, was trying to choke them.

There were two stages, the main stage upstairs and a smaller more intimate one downstairs in the dance reception area; however, the latter was only used during Saturday afternoon shifts, and sometimes for auditions. The main stage was an area where dancers performed erotic dances for customers in the audience. Dancers, on a rota, took it in turns throughout the night to perform on stage, each performance lasting for approximately six minutes, with two separate pieces of music; it was during the second track that dancers removed their tops to reveal their breasts. While the dancers were on stage, customers were not permitted to approach them in any way. Managers saw stage performances as an opportunity for the dancers to advertise their bodies and dancing abilities to customers. In relation to this, the dancers had mixed feelings about performing on stage; some seemed to love the experience, whereas others appeared to dread it. During a performance, a dancer's attitude to the use of this space could be easily interpreted. Some looked involved, attempting to dance erotically and connect with their audience, whereas others seemed uncomfortable and bored, avoiding customer eye-contact. Janine, who always seemed excited about performing on stage, explained: 'I love it. Getting out there. I could do it all night if they asked me', whereas Kerry made more negative remarks about the experience of dancing on stage: 'I hate it. I feel sick every time I go on. I can't wait 'till it's over.'

At 11 pm and 1 am 'the parade' took place, and as the DJ announced their names, the dancers walked around the stage, advertising their bodies for the 'two-for-one' private dance offer that directly followed. As the dancers queued backstage waiting to take their turn on stage, the small backstage area would become overcrowded. This usually solitary area transformed into communal chaos with dancers spilling out of the doorway; all chatting, laughing and sometimes singing along to the parade song 'We Will Rock You' by Queen. There were mixed feelings about the parade: some dancers seemed nonchalant, others despised what, for them, it represents: 'It's like we're cattle or something' Stacey once commented. Other dancers would joke about the 'two-for-one' offer, comparing it to those offers advertised by various supermarkets and department stores, which although it gave rise to amusement was nevertheless an indication of their being made to feel like commodities, a theme which has been acknowledged by other researchers (see for example Wesely 2002, 2003).

Dance reception

... This afternoon the club was busy with customers, by 2pm the dancers all looked sweaty and exhausted. At this point while most of them were sitting at the bar smoking cigarettes and talking, others were trying to get as many dances as possible before the shift ended and customers left. Stage performances were still taking place, but the customers seemed disinterested and were starting to make their way out of the club. Some were more interested in watching the screen than the dancers on stage; this was not unusual during a Saturday afternoon shift in Starlets. It was often the case that the football matches screened seemed to take priority over half naked lap-dancers[18] ...

Walking down the spiral staircase with its showy brass banister, from the main floor, on the way to the dance reception area (see Figure 4.2) it was possible to feel the temperature drop from warm to icy cold. At the bottom of the stairs there was a short open corridor leading to the reception dance area. In this corridor there was the ladies' washroom and gents' washroom and although they were intended for customers, dancers would often favour the icily cold 'ladies' to the single cubicle allocated to them in the changing room. Firstly there was never a queue and secondly this isolated area was an ideal place to snort cocaine, away from the risk of interruption. Although cocaine was not taken by all dancers the use of this drug was nonetheless quite prolific in Starlets, something which is discussed throughout the book.

Past the washrooms the corridor opened out into the reception dance area. A bar stretched across the back wall of this space, directly opposite the reception area. At each side of the bar was a door, both leading to the corridors that ran around the back of the building to the various staff areas. To the far left of the bar there was a long dark stage with a single brass pole at either end; behind the stage, its back to the wall, was a large television screen, on which football matches were screened during the Saturday afternoon shifts. In sharp contrast to the dimly lit main floor, the lights in the dance reception were bright. Dancers tended not to favour the lighting in the dance reception, as Davina would often exclaim: 'It's awful. You can see all my cellulite!' In contrast the dance reception stage area itself was always dark, sometimes making it difficult to see the movements of the dancer performing there. At the other side of the room, in each of the opposing corners was a brass pole set on a small raised dais on which there was only enough room for a single dancer. These were rarely if ever used, and became part of the club decor. The walls were painted red, and under the glare of the bright light the decor seems much starker than that of the main floor. Unlike the busy backdrop of the walls on the main floor there were no framed pictures or mirrors. There were, however, both a cigar dispenser and a standard cigarette machine mounted on one of the walls. The floor of the dance reception, unlike the main floor, was not carpeted.

The dance reception area, like the main floor, was a place in which dancers and customers could interact. Although the main floor played a more central role for the participants in Starlets than this space, it was nonetheless important. During Saturday afternoon shifts, the dance reception was where dancers conducted most of their business. Although stage shows were performed in this area during this shift, customers were also taken upstairs to the main floor for private lap-dances. The atmosphere in the reception area seemed less mysterious and upbeat than that of the main floor. The music, for example, during the Saturday afternoon shifts was loud, the lighting bright and glaring; the crowds were there not just to watch semi naked dancers gyrating to music but to watch the football. Often dancers would complain about the lack of attention customers paid to them, as reflected by Kerry: 'I went up and asked him for a dance and he told me to get out the way of the screen, coz he couldn't see the game!' In many ways the atmosphere was similar to that found in some of the sports bars that played host to strippers during football matches; in addition, during this particular shift at Starlets, dancers were permitted to collect money from the customers for their stage shows. The only time other than the Saturday afternoon shift that the dance reception was used was on Friday and Saturday evenings. However, during these last two periods, customers were permitted only to drink and talk to dancers; stage performances and private dances did not take place in this space on these occasions.

Conclusion

Rich descriptions of the setting in which this ethnography is based have been provided, forming part of the foundations on which discussions about the research findings can be built in the following chapters. The various spaces discussed in this chapter are central to this ethnography as they help locate the various social interactions that take place in the lap-dancing club setting. The changing room, for example, as a place of private solitude for the dancers, played a significant role in the bonds they developed between one another. It was a place from which customers and other staff members were excluded; dancers could therefore interact with one another freely and in some ways were almost forced to find common ground. The main floor and reception dance area, in contrast, although equally significant, offered a different meaning. They were, for instance, the only areas in Starlets in which dancers, customers and staff could simultaneously interact with one another. In these spaces dancers conducted their business but were also able to socialize and act out aspects of the lifestyle with which lap-dancing in Starlets was associated. The decor and various layouts of these settings, to some extent, appeared to influence the conduct of the social actors; this is something echoed by Liepe-Levinson (2002). For example, there was an air of sensuality created on the main floor, encouraging customers to spend money and dancers to engage in flirtatious interactions. In contrast, it has been suggested that informality and a relaxed atmosphere were encouraged in the changing room and manager's office by the cluttered and lived-in appearance of these areas.

Now that the scene of Starlets has been set, Chapter 5 departs from these discussions and begins to delve into the stories of the dancers observed in Starlets. The following chapter examines the different entry routes into lap-dancing and also explores the initial audition process women experienced in order to work in this club.

Notes

1 All observational data presented in this ethnography was recorded in a field diary between November 2003 and February 2006
2 This, in particular, refers to some media and film sources widely available to the public. See for example Dispatches documentary aired in October 2008, *The Hidden world of Lap-dancing*.
3 Local feminist academics along with members of the Christian Institute protested against the opening of Starlets.
4 It is common, in the North of England for social clubs to play host to 'Sunday strippers'. A stripper's spot usually involves a 6–9 minute striptease performance on a club stage.
5 This does not extend to managers and bouncers who are free to form romantic and sexual relationships with dancers.
6 Also see Hobbs *et al.* (2003) for a general discussion about bouncer culture.
7 Field diary extract.
8 Slang for semen.
9 Field diary extract.
10 Gerard and Ken are the managers of Starlets.
11 Field diary extract.
12 This is prior to the smoking ban in the work place.
13 Masturbates.
14 Prior to the imposed UK smoking ban.
15 Field diary extract.
16 Prior to the imposed UK smoking ban
17 Field diary extract.
18 Field diary extract.

Karen's story – Part 1: starting out

... I started dancing when I was 17... how I got into this was, I was living in a flat on my own, and I hardlies [sic] had anything. Not even like the bare, bare essentials like [a] fridge, cooker, carpets, [or] anything like that. My mum had just kicked us out [of] the house. It was nearing to Christmas time, it's really cold, I'd just got sacked from my job, and I had nobody really. So I started hanging around with different people and then before I knew it I met this girl called Judith. And Judith was like a friend of a friend ... I was in a shopping centre and she approached me and she was like: 'Hi, I was wondering if you'd like to dance. Coz I work for this 'Stars' dance agency,[1] and they like need some new people to work for them'. So I took it from there on, and I was like: Yeah I might as well, don't know what the hell I'm getting myself in for but I might as well try. So I started working for the dance agency ... but it got to a point where I thought: Oh my God, this is my life, this is it! So I thought: Right I need to make a choice. I don't think I was actually strong enough to think: Right, stop doing it, get an education, just get away from it, cut all ties. So I thought: Right I'm gonna stop working for this agency even though it was like supposed to be one of the best around here ... So I stopped working for that agency and worked for another one ... I guess the main reason was because me and Judith went our separate ways. I just realised after a while that she wasn't really that intelligent ... she's never actually learned from her mistakes and the reason why I actually stopped hanging around with her was because, she was like you know ... She turned out to be this little bitch really ... So anyway moved on and anyway worked for this [other] dance agency ... didn't

like it there so moved to 'Glitter Girls' [dance agency]. And yeah, the girls were a bit sleazy but it wasn't like I was going to be ... obviously this is my third [agency] in three years, and I thought: Third and last, if it doesn't work out here, then that's it. Then you stop dancing ... In the end I only actually worked there for three months and I met my boyfriend ... Really got sick of it then. I didn't even think of dancing. I regained a lot of confidence to be quite honest and got myself on the straight and narrow. Got a job. God! 'Straight and narrow', you'd think I was a drug dealer! Or a pimp! Jesus, what am I saying! So got myself on the 'straight and narrow' and worked like in a normal job, in a call centre, and I was actually fulfilled working and like making an honest living. Waking up in the morning, it was hard at first; it was quite scary, coz obviously since leaving school I only had like one job, which I kept for like a year. I worked as like a clerical assistant for one year, packed that in and had little silly factory jobs three months here and there, a month off, doing nothing and eventually got into the dancing. But going from that [dancing] to like [call centre] you know, [it] was quite nerve racking but fulfilling ... I like stuck in, definitely stuck in, never had any days off, [I] was there for nearly three and half years, I had 0.0 per cent sickness. I really, really liked it ... I felt so proud of myself, like so happy and I was like, I would never dance again, never. And then me and my boyfriend finished, like I'd been with him for years. But just before we'd finished I was still working at the call centre and I was like: Look! I'm really, really skint and I'm gonna have to start working at Starlets ... But my boyfriend didn't really want us to do it and he was like devastated, and he was like: 'No! No! No! You can't do this!' I was like the breadwinner, I was like the main one working and he was like doing his degree, and he'd packed his like part-time job in coz I said to him: You pack your part-time job in and I'll just support you, like I know it doesn't really matter, I know you would do the same for me. And you just study, you use your time studying ... I got in touch with my friend Stella who worked at Starlets, and I was like: Can you put a good word in for me? And I was so nervous, I was like thinking: no I shouldn't do it, I shouldn't do it! Went back to dancing anyway after all that time, it felt really strange. In a way I think I'd missed the sort of, dunno what it was? I think most people have, I dunno a bit of an exhibitionist in them ... I think in certain ways [when you dance] you are the centre of attention, you are the act, therefore everyone is looking at you, you have absolute control, so therefore it makes you feel good. Well it does ... I think if you've danced, you feel like, I can do that, yeah, the way I can express myself is through dancing ... It's *weird, it's like you can say something about who you are this way ... But I guess maybe everyone does it for a different reason ... God, I don't really know what it was ...*

Note

1 The 'dance' agencies referred to in this prologue are in fact stripping agencies.

Chapter 5

Becoming a dancer

... There seem to be many reasons for entering an occupation in dancing, as I have discussed in previous fieldnotes, but one thing I have noticed is that the dancers I have talked to about this either struggle to provide a reason or, over a period of time, when re-questioned, contradict previous explanations. I discussed this with Karen [a dancer], who claimed: 'I don't think it's straightforward, as in I need money, I need a job. It's hard to put your finger on.' That makes sense, and is perhaps why dancers give me different answers when I ask them ...[1]

The career choice of stripping was largely explored in the early literature produced in the 1970s, when the popularity of regulated strip clubs in the US was first brought to academic attention (Boles and Garbin 1974a; 1974b, 1974c; Carey *et al.* 1974; Skipper and McCaghy 1970). This focus, in one way or another, has continued to be an important theme within more recent American and Canadian accounts (Barton 2002, 2006, 2007; Egan 2006a; Forsyth and Deshotels 1998a; Scott 1996; Sweet and Tewksbury 2000; Wesely 2002) with an absence of material on the participation of dancers in UK-based lap-dancing clubs. Economic motivation has tended to be the overriding explanation put forward to make sense of women's participation in the stripping industry, although some authors have questioned this position and drawn attention to the actual complexity of dancer motivation. Sweet and Tewksbury (2000) suggest there are several types of dancer based on their motivation to continue to dance. These include (1) the career dancer, who dances primarily for the financial rewards; (2) the party dancer, who dances for the 'social' experience and will usually consume drugs and alcohol as part of this; (3) the power dancer, who dances in order to feel sexually desired. Forsyth and Deshotels (1998a) were the first to challenge economic explanations, despite the dancers in their own research sample citing this as a main reason for their participation. These researchers draw attention to the contradictory information their participants offered and argue that this can only indicate that dancer motivation is more complex than first suggested through traditional explanations of economic motivation. Indeed, there is a wider literature which demonstrates that economic factors play a less important role in explaining work motivation than is often assumed by both the public and by influential 'rational choice' theories of labour supply (Bradley *et al.* 2000; Duncan and Edwards 1999; Dunn, 2010). The research findings generated from this ethnography reiterate this clearly, and suggest that beyond superficial explanations of easy economic gain, there are in fact other more significant reasons for women becoming erotic dancers. This is something I have discussed elsewhere (Colosi 2010b forthcoming) and reflects the complexity of motivational strategies suggested in the work of both Forsyth and Deshotels (1998a) and Sweet and Tewksbury (2000). As illustrated by Karen in the opening extract, dancer motivation cannot be simplified, and this is something which the dancers concerned sometimes struggle to articulate. This often results in contradictory accounts of their career choices.

This chapter specifically addresses the motivation for the career choice of lap-dancing, through exploring some of the women's entry routes into this occupation identified as part of this ethnography. Further to this, the audition process at Starlets is also explored, thus developing a detailed picture of the overall process of becoming a dancer.

Entry routes

The entry routes applicable to the dancers at Starlets fall into two main categories: those which are practically driven and those which are emotionally driven. Within these categories there are several different patterns of choice. Practical entry routes include those that relate to economic factors, occupational association and progression (for example, moving from stripping agency work to lap-dancing club work) and flexibility (which refer to the flexibility of working hours). The more practical routes tend to overlap with the findings generated by other researchers (Boles and Garbin 1974a; Carey *et al.* 1974; Forsyth and Deshotels 1998a; Scott 1996; Skipper and McCaghy 1970). Alternatively the more emotionally driven entry routes include thrill-seeking and sexual attention. As will be discussed, what is interesting about these two categories is that most of the dancers involved in this research primarily expressed a practical reason for entering this occupation; however, what became obvious was that, beyond this explanation, the behaviour and subsequent informal conversations with dancers suggested that emotionally driven entry routes, were equally if not more applicable to the same dancers.

Economic motivation

The potential and desire to make large amounts of money in a short space of time is something that was clearly accounted for as an entry route into lap-dancing. More generally lap-dancing has been associated with a high income generation. This is something that other researchers have argued is a central motivation for women becoming involved with the stripping industry as dancers (Boles and Garbin 1974a, 1974b; Barton 2006; Forsyth and Deshotels 1998a; Lewis 1998; Scott 1996; Skipper and McCaghy 1970; Thomas and Harred 1992) and suggestive of the 'career dancer' identified by Sweet and Tewksbury (2000). Initially, economic gain was the most cited reason for entry into lap-dancing at Starlets. As Ruby explained: 'I think the money was definitely the main reason I got into it'. Similarly Jan explained that the money was a deciding factor: 'There's a lot of money to be made, even more than in stripping.[2] It's hard work but I'm here for the money.' Dancers rationalized this: 'I could be stuck working 9–5 for nothing or in here for less time and make more in a night than I would in a week.' However, despite the emphasis on a financial route, a high proportion of dancers admitted that making money in a lap-dancing club was not guaranteed. Furthermore, some of the dancers who emphasized economic motivation seemed to be primarily engaged with the social side of lap-dancing and making money did not always appear to be a priority (Colosi 2010b forthcoming). For example, Karen, in her story, suggested it was financial difficulties which led her to work at Starlets; however, despite this, at a separate time, she explained: 'you're going to work, having a laugh, having a good time, I'm not arsed if I don't make any money … just having a laugh, thinking I may as well just have a laugh'. Thus the complexity of dancer motivation is suggested in

Karen's changing sentiment about her work. Despite the sentiment of this statement, making money *is* important to Karen, but, it is clearly not her *only* motive for dancing.

Although the extent to which dancers adopted this route is questionable, this is not, however, to suggest that money is not a factor for women entering a career in lap-dancing, or that for some it is not their main motivation. Neither does it imply that dancers at Starlets were not in a position to make money, as there was evidence to suggest that a high income could be gained from lap-dancing, and that this is certainly a source of pleasure for dancers at Starlets:

> ... At the end of the night, spirits were high as it had been a good night for everyone, including dancers, managers and customers. Saturday nights are usually busy but tonight the customers seemed to be spending their money. It was, after all, the stag party season. It had been a busy night for the dancers. This was reflected in the general mood in the changing room, the dancers looked tired but were laughing and joking more than usual. Kitten pulled a large wad of money from her garter and started counting it; similarly around the room other dancers were counting large amounts of money. Charley was talking to Phoenix, her voice drowning out any of the other conversations taking place in the changing room: 'What a belter! I've not stopped all night' ...[3]

However, there are also periods in which dancers were faced with less financial opportunity. As indicated in Chapter 3, the money-making potential was dependent on a number of factors which can sometimes be outside of the dancer's control. This might include the time of year and the type of customer present in Starlets, as reflected in the following field diary extract:

> ... January is the worst month to work; this one so far has been no exception. Customers are limited, apart from Saturdays and even then they don't seem to spend much money. Not only are there fewer customers, but fewer dancers ... It's a Monday night and all the dancers were sitting around on the main floor for the first two hours drinking wine and playing 'who am I'[4] ... everyone seemed to be in good spirits, despite the lack of money, but this probably had more to do with the free wine Gerard had supplied and the fact he closed the club at midnight ...

Egan (2006a) conceptualizes the unpredictable money-making trend by referring to 'good night' when dancers make money, and 'bad nights' when they make no or little money. The unpredictability of money-making opportunities in the lap-dancing club again brings into question the reliability of the economic explanation offered by dancers, particularly for those who suggest that the money is something that continues to fuel their motivation to dance. For example, it is perhaps unlikely that dancers who claim to be solely motivated by money would remain in an occupation which they are aware is, in fact, financially unstable. It could be argued that the popular economic explanation offered by dancers at Starlets was a reaction to the social and moral questioning surrounding lap-dancing. Offering a financial explanation enabled dancers, to some extent, to neutralize the stigma associated with their choice of job by offering what might be perceived as an acceptable set of reasons. This process of neutralization is reflective of the stigma management strategies defined by Sykes and Matza (1957), and something which will be discussed further in the process of stigma management by the dancers at Starlets in Chapter 7. Furthermore, as well as offering dancers a means of self-protection, the use of an economic explanation simultaneously reinforces perceptions that women turn to lap-dancing out of financial necessity (Bindel 2004), presenting dancers as victims.

Occupational association and progression

This refers to those who began dancing as a result of working in an occupation closely associated with lap-dancing. For example, this was applicable to those who worked as agency strippers, podium dancers[5] and lap-dancing club waitresses. Where this was applicable, the dancers in question saw lap-dancing as a convenient career move or as an occupational advancement. For many of the dancers who initially worked at Starlets when it first opened, occupational progression was a key motivation. From my own story, described in Chapter 1, it is apparent that to some extent I fall into this category, having made the progression from agency stripping work to a career in lap-dancing. This type of occupational progression has been accounted for in the work of Boles and Garbin (1974a), Forsyth and Deshotels (1998a) and Skipper and McCaghy (1970), who have emphasized that association with, or involvement in, the industry is a factor in women becoming dancers.

Phoenix was an example of a dancer who had previously worked in an associated occupation; prior to Starlets she had worked as an agency stripper and glamour model. When she started dancing at Starlets, she was taking a break from glamour modelling and lap-dancing proved to be convenient, providing her with what she wanted:

> ... *Image is very important to Phoenix; in the club this is apparent from the costumes she wears, the music she dances to on stage and the dancers she associates with. Phoenix is very in vogue ... After leaving glamour modelling Starlets has offered her a similar lifestyle, something that stripping as an agency worker cannot match ...*[6]

For Phoenix, the 'lifestyle' differences between 'stripping' and 'lap-dancing' related to there being a higher proportion of wealthy customers frequenting Starlets, as opposed to the majority of the clients she encountered when working for a stripping agency. Like Phoenix, Jan had also previously worked as an agency stripper. After working in this capacity in Spain, on her return to the UK she decided to audition for a job as a lap-dancer at Starlets. Jan explained that the club had just opened on her return from Spain and seemed like a logical option: 'I was back and this club just opened so I went along for an audition. It was not too far from where I was and it was convenient.' Even Karen, as she explained in the first part of her story, worked as an agency stripper before becoming a dancer at Starlets. Her friend Stella, with whom she had previously worked at 'Stars' stripping agency, arranged Karen's interview and audition at Starlets.

Although there are different skills involved in stripping and lap-dancing, these skills are transferable; it is therefore easy and logical for agency strippers to enter a lap-dancing occupation. Further to this, as Karen explained to me: 'It's easy for dancers who have never done anything else to just stick at this type of job. Look at Stella, what else is she going to do? She's been stripping since she was 16.' The suggestion Karen makes here is that lap-dancing is not only a natural progression, but that some dancers do not have enough experience and/or skills to pursue other careers, thus limiting their wider job opportunities. The idea that the stripping industry is confining and has a tendency to 'trap' women has been previously articulated (Barton 2006; Maticka-Tyndale *et al.* 2000). This appeared to be true for some, although not all, of those dancers at Starlets who had worked in the stripping industry from a young age, and who had few qualifications or alternative work skills and/or experience to move out of the stripping industry with ease. Stella, for example, as illustrated by Karen, had worked for stripping agencies since she was 16; she not only lacked any other occupational skills but also had left school with no qualifications. For Stella, working at Starlets as a lap-dancer was a more attractive option than stripping for an agency; as she explains: 'When you're stripping you've got men touching you, the customers are all horrible, at least here you're safe coz the bouncers look after you.' Similarly, Alicia, who had worked for various stripping agencies for a number of years before working at Starlets, had expectations about how much better working as a lap-dancer would be: 'I don't have to go fully nude any more. I don't have to put up with men trying to touch me ... and the money is so much better.'

Other dancers started after spending time working as waitresses in the club; Jenna and Terri both worked in this capacity before becoming dancers. Terri was a waitress at Starlets for almost six months before taking up dancing:

> ... Terri had talked about becoming a dancer for some time before she actually auditioned. She was very friendly with most of the dancers and would often go out with them and the managers on a Sunday night. This close connection was probably what encouraged her to change from a waitress to a dancer ...[7]

In a similar way, Jenna, who only waitressed for a few months before becoming a dancer, also socialized with the dancers. When Jenna announced she was going to audition, her friends at Starlets were very encouraging. In some ways, becoming dancers made it easier for Terri and Jenna to continue to socialize with their dancer friends while at work; waitressing had previously made this more difficult.

Job flexibility

Job flexibility refers to the flexible nature of lap-dancing women at Starlets experienced while dancing and relates to the suitability of working hours and the self-management of shift patterns. This was often applicable to those who already worked in another occupation during the day and/or were university and college students. The association between 'sex work' and students is not unfamiliar and argued to be increasingly common (Roberts *et al.* 2007). Ruby, for example, as a college student, started working at Starlets not only for the financial rewards but also found the working hours were suitable: 'Because I'm studying, like, the hours that you do [at Starlets] are good, it's so flexible that you basically tell them when you want to work, and you can, if you've got an assignment due in, have a week off without any questions asked.' Increasingly, students are attracted to lap-dancing as a flexible occupation, and this certainly became evident in Starlets as time progressed; other researchers have also acknowledged this (see Spivey 2005). Dancers who also worked in different occupations during the day would fit lap-dancing in around their work schedule by working in Starlets during the evenings. Sally, for example, worked as a bank clerk during the day and as a dancer at Starlets during the evening. Other dancers, like Sally, claimed that it was the flexibility of the working hours that was appealing about Starlets. Emerald, for example, who also worked as a dancer in the evenings and a hairdresser during the day, explained: 'I couldn't fit many other jobs around my hairdressing.' Although there were some restrictions, as reflected in Chapter 3, dancers were able to choose their shifts and were not restricted to the number of days they worked. This was not only advantageous to those for whom lap-dancing was a second job, but it appealed to dancers who were able to fit shifts around their lifestyle. This route is also applicable to those who are interested in pursuing an occupation that enables them to live their lives without the constraints of regular working hours and shift commitments.

Thrill-seeking: the pursuit of 'excitement' and 'adventure'

This route is applicable to those dancers at Starlets who were drawn to lap-dancing due to the sense of 'excitement' and 'adventure' associated with this occupation. Price (2000) similarly discovered this connection between stripping and pleasure: 'A number of strippers suggest their work provides a sense of adventure, excitement ... unavailable in other jobs women tend to hold' (p. 16). On entering this occupation, the pursuit of 'adventure' and 'excitement' relates to preconceptions about the nature of the job and/or lifestyle associated with lap-dancing, both of which are often linked with various forms of risk-taking. Firstly, in relation to the nature of the job, by using flirtation and nudity to titillate men sexually, it has been suggested that dancers are inevitably exposing themselves to an element of risk by potentially encouraging unwanted sexual advances and/or harassment (Holsopple 1999). Secondly, in relation to the 'lifestyle' connected with lap-dancing, 'excess' in the form of drug-taking and heavy alcohol consumption in particular has been closely associated (Barton 2006; Forsyth and Deshotels 1998a; Maticka-Tyndale *et al.* 2000), reiterated in the findings of this ethnography. Overall, it has been argued that the dancer is placed in a vulnerable position by exposing herself to both psychological and physical dangers (Barton 2006; Holsopple 1999; Maticka-Tyndale and Lewis 2000; Wesely 2002, 2003). It is from the pursuit of risk in this way that dancers gain a sense of 'excitement' and 'adventure', in the same way someone who practises extreme sports might gain an intense emotional arousal (Lyng 1990). In this sense, this route then can be understood through Lyng's (1990) concept of 'edgework', in which the pursuit of risk-taking activities relates to thrill-seeking. Lyng (1990) contends that this intense arousal brought about by risk-taking is an effect of a conflict of negative and positive emotions simultaneously experienced by the person in question. This is something conveyed by some of the dancers at Starlets, who have accounted or displayed feelings of intense mixed emotions. For example, Melissa, before she embarked on her first stage show performance, explained to me: 'I feel sick but I'm excited. I can't believe I'm doing this ... They're going to see my tits!' Talking to Melissa I could sense her apprehension but at the same time she seemed excited. It is reminiscent of the accounts described by those in pursuit of an adrenalin rush from skydiving and other extreme forms of activity (Lyng 1990). In a similar way to Melissa, other new dancers have demonstrated that they draw a similar sense of pleasure from dancing on stage:

> ... *I watched Kate dance on stage for the first time; I was sitting next to the stage with Kitten and a few other dancers. As Kate walked on the stage her face looked expressionless as she stared over the heads of the customers. I could see her hand shaking as she gripped the pole and when she walked around the stage. Soon she started to get into the music and something changed in her manner. Kate was still shaking but she started making more eye contact with the small crowd, including the dancers sitting at the front of the stage. Some of the dancers smiled as they could see she was starting to enjoy it ... After she'd finished, Kate came back onto the main floor and sat down with the girls at the front of the stage, she was shaking but her face was beaming: 'That was the scariest thing ever. But I loved it!'...*[8]

This is something to which, during my time spent as a dancer, I could also relate. For example, stage performances at Starlets in particular fuelled a mixture of apprehension and excitement which seemed to produce an overall sense of exhilaration, something which, to some extent, continued to motivate *my* participation as a lap-dancer.

The preconception of risk associated with lap-dancing is echoed in media reports and social conjecture, something prospective dancers, before spending time in the stripping industry, might internalize. For example, Sarah and Julie, two customers in Starlets, who expressed an interest in lap-dancing, asked about the risks involved:

> *Sarah: Is it scary? Do the customers try and touch you?*
> *RC: Some try. But not all are like that.*
> *Sarah: I don't know what I'd do if anyone tried to touch me. I'd love to do it though. It must be exciting meeting all those rich men.*[9]

Despite Sarah's acknowledgement of what she considered to be the potential risks involved in lap-dancing, she nonetheless seemed to draw excitement from the idea of putting herself under threat. As well as feeding her curiosity further, her acknowledgement of these perceived risks appeared to increase her desire to dance. In a similar way Jane and Lucy, who visited Starlets as customers, previously having never entered a lap-dancing club, expressed the same expectancy about the 'fun' they thought could be gained from this occupation:

> *… I approached Jane and Lucy at the table where they were seated and asked them what brought them to Starlets. They explained to me that they were interested in becoming dancers and hoped to audition. I was curious to find out what had made them interested in this occupation. Jane explained: 'I just think it must be great fun, everyone seems to be so friendly', then Lucy remarked: 'And you must get to meet loads of famous people'. They were looking at me expectantly, as though they wanted me to confirm what they were claiming …*[10]

Some dancers seem to draw a sense of excitement from the thought that they are engaging in a 'forbidden' occupation. Leila, for example, who was from a strict Catholic background, explained: 'It's not the kind of thing that good Catholic girls are expected to do. That makes it feel good.' Likewise Dana, who was from a similar background to Leila, explained that her parents were not satisfied with her decision to dance: 'It's against everything they believe in. They probably think I'm a slut.' There was perhaps an element of rebellion in Dana and Leila's decision to become lap-dancers, and certainly in Dana's case she seemed to draw a sense of satisfaction from this.

Sexual attention

This entry route is relevant to dancers who demonstrated an attraction to lap-dancing based on the need for sexual attention. To some extent this has been accounted for by some of the earlier pieces of research about the lap-dancing industry. It was suggested by Skipper and McCaghy (1970) and Boles and Garbin (1974a) that dancers demonstrated exhibitionist tendencies. Further to this, there are obvious parallels between this route and Sweet and Tewksbury's (2000) 'power dancer'. Although Scott (1996) suggests that the financial rewards are what fundamentally motivate the majority of strippers, he also suggests that 'ego gratification' (p. 26) is also an important reward gained from dancing. In light of this, Karen, in the first part of her story which forms a prologue to this chapter, suggested that lap-dancing is appealing to those who consider themselves to be exhibitionists. She goes on to suggest that dancing, by putting her in the spotlight, makes her the centre of attention. This attention Karen talks about is sexual by nature, and is something other dancers find attractive about this industry. For example, some of the dancers at Starlets openly expressed an attraction to lap-dancing based on the need to gain sexual attention. For example, Princess explained: 'It makes me feel really sexy when I can see them [customers] getting off on me dancing ... sometimes you'll catch their eye and there's something there ... I start feeling horny.' Similarly other dancers have described the love of sexual attention from customers. As Leanne explained to me: 'I love it when you're walking out onto that stage, and you see them all watching you with their tongues hanging out. I don't care what people say, it does make you feel sexy'. Sexual attention was perhaps important to these dancers at Starlets, because feeling desired increased their confidence and self-esteem. Princess, for example, explained: 'If guys [in Starlets] didn't look at me like they wanted to fuck me I think I'd hate it. In fact I don't think I could do this job. It sounds stupid but I need it.'

Of the other researchers who acknowledge this desire for sexual attention or approval (Barton 2002, 2006, 2007; Scott 1996; Sweet and Tewksbury 2000; and Weseley 2002), Barton (2002, 2006, 2007) suggests that as well as the incentive of money, the level of sexual attention dancers receive can also cause them to break personal boundaries in pursuit of more attention. This was not, however, something echoed by the participants involved in this piece of research. Dancers would work within their own personal boundaries, making it clear to customers and other dancers that they were not willing to compromise, as Elle demonstrated: 'He [customer] kept trying to touch my tits! So I stopped dancing and told Gordon [bouncer].' It is important, however, to point out that there was, of course, some variation in the personal boundaries dancers set for themselves, regardless of the house rules (see Chapters 7 and 8). For example, in contrast to Elle, Charley, a dancer at Starlets, was known to allow customers to touch her. It was not something that was openly talked about, but neither was it something she ever denied (see Chapters 6, 7 and 8).

Some of the dancers explained that the sexual attention they received was addictive; Linda discussed this with me: 'You'll have nights when guys are saying how sexy you are and it gives you a real lift. It's kinda addictive. It gives you a buzz.' Karen also echoed this in an interview I conducted with her: 'It feeds like sort of an addiction ... wanting to be adored, wanting to be loved, just showing your body off.' Other dancers have suggested that this need goes beyond just gaining sexual attention, as Princess explained: 'It makes you feel in control, when you're dancing for them [customers] and you can see they really want it.' The sense of control a dancer feels over a customer is visible in the first part of Karen's story. The role of power between dancer and customer in the lap-dancing club is something that has been discussed by a number of researchers in this field (Boles and Garbin 1974b; Frank 2002; Salutin 1971; Holsopple 1999; Pasko 2002; Price 2000; Rambo-Ronai *et al.* 1989; Wesely 2002; Wood 2000). More specifically, Pasko (2002), Price (2000), Wood (2000) and Wesely (2002) consider the dancers' use of their sexuality to draw the attention of customers in an attempt to empower themselves.

The complexity of dancer motivation

Some of the examples of practical routes, particularly the economic, as discussed in this chapter, have frequently been acknowledged and accepted by other researchers as viable explanations for dancer motivation. In relation to economic motivation, although this was frequently offered by many of the dancers at Starlets as the reason for their entry into this occupation, this was often contradicted by the dancers' behaviour and by subsequent conversations, in which they offered alternative explanations for their initial entry into the industry. Further to this, rather than being seen as a solitary explanation, it is more likely that economic motivation is part of a number of routes simultaneously applied by dancers at one time. An initial example presented is reflected in the first part of Karen's story, in which she talks about how she moved from working as an agency dancer[11] to a lap-dancer at Starlets. Her motivation for entering this industry is complex, involving a combination of practical and emotional routes. For example, on a practical level, Karen was drawn to stripping, both as an agency stripper and lap-dancer at Starlets, for financial reasons. However, she also admits that there are other more emotive reasons driving her to dance: the need for attention and to feel in control. Despite this she still claims to be uncertain about what exactly led her to work as a dancer. It is Karen's tangled account of her entry into dancing that is significant for understanding stories of how the other dancers came to work at Starlets. It is also important to take into account the possibility that an economic explanation offers the dancer a way of legitimizing her entry into dancing and therefore plays a role in neutralizing the stigma associated with this form of work, hence why it appears to be such a popular explanation. Although there have been a number of similarities between the entry routes identified and those accounted for by other researchers, this ethnography draws attention to emotionally driven routes, such as thrill-seeking and sexual attention. The need for sexual attention among dancers has been explored previously (Pasko 2002; Price 2000; Sweet and Tewksbury 2000; Wood 2000; Wesely 2002) but not in relation to the *initial* entry routes of women moving into lap-dancing. Sexual attention is seen more as a factor which can fuel dancers' continued participation after initially starting out in this occupation. There are, despite this slight difference in focus, similarities between the findings presented in this chapter and previous discussions, in particular that the dancers' desire for attention is underpinned by the need to feel in control, and that this is closely related to enhancing their sense of self-empowerment (see, for example, Pasko 2002; Wood 2000; Wesely 2002). However, unlike sexual attention, thrill-seeking through the voluntary engagement of risk, has not previously been accounted for as a motive for women entering the lap-dancing occupation. Socially motivated reasons, such as the pursuit of 'adventure' and 'excitement', were also particularly significant in dancers' continued participation in lap-dancing (see Chapter 9 and Colosi 2010b forthcoming). Alternatively, it is the dancers' voluntary engagement with risk and the potential pleasures that risk-taking can offer a lap-dancer that are rarely taken into account. The work of Lyng (1990) provides a useful basis for understanding the way in which the pursuit of 'adventure' and 'excitement' through engaging with risk draws women to lap-dancing. This again proves to be a significant theme throughout the dancer's career and cultural engagement, for instance in relation to recreational use of drugs and alcohol consumption, which formed a significant part of the dancer's 'social rituals' in Starlets (see Chapters 6, 7, 8 and 9). Thus the pleasure derived from 'risk-taking', beyond being a motivational factor for the initial entry of dancers, has proven to be a prominent aspect of dancers' engagement with lap-dancing club culture.

Getting in: the audition

> ... Mel came into the changing room after her audition; she was still carrying her dress, which she was clutching against her semi-naked body. Davina turned round and asked her how it went. 'I was really nervous. But I got in' Mel confirmed. The other girls in the changing room remained cool about it and Davina simply said, 'I told you it would be fine' ... The other dancers started teasing Mel, Beth joking: 'We were all going to stand around the stage jeering and throwing tomatoes at you'. Mel seemed amused by this and returned to putting her dress on. Auditions were usually straightforward and it was rare for prospective dancers to be rejected ...[12]

Although dancers have expressed some variation in their experience of the audition process at Starlets, there are several similarities. Firstly, all auditions were held in the club and involved some form of performance, either on the main stage or the one downstairs in the dance reception area. Secondly, the prospective dancer was observed during her audition by at least one member of the management team. Finally, if accepted, she would then be asked to fill in and sign a dancer's contract (see Chapter 3). Most auditions were arranged over the phone; however, other women would visit Starlets in a customer capacity with an interest in becoming lap-dancers, and then enquire about auditioning which would be arranged there.

Jan, as mentioned earlier, was one of the first lap-dancers to work at Starlets when it opened. She describes, in the following extract, the original auditions held by the club:

> ... I went for the audition, and that was quite daunting because with it being a brand new club, there were loads and loads of girls there ... so I went along ... there was over 100, 150 girls, but they'd even been girls there before. It was staggered, during the day I actually done my audition, it was a chat in front of the house mother,[13] at the time, the manager, and a guy from another club, we had to do a little chat

and then do a lap-dance for just a random guy that they got while they watched and it was a bit like a judging panel. A bit like the X Factor coz there were three of them. They were sat there and they had their little notepads, the clipboards with the pen and paper, making comments, and you could hear the comments in the background ... I got the job to cut a long story short ...

In some ways, Jan's rather formal experience of the audition process was something I also encountered on entry into lap-dancing at Starlets. My audition was also carried out in front of a number of managers with clipboards, all of whom seemed to take the process very seriously. However, this level of formality was not a common experience for many of the dancers who joined Starlets subsequent to my own and Jan's auditions. In fact, the audition process gradually became increasingly informal, despite the contractual process becoming increasingly formal.

Prospective dancers were not expected to demonstrate skilled performances on stage during auditions, as it was accepted that some new dancers were not necessarily from dancing backgrounds. Because some of the women auditioning had previously never worked as lap-dancers, these auditions could be based only on the visible potential demonstrated during the audition, as well as the way in which the dancer physically presented herself. It was expected that the appropriate skills would be developed over time. The presentability of a dancer is important to the managers, and again is a theme discussed later in the book. Managers were keen to emphasize this by monitoring dancers' appearance throughout their dancing careers. Ken, for example, would spend time attempting to direct the way in which dancers dressed and generally presented themselves:

... Sandy walked into the changing room; her face was contorted with frustration. As she approached the dressing table bench she began to rant about Ken: 'He's a fucking wanker! He's told me if I come to work looking like this again he's going to send me home!' I asked her why and she explained that he was unhappy about the way in which her fake tan was applied: 'He said I look unwashed! Fucking wanker!'...[14]

The unprofessional and insensitive tone of the managers when approaching the dancers about their appearance is indicative of the wider negative treatment these women are subjected to as workers (see Chapter 10). This attention to the dancer's appearance was something Ken and Gerard made clear to some of the new dancers, directly after their auditions:

> ... I was outside the office waiting to pay Ken [commission], the door was open, he had a new dancer in the office and was explaining some of the house rules to her ... He looked disdainfully at her shoes: 'You'll have to get some different shoes ... it's important to look the part'...[15]

Within the established group of dancers, these women were often very vocal about the suitability of a particular new recruit to Starlets. For example, when Kristy started working at the club, many of the dancers criticized her physical appearance and ability to dance. Over the short period of time in which she worked at Starlets, she was criticized for having made little improvement in performance or appearance. It was on this basis that dancers questioned management's judgement and led to speculation about her recruitment:

> **Davina**: Have you seen her on stage? I'm not being nasty but she looks possessed.
> **Phoenix**: She can't dance and she dresses like some 80s glamour girl.
> **Charley**: How did she get a job here? She must have been sucking Gerard off.[16]

Most of the auditions were held before the start of a shift, many of those auditioning would be in the changing room as the dancers prepared themselves for the shift ahead, so quite often those already working at Starlets would witness the reactions to auditions. It was not uncommon for prospective dancers to appear anxious before and after the audition process, particularly those who had no or very limited experience of lap-dancing. In a conversation a week after she started working at Starlets Gina described how she felt nauseous during her audition: 'It was really scary, I kept wanting to be sick.' In contrast, more experienced dancers, for example those who would regularly work in a number of different lap-dancing clubs, including Starlets, as expected, demonstrated calmer reactions:

> ... Katrina and Mazy had never worked in Starlets before, tonight was the first time I had ever seen them working. Both dancers had come from a lap-dancing club in Birmingham, where they were regular dancers ... I was surprised by how relaxed they were considering it

was their first night in a new club. As they were getting ready to go onto the main floor they laughed and talked as though they had been working in Starlets for years, this caused some of the regular dancers to glare at them ...[17]

In a similar way, and demonstrating an exception to the rule as she had never danced before, Lisa illustrated the same relaxed manner directly after her audition; despite never having worked in a lap-dancing club prior to her audition at Starlets:

... Lisa was one of Candy's friends and had never worked as a lap-dancer before joining Starlets. However, I was surprised by how at ease she seemed, as she casually strolled in the changing room following her audition. She was not due to work that night, but talked to Candy as she changed into her clothes. Candy was asking her how it went and Lisa appeared relaxed in her response 'It went well. I'm starting at the weekend' ...

Following the audition prospective dancers would be quickly informed if they had been successful; on many occasions these women would start working on the same day. After the initial entry process, dancers, starting out as 'new girls', embark on a occupational but also cultural journey, in which, I argue, they experience three distinct career stages also known as status roles. These significant stages are discussed over the following three chapters.

Notes

1 Field diary extract.
2 Refers to agency stripping work.
3 Field diary extract.
4 A guessing game, where one person thinks of a celebrity and the other person or group have to guess who they are by asking questions that can only be given a yes or no answer.
5 This refers to dancers who worked as paid dancers in various nightclubs. Podium dancers will often dance on a small stage or caged area elevated from the main dance floor of the club.
6 Field diary extract.
7 Field diary extract.
8 Field diary extract.
9 Field diary extract.
10 Field diary extract.

11 Also referred to as 'agency stripper'.

12 Field diary extract.

13 Starlets originally employed a housemother who was responsible for the dancers, including the shifts they worked and the commission they paid. However, the role of housemother only existed for a short period of time.

14 Field diary extract.

15 Field diary extract.

16 Performing fallatio.

17 Field diary extract.

Karen's story – Part 2: working at Starlets

... What did I actually think about it [working as a lap-dancer) when I got there [Starlets)? It was a bit nerve racking ... like on my first day, there were these girls who came in [the changing room], Ruby and Eliza ... Within a few minutes they came in, I had my bag on the side; this girl with brown hair she actually moved her bag and went somewhere else and the other girl didn't even speak to me. I was like: That is actually really strange. Do I smell or something? ... I was like Oh my God! They [other dancers] actually think they're like It! ... I was like fucking hell who the hell do they think they are! But I thought: Just take it on the chin Karen ... I don't think I come across like a lap-dancer ... I think they're some girls who are like lap- dancer people who don't have to work very hard and they can just get dances, they're very, I dunno, they're in demand. I don't think I am the girl who has that look. Like to me your typical lap-dancer has long blonde hair, nails done, you know that kinda thing ... But like you do what you can, I might not be your 'typical' dancer but I still have to make money out there [on the main floor] ... it would depend what mood I was in, how well I worked ... you'd get there [Starlets] and think: Right OK am I gonna make any money tonight or am I not? Obviously you're like self-employed and you've gotta motivate yourself to dance ... sometimes it's [a] battle ... You're there and you try and psych yourself up: OK, right tonight is gonna be a bit different ... it's all in your mind, you pretend you've never worked here [at Starlets] and try and be enthusiastic, like you were the first time you worked. And it's like, you look at yourself in the mirror and you're like: Yeah I'm all right. But then you get out there [on the main floor] ... and

it's not as easy as you thought. Like you've gotta sit there and talk to them [customers] so it's actually not easy money. It's not money for nothing ... You've gotta contend with the girls, the whole thing, so it can be draining. Emotionally draining. Some people can find it really easy ... there's some things I'll do for money and some things I won't do, you know what I mean ... everyone has boundaries, depending on the person ... but I wouldn't do something I didn't want to ... Like I won't sell my soul ... I wouldn't have a battle over some money with another girl over a customer ... If there's like one guy who is say gonna give you £200 I'd just let another girl take it, I can't be arsed with that shit. I'd be like: You take the £200! Really seriously, honestly I'd rather go home with £10 than battle like that, but some girls are like that ... After a while of being there [at Starlets] I was like: I think I'm getting sucked into it more! Like the lifestyle and stuff. I'm thinking: Oh God Karen don't get ahead of yourself! ... One of the girls asked me: 'Oh would you and your boyfriend like to come to like a party? My boyfriend's got like some decks?' ... I remember going home and saying to my boyfriend: Oh do you wanna go to Kelly's party? Her boyfriend's got decks. My boyfriend straight away is like: 'Karen honestly I really can't be bothered, you go. I really actually don't want to go. Pretentious people, decks, oh my God' And I was like: God he's so boring. Like God I'm sick of this ... But I didn't want to be like her, like she's in with the managers and stuff. You know she'd sit in the office and stuff. And speak to them and stuff and a few of the girls would do that ... you'd see new girls starting and you know they'd start off really nice, sweet and innocent and within a few months you'd see them changing. Bit by bit ... they get sucked in by it all. Like they'll come in one day ... and they've spent £50 on beauty products and it's like oh my God can you afford that? And they get their nails done. It's like £30 for their nails and stuff ... they'll go to an expensive hairdressers and get their hair cut, and next they're doing lunch and stuff ... I'd sometimes think this is all a bit too much. Do I really want to fit in with these people? But before you know it you're there doing it, the lifestyle and stuff ... I think it was just a case of, well do you know what Karen: You're 25 now and you might as well enjoy yourself, if you can't beat em join em. Join them. It's acceptable stuff. Don't be silly. Enjoy yourself ... But then it becomes difficult to separate the two [work and lifestyle], especially when you feel you need a bit of excitement in your life ... I'd never ever tried cocaine before dancing. No, never ever. I used to think it was like a dangerous drug. I'd heard you could get hooked on it. I thought: Don't try it. ... but I'd tried speed.[1] Me and my mate would just have speed and stuff, now and again if we were doing [stripping] jobs where you know you're gonna be like a few hours away from home. Just like on the night time, and I'd probably do like pills[2] and stuff like, like when I went clubbing and stuff ... My friend who I haven't seen around for a while, Cindy, was working at Starlets would invite me to her place. I started going round to her flat ... And she offered me a line of coke one night ... I used to just go to work on a night and have a few glasses of wine, I never used to get pissed or anything, I would do all right and stuff. And then one day I thought: Oh God I can't just drink all the time, I can't, it's just not me ... Erm, so in the end my friend [Cindy] asked me if I wanted a few lines, well a line. I was like yeah why not. I'll try it ... and then it was like on a Saturday when it was really busy I was like: Can you get us some [cocaine]? And then it would just be a constant battle ... And then it was like a case of, if I work Friday I'll have some, well if I work the Monday or Tuesday and Wednesday I may as well just get some then really ... I'd be like: Shit, oh God how much have I done tonight? 60 quid, oh God I'm gonna have to give my friend 40 quid [for cocaine] and then pay my house fee and go home with nothing, it's alright I'm working like Friday. Tonight I'm gonna have to work really, really hard. And before you know it, it's like your lifestyle ... I think I was like using that [cocaine] as a way of escaping really ... but also for something to give me a little 'kick' ...

Note

1 Amphetamine.
2 Here Karen is referring to ecstasy pills.

Chapter 6

Learning to lap-dance:
an apprenticeship

Through focusing on the relationships between dancers at Starlets, it became apparent that there was a hierarchy of dancers, comprising three status roles (which I also refer to as career stages): including 'new girl', 'transition' and 'old school'. Other researchers have also identified dancer typologies (see, for example, Lewis 1998; Sweet and Tewksbury 2000); however, these typologies have been based on dancer motivation rather than status. The second part of Karen's story which forms a prologue to this chapter, in which she revisits some of her experiences of working at Starlets, is indicative of some of the themes to be discussed in the following three chapters and, more crucially, suggestive of the career stages identified at Starlets, as discussed below. Prior to this focus, the power relations *between* dancers have been underexplored. Price (2000) provides an exception by making some acknowledgement of the power relations between non-regulars and those whom she calls house girls (regular workers in a particular club). The status roles identified in this ethnography offer a unique insight into lap-dancing per se, but they also help place the different behaviours, adopted by the dancers, into the context of a dancer hierarchy and occupational culture. In particular, it is suggested that the dancers at Starlets participated in their own unique occupational subculture (Colosi 2010a), characterized by the different roles and rituals discussed across the three subsequent chapters. The status roles under discussion were acknowledged in various ways by the dancers, but were not officially recognized stages of a dancer's occupational development. Each stage involved a set of different and important experiences which reflect the lifecycle of the lap-dancer, all of which are explored over the next three chapters. Although the dancer hierarchy identified in Starlets relates to the ability of the dancers to immerse themselves socially with their peers and develop the necessary skills to be accomplished at their job, it is, however, more complex than this. For example, it is through the club's 'tacit rules', which were maintained and circulated among and by the dancers, that the different status roles were characterized and sustained. These rules remained unspoken, acting as an implicit form of knowledge of which the dancers in the club learned to make sense and, in turn, helped recreate. The tacit rules of the club were an important source of power/knowledge (Foucault 1977, 1980) through which the club, for the dancers, functioned. In addition, the 'social' and 'emotional rituals' in which dancers engaged played a significant role in enabling the dancers to advance through the hierarchy, which will be given a greater focus in Chapter 7. This chapter specifically focuses on the position of the new girl, as applied to a new dancer starting out in her career. In Starlets the new girl was the lowest ranking of the three status roles and a period in which a dancer learned to *do* the job, make sense of her surroundings and adapt to her new role.

The apprenticeship

... Tonight two new girls started at Starlets, Annie and Carmen. It was their first experience of working in a lap-dancing club and it was clear to me they were feeling extremely anxious. I approached them on the main floor; where they were sitting close to each other looking nervous. I introduced myself and asked how they were feeling. Annie replied, with Carmen nodding in agreement 'Really scared!' She went on, 'We don't know what we're doing really. We've been watching the other girls on the stage and they are all so good.' I asked them about what their first impressions of the club and how they found the other dancers. 'Everyone seems really nice'. However, Annie didn't seem as convinced 'We haven't really spoken to anybody but you yet' ...[1]

The feelings of anxiety and the sense of separation from the existing dancers, as depicted in the opening extract, was common among new dancers. This was certainly something I experienced when I first began working at Starlets; I was apprehensive about the stage shows, the other dancers, the customers and whether I would be accepted, despite having worked as an agency stripper for some time prior to this. Throughout the period I conducted research in the club, I witnessed many new girls step out onto the main floor showing the same sense of apprehension and awe displayed by Carmen and Annie. In her story which forms the prologue to this chapter, Karen also reflects on the sense of isolation being a new girl can cause. For example, Karen described how two old-school dancers, when she first started working at Starlets, were openly hostile towards her, making her feel like an outsider.

The title of new girl, which was regularly used in Starlets to describe new dancers, suggests an acknowledged divide between different dancers. These differences were apparent in the sets of behaviours associated with the new girl, and which help us recognize it as a definitive stage. In the role of a new girl, the dancer would be given her first introduction to the social and occupational experiences that were central to being a lap-dancer in Starlets. Part of this not only involved learning to readjust to a new occupation, but also learning about the work environment and people with whom the dancer in question would be expected to interact; this included customers, other dancers, managers and staff members. In many ways this first stage served as a lap-dancing apprenticeship, during which the dancer learned those skills needed to advance both occupationally and 'socially' in the lap-dancing club setting. On a fundamental level part of this involved learning how to increase the sensuality of her dance and improving her social interactions with customers. This was usually achieved through the informal tuition of and by the observation of established dancers from the old school and sometimes transition stage. This reflects the process of socialization witnessed among strippers by Lewis, in which she suggests that 'becoming an exotic dancer requires a process of socialization ... achieving job competence involves getting accustomed to working in a sex-related occupation ...' (1998: 51). In Starlets, this was not a formal process; the apprentice dancer learned by example and relied on the advice of others. In addition to learning the basic skills of lap-dancing, the new girl would also begin to develop an awareness of the tacit rules of the club. These tacit rules were important as they guided the lap-dancers' behaviour, helped create and reinforce the different roles in the club and maintained a sense of order. Finally, during this apprenticeship, new girls would start to form relationships with other dancers. In Starlets, these relationships were important as they influenced, to some extent, the progression of the new girl through the dancer hierarchy.

New and under scrutiny

... It was Melissa's first shift in Starlets; in fact it was her first time in the club since her audition. It was interesting to watch her and the other dancers' reactions as she entered the busy changing room. It was a Friday night, so as usual we were all struggling for space, and with everyone talking the noise level was high. Melissa entered the changing room and although many chatted, there was a noticeable reduction in volume. Most of the dancers were watching her, trying to read her face, sussing her out. I heard Kitten, who was sitting next to me, telling Candy: 'She must be new?' and Candy responded, 'Must be. She needs to do something about her hair though.' This wasn't the first time I'd heard remarks like this when new girls had started ...[2]

On entering Starlets' changing room for the first time, a new girl was likely to experience the scrutiny of other established dancers in the club; Melissa, in the example above, was no exception. There were perhaps two main reasons that new girls encountered this attention. Firstly, and perhaps inevitably, new dancers were seen as potential competitors, as Lisa confirmed: 'You can see them [dancers] checking out the competition. Others [are] looking to see what's wrong with them [other dancers].' The competitive relationships between dancers has been explored elsewhere (see, for example, Price 2000; Lewis 1998) and is therefore not considered to be unusual. Secondly, dancers would attempt to establish whether the new girl in question could easily integrate with the others, or if in some way she offered a challenge to the other workers and the rules they followed. Charley, one of the more outspoken old school dancers, would often make her initial impressions available to the other dancers by openly remarking, 'She's not one of us. She ain't got no chance' or alternatively show her approval by insisting: 'She's one of us'. Clearly, it was important for a new girl to be considered 'one of us', to quote Charley, if she wanted to be accepted by the other dancers and not encounter hostility. Ultimately, new girls, as far as the more established dancers were concerned, were on an unofficial trial period, during which they must gain the acceptance of their fellow workers. It was those with greater status in the club, usually old-school dancers (discussed in Chapter 8), who played a central role when it came to observing and 'assessing' new dancers.

Physical appearance was inevitably the first aspect of the new girl that was assessed in relation to her body shape, hair, facial features and clothing – both work and non-work attire. Physical appearance was one of the first principal talking points among the 'assessors' and was clearly reflected in the previous fieldnote extract in which Candy and Kitten criticized Melissa's hair style. This type of critique was not uncommon; established dancers could be heard remarking 'she's too fat/thin', 'she looks like a tramp', 'she might have a nice body but she's got a rough face'. Reflecting on my own initial entry as a new girl, despite only starting two weeks after the club opened, I was, compared to those who started on the club's opening night, a new dancer and therefore faced their scrutiny. I felt too pale, a bit too raw and unkempt for 'lap-dancing' standards, which as a stripper did not seem to matter. I quickly tidied myself up, cut my hair, got a few highlights and bought some new outfits for work; my change was acknowledged by the others who quickly commented on my physical improvement. Although critiques of a dancer's physical appearance were not always articulated to the dancer they concerned, old-school and transition (see Chapter 7) dancers would, however, sometimes advise new girls on the changes they should make to their appearance, with these more established dancers sometimes offering 'new girls' their own clothing as a way of improving the dancer's appearance. This often came into play when established dancers became the unofficial mentors to new girls, something which is discussed later in this chapter. Physical appearance is clearly valued in the stripping industry (Bradley 2008); it is argued that women's bodies are transformed into commodities and sold to customers in their performance (Wesely 2003). This results in dancers feeling compelled to offer themselves as physically attractive 'packages' to the 'consumers' (customers), hence their preoccupation with physical appearance. Karen, in her opening story, for example, described how appearance can begin to take priority, as dancers spend lots of time and money on their personal presentation. She provided the examples of dancers frequently buying expensive beauty products and regularly having their hair and nails done, despite the extra costs. There were a high proportion of dancers who underwent or became accustomed to the idea of having various body augmentations. Breast augmentations, in particular, were very popular with several of the dancers having these procedures after becoming lap-dancers, a trend documented in other strip clubs (Wesely 2003).

The dancers' emphasis on physical appearance in Starlets was perhaps further influenced by the pressure managers placed on these women to look a certain way. In relation to this point, Bradley argues that 'Gentleman's clubs promote an image of upper-class … Dancers must adhere to exceptionally high beauty and show expectations to maintain the image of the "fantasy girl" ' (2008: 509). Both Gerard and Ken (the main managers) would often demonstrate their need for physical perfection by comparing dancers' appearances and criticizing the way in which they presented themselves. In addition, it was not uncommon for managers to punish dancers, through fines, for not meeting their standards. In relation to this attempt to manipulate and control a dancer's appearance, Wesely (2003) describes how lap-dancers in certain clubs in the US are subjected to weekly weigh-ins instructed by management. Although these extreme measures were not taken in Starlets, weight was something that managers would nonetheless occasionally monitor. For example, Gerard temporarily suspended Sandy, one of the dancers, from working for being underweight; she was only allowed to return after reaching what Gerard deemed a 'healthy weight'. It was incidents such as this which deepened the dancers' need to monitor and improve their own appearances, something which was then passed down from the experienced dancers to new girls.

As well as making evaluations of a new dancer's physical appearance, the dancing ability and interactional skills of a new girl was also given some focus. For instance, established dancers would pay attention to a new girl's stage performances and the private dances she provided customers with. As well as assessing the level of competition, perhaps more significantly, observing a new girl while she danced allowed the others to monitor the extent to which she performed in accordance with the tacit rules of the club. Ensuring that dancers obey the special code of conduct held within the strip club is acknowledged elsewhere (Rambo-Ronai and Ellis 1989; Price 2000). Other important observations include those of the interactions between the new girl and a customer, including the time she spends sitting with a customer. In making an 'evaluation', as well as making first-hand observations, established dancers would sometimes question customers about new girls and ask other workers about the dancer in question. As far as the established dancers at Starlets were concerned, the way in which a new girl interacts with both customers and the other workers would tell them a great deal about the role she would play in the club alongside other dancers, as well as what kind of competition she might pose. In terms of the suitability of the new girl's performance, established dancers would watch out for what they called 'dirty dancing', an expression identified in other lap-dancing clubs (AEWG 2006). Although the term 'dirty dancing' was somewhat ambiguous in Starlets, more generally it referred to a private dance which involved some form of sexual contact. Examples might have included anything from sitting on a customer's lap, allowing a customer to touch the dancer's breasts, bottom or vagina, or simply making repeated contact with the customer's body. The process of monitoring and the identification of 'dirty dancing' are reflected in the following field note extract:

> **Charley:** *I was talking to Rick [customer] and he reckons she [dancer] lets the guys touch her.*
> **Phoenix:** *Never! Sneaky.*
> **Charley:** *I tell you what; if I catch her I'll be having words.*

What is particularly interesting about dirty dancing is that its meaning seemed to change over time. This was inevitably a result of changes in rules associated with both 'tacit' and 'house' rules, along with the influence and influx of different dancers. A good example of this relates to what dancers in Starlets called 'grinding', in which a dancer, during a private dance, would gently rub her rear area in a customer's lap. When the fieldwork for this project started, the majority of dancers classed this as a form of dirty dancing; however, towards the end of my time in the field grinding soon became an acceptable form of customer–dancer interaction among dancers. What is also significant about dirty dancing is the way in which it was applied. For example, old-school dancers, as is further discussed in this chapter and Chapter 8, were often exempt from this label, and therefore more often than not able to freely engage in what might for newer dancers be called dirty dancing. Even when old-school dancers were accused of dirty dancing this information was rarely taken to management or used against them. This emphasizes the power divide between the new girl and the old-school dancer. This type of provocative conduct with a customer, from a new girl, was not considered acceptable and could potentially jeopardize her position as a permanent dancer in the club. For example, it was not uncommon for other established dancers to ostracize those who did not follow the accepted rules or even report 'bad' behaviour to management.

Forming relationships with other dancers

Successful social interaction between dancers was important for a number of reasons. Firstly, it ensured that the dancer has emotional support in the lap-dancing club environment as trust between the dancers was established (see Barton 2006). Secondly, it enabled the dancer to become in tune with the tacit rules of the club. Through connecting with other dancers, she would more easily be guided by the behaviour and conduct of her companions (see Rambo-Ronai and Ellis 1989). Finally, it secured her role as a permanent dancer in the club; this was related to gaining the trust and respect of other dancers.

Those who isolated themselves found it difficult working in Starlets. Lotti, for example, who remained distant from her work colleagues, experienced a negative reception from her fellow dancers and was generally treated as an outsider. Lotti was European and although she spoke English well her nationality also seemed to set her apart from the other dancers. This sense of isolation this dancer experienced while working in Starlets was evident by the fact that she would often sit alone in the changing room and on the main floor. Other dancers acknowledged this divide by gossiping about her and not including her in conversations, an example of which was observed during a conversation with Candy, Kitten and Davina:

Candy: *We never invited her [Lotti] out, she just turned up! We couldn't tell her we didn't want her there, so she just tagged along. Anyway, she just kept laughing at weird things.*

Kitten: *Like what?*

Candy: *I don't know. We were just talking amongst ourselves and she just kept laughing. So I got sick of it and asked her what was so funny? And she said: "You are so funny!" I didn't have a clue what she was talking about so I just ignored it.*

Davina: *But then she took out this carrot and started eating it. In the middle of a [night] club! She is so weird!*[3]

This type of discussion was not unusual and was often aimed at dancers who were seen as 'outsiders'. Tiger, for example, in a similar way to Lotti, isolated herself from the other dancers; she explained to me: 'I'm not here to make friends. I'm here to make money.' Unlike Lotti, however, Tiger was far more confrontational, something which caused resentment and led to her being repeatedly taunted by the other dancers, some of whom used verbal and sometimes even physical forms of bullying. For example, on one occasion, Tiger was accused of stealing another dancer's customer; this caused an argument which erupted into a physical scuffle between her and Davina. Following this, Charley deliberately damaged Tiger's property including a stereo and some clothing which Tiger had stored in the changing room.

New girls, through observing negative relationships in the club and indeed from getting to know the different 'personalities', would quickly become aware of the importance of having positive relationships with the other dancers. In relation to this, Eva, a new girl, described to me her relationship with Charley: 'I was really scared of her at first. She's not the sort of person you want to get on the wrong side of. A few girls warned me about her, but we're friends now and she's been good to me.' Eva, aware of Charley's established role in the club, along with her threatening 'reputation', saw value in befriending her.

It was common for new girls to interact with a number of different dancers until they found a specific group of dancers they felt comfortable with; this usually occurred as they entered the 'transition' stage (see Chapter 7). In relation to this, some old-school dancers opted to mentor new girls in order to draw them into their clique; this was the case with Eva who was guided by Charley and Leanne. Beyond these workers being grouped by the three different status roles, inevitably dancers would also socialize with dancers with whom they naturally formed friendships, as Lisa, a dancer, clearly described to me:

> ... You've got your little cliques. Bit like school. You've got your pushy type of girls, then you've got your pretty popular girls, then you've got your girls that like, work really hard. I think it just depends on which group you fit into ...

Despite the formation of these groups, in the lap-dancing club environment, the three status roles took precedence over individual relationships which were based on common interests; again this is emphatic of the importance these career stages held in Starlets.

Making adjustments

> ... When I first started doing it [dancing], because it was something new, I don't know what I felt like. I just thought: oh wow this is like, amazing. This is like definitely what I wanna do like forever, kinda thing. I was only like 18 when I started, just before my 19th birthday. So I was still like really young, although I was quite grown up for my age, being 18. I still didn't really know that much. Like even when I look at photographs of myself I think like: oh my God, like, I looked like that!? I was just really young and see like those other girls starting and I think you've got all this to go through...'[4]

The experience of working in Starlets, for new dancers, was, as Ruby described, difficult to convey to others. The new girl would regularly be overwhelmed by feelings of excitement and apprehension; this was common for those who had never worked in the stripping industry prior to joining Starlets. Barton (2006) also acknowledges this is the case for novice strippers starting out in this occupation. In these cases the lap-dancing club environment may be far removed from anything they previously experienced. In Starlets, three areas, although with some overlap, can be identified in which 'new girls' appeared to be affected. The first relates to the atmosphere of the overall working environment of the lap-dancing club. The second relates to the nature of the job, with regard to income, partial nudity and displays of overt sensuality with customers. Finally, the third area relates to dancers' personal autonomy, by which is meant their freedom to manage working hours and the manner in which they were able to conduct themselves while at work.

Inarguably, the atmosphere of the lap-dancing club is a highly sexually charged environment (Brewster 2003; Liepe-Levinson 2002). Part of this was created by the decor of the main floor (see Chapter 4). However, beyond this, the sense of sensuality was more obviously influenced by partial nudity and the flirtation between dancer and customer. Every dance performed, whether stage or private, despite the meaning for the dancer, was nonetheless an act of eroticism which aimed to create a sense of sensuality (Barton 2006; Boles and Garbin 1974a, 1974b; Dragu and Harrison 1988). With the flow of alcohol and other potentially intoxicating substances, there was also a sense of energy and excitement which helped ignite the atmosphere. Melissa, as a new girl, commented, '… it's like being out with your mates, but not. You're making money on a night out type thing.' Ruby conveys how initially working as a lap-dancer can be a shock to the system: 'It's mad when you first walk in and all you can see are girls half naked. Looking dead sexy, talking and dancing … It's dark and there's R and B playing, it's hard to describe how it makes you feel.'

Prior to working at Starlets or in the stripping industry more generally, some of the dancers had worked in jobs such as nursing, teaching, accountancy, banking and customer services. Jan, for instance, before working as an agency stripper, had worked as a teaching assistant in a primary school. During an interview, I asked her how she felt the two occupations (teaching and lap-dancing) compared. In response Jan explained that although she considered both 'people-based', she acknowledged that they were very different.

In relation to these differences she admitted: '[I] never thought that for a minute that it would be stripping that I'd end up doing.' It was these distinct differences that prevented Jan, in her role as a teacher, from initially considering a stripping occupation. Although, like lap-dancers, workers from other occupations may engage in their own form of occupational culture, something, for example, which has been indentified among teachers (Hargreaves 1980), there are still obvious differences in relation to the purpose and nature of these different occupational roles, including the environment in which employees work and the ways in which these jobs are portrayed and perceived. Unlike teaching, banking or accounting, for example, like other forms of sex work, lap-dancing is still portrayed as a 'deviant' occupation which faces opposition and remains on the periphery of social acceptability (Lewis 1998; Thompson and Harred 2003). This is clearly reflected in the recent inclusion of lap-dancing clubs in the Policing and Crime Act 2009, which followed the high-profile campaign led by the feminist group Object, to relicense lap-dancing clubs as 'sex encounter establishments' (see Chapters 3 and 10).

The prospect of performing for a customer (during a private dance) was found to be intimidating for many new girls. Paula, for example, explained: 'I took my top off and just felt my face going red. He [customer] must have been laughing.' Although many of the dancers at Starlets claimed to be exhibitionists, new dancers experienced feelings of apprehension about taking off their clothes, something which is inevitable in an environment where the dancers are judged on their naked 'goods'. In addition, the amount of money earned, for the time spent working, could also initially be overwhelming. For many girls, the reward for 30 minutes private dancing in Starlets equated to £100. As Lisa pointed out, 'You get the new girls coming in, totally impressed by how much money you can make for such little work. It's not something they've ever experienced before.'

Finally, working in the lap-dancing club offers dancers a level of autonomy they may not have experienced in previous occupations. As Lisa suggested, working in Starlets and other clubs was as much about engaging in a sense of fun as it was about making money: 'I think dancing is more of a social thing than other jobs. Like I don't know many jobs where you can smoke and drink. You can get away with just sitting around and having a laugh. And half the time some girls have their mates come in.' Ruby described how she became engrossed in the social aspects of the job: 'When I first started it I did get caught up in the whole like thing, I used to go out drinking, ya know, meet all the footballers and stuff, on a night out and they'd buy us champagne and that. And I did get caught up in it.' Lisa also argued that new girls routinely had similar responses: 'They have silly ideas about the whole glamour side of it. They just can't accept the money, the drink and social thing is part of the same thing. You see them spending money, not saving … you've got to make a few mistakes to realise what you're doing and what it's about.' This is something emphasised by Skipper and McCaghy (1970) and to some extent Sweet and Tewksbury (2000), where new dancers have been found to engage with this occupation as a form of leisure, an argument I have developed elsewhere (Colosi 2010b forthcoming). In relation to this final point, it was through engaging in this social experience that dancers were able to start making sense of the lap-dancing club environment. Following a period in which the dancers would become absorbed by their surroundings and take advantage of the freedom offered, these women quickly adapted to the culture associated with this occupation and would soon start taking it for granted.

The tacit rules

… With like the rules, when I started at Starlets it was a case of working the rules out for myself and certain things dancers told me about … Truthfully, with the rules, it was a case of what I observed, what the girls have told me and the questions I've asked … the thing is, it's not that straightforward. Coz for example, it says in the club rules [house rules] that you're not allowed to go down on your knees (during a private dance), but all dancers do …'[5]

As was discussed in Chapter 3, on a very fundamental level there were official 'house' rules which managers and club owners put in place to guide and control, to some extent, staff members, but also to ensure the safety of the customers and dancers. However, beyond this the club played host to another set of 'tacit rules' (also see, for example, Colosi 2010a) which, for the dancers in particular, took precedence over the house rules. These rules not only governed the dancers' interactions with customers and other workers, but also helped bring into existence, shape and maintain the hierarchy identified. Rambo-Ronai and Ellis (1989) have also identified sets of tacit rules in strip clubs in their research conducted in America. In Starlets there were distinct differences between the way in which the tacit rules and house rules were presented and functioned. The tacit rules were not 'rules' listed as 'dos and 'don'ts', but were more nuanced and implicated by the interactions between social actors in the lap-dancing club environment. They influenced the conduct of the dancers, framed the relationships between these women and helped to create and maintain the different status roles. These rules can also be described as what Price (2000) refers to as the 'mutualistic ethical code' (p. 22). The tacit rules were almost like a way of life, and existed as an implicit source of power-knowledge, as indicated by Foucault (1977, 1980). Foucault suggested that there was almost a symbiotic relationship between power and knowledge, with a connection between the two always apparent, explaining that:

> ... *power and knowledge directly imply one another ... there is no power relation without the correlative constitution of a field of knowledge, nor any knowledge that does not presuppose and constitute at the same time, power relations. (Foucault 1977: 27)*

In this way then, the tacit rules as knowledge become an implicit 'truth', therefore simultaneously being a product and form of power among the dancers and within the club. Furthermore, it is clear now how these tacit rules played a significant role in the cultivation and maintenance of the subcultural hierarchy to which the dancers at Starlets belong.

The tacit rules evolved over time and were always subject to change, as ideas shifted and changed with the influence of different dancers moving in and out of the club. These rules were implicit in every aspect of the dancers' working lives, and central to the dancer's understanding of the occupational subculture evident in Starlets (see Chapter 8). For instance, these tacit rules underpinned the 'social' and 'emotional' rituals (see Chapter 7), but also dictated what emotional and social engagement was deemed acceptable and likely to be rewarded. In this instance, the reward for dancers is hierarchical, with the favoured social conduct, as outlined by these rules, leading to improvement in a dancer's status.

In relation to the superiority which the tacit rules have over official club doctrine outlined by managers and owners, there are a number of examples where this was particularly evident. For instance, despite the prohibition of sexual contact between dancer and customer, the tacit rules changed the boundaries for this type of interaction, as previously indicated earlier in this chapter in relation to dirty dancing. To reiterate the point made earlier, while it was not acceptable for new girls to make any sexual contact with customers, for higher status dancers such as old-school, this was judged differently. Where contact was made between an old school dancer and customer, this interaction would often be overlooked and go unchallenged. This is suggestive of how the tacit rules were influenced and somewhat constructed by workers of a high status, such as the old-school dancers, as they would often work in their favour. The success of these rules, however, relied on other lower status dancers, who had to learn to comply with them and gradually understand them as 'truth'.

This was a gradual process, and something a new girl would only understand over time, as new starters were initially only made aware of the house rules and were therefore unaware of the extent to which the tacit rules were at the heart of the club and its culture. As suggested in the opening discussion of this chapter, new girls would initially be seen as outsiders. It was therefore important that they eventually did adopt the tacit rules if they were to be accepted in the long term. The need to comply by sets of rules in order to fit in and not be labelled an 'outsider' is reflected comprehensively by Becker (1963). The role of the mentor figure, discussed in the following section, was important in providing the new girl with her first meaningful introduction to these rules. Through following and watching the mentor's conduct the apprentice would develop some understanding of how to work and socialize in the lap-dancing club.

Developing dancing skills

> ... I remember watching the other girls, looking to see who was doing the most dances. So I took note what was working for other girls ... I do think you do learn a lot from other dancers, but then again when you do start getting into it, you work out what works for you ...[6]

There are many skills involved in being a successful lap-dancer; for a dancer to be competent at her job in Starlets it was important for her to understand how to interact with customers, perform both private and stage dances and be able to manage their appearance. Although a proportion of dancers entered the lap-dancing club with some previous experience of dancing as podium dancers in nightclubs or indeed working as agency strippers, lap-dancing involves a new set of skills. As Jan explains:

*It's easier being a stripper because the job is already set up for you …
You're not actually involved with the crowd, you don't have to speak
to any of them. You don't have to please any of them … lap-dancing's
different coz you've got to sit and talk to them [customers] first, and
then you're not guaranteed your money, if they don't want a dance.*[8]

Therefore, even for those who had previously worked as erotic
dancers, it was a new learning process. As suggested earlier in
this chapter, part of the learning process new girls experience was
aided by informal tuition and by observing other more established
dancers. This kind of tuition was important on the dancer's initial
entry into this occupation and became less necessary after she moved
from being the new girl to the transition stage. The tuition of a new
girl usually followed when a more established dancer befriended
her then acted as her unofficial mentor. As was discussed earlier in
this chapter, crucial areas, including appearance, dancing ability and
interaction, were all informally assessed by more established dancers
when a new girl first started dancing. This informal assessment was
useful for the old-school dancer tutoring the new girl, as from this
she could identify the areas in which improvements were required.
As mentioned earlier, when Eva first started working at Starlets, both
Charley and Leanne befriended her and both acted as her 'mentors'. It
was under Leanne's tuition in particular that Eva learned some of her
basic stage skills. In relation to this, during an informal conversation
with Eva, I asked her how she felt about the stage shows:

> **Eva:** *I was really terrified at first. But I feel more confident and
> Leanne's helped me with the pole.*
> **RC:** *Do you think you'd have picked dancing up as quickly without
> her help?*
> **Eva:** *Probably not. She taught me to hang off the pole but I can't
> dance like her. She's amazing.*[8]

In relation to private dances, sometimes the 'mentor' would ask her
'apprentice' to sit and watch while she performed for a customer;
others would demonstrate by actually dancing for the new girl
under tuition. This form of tuition is also suggested by Lewis, who
explains: 'Learning occurs through observing and interacting with
strip club employees, especially more experienced dancers' (1998: 65).
This was also highlighted earlier in this chapter. Price (2000) similarly
acknowledges that most new strippers learn to do their job by being
'taken under the wing' of a more experienced worker. Beyond

learning the skill of dancing both privately and for stage shows, new girls must start to understand the art of flirtation. Learning how to interact with customers could be initially difficult for the new girl to grasp. Simone, on her first night at Starlets, explained to me how she was feeling about this part of her dancing experience:

> **Simone:** *I feel really stupid just going up to them. I just go all quiet. They just look at me as if I'm weird.*
> **RC:** *Do you ask them for a dance?*
> **Simone:** *Not at first, I say hello and then don't know what to say.*
> **RC:** *Have you asked any of the other girls what you could do?*
> **Simone:** *Yes, but it's not easy making conversation with a complete stranger.*[9]

Through watching and listening to others, the new girl could gain a basic understanding of how to interact with a customer, for example how to approach and make initial conversation with her clients. Ruby in relation to this suggests: 'It wasn't until I started watching other dancers who'd been doing it for ages, that I started to understand what I had to do.'

Some new girls were naturally better at interacting with customers than others, regardless of whether or not they were from an erotic dance background, as demonstrated in the following extract taken from a conversation in the changing room of Starlets between Leanne and Eva, only a few weeks after Eva started working:

> **Leanne:** *You seem to be doing well tonight.*
> **Eva:** *It's been really good. I've just got a sit-down with that computer guy.*
> **Leanne:** *Eddie! He's really picky.*
> **Eva:** *Well I just batted the eyelashes and put on the charm.*
> **Leanne:** *Good for you.*[10]

Although some dancers were naturally more flirtatious than others, this did not ensure the dancer was equipped to hustle[11] with the customer, although in Eva's case her flirting was successful. The skill of hustling was something a dancer would develop over time and it was not until she reached the transition stage that she started to perfect her technique (see Chapter 7).

Finally, in relation to the dancer's appearance, as has already been suggested earlier in this chapter, new girls were often censured for the way in which they presented themselves. Paula, for example, was criticized in a number of areas, including her makeup, clothes and hairstyle. Leanne explained: 'She's starting to look better now she's bought a new dress, and I showed her how to put her make-up on.'

These important lessons are all guided by the tacit rules of the club; it was therefore necessary for new girls to learn by example from established dancers. In relation to these rules, as well as learning the correct form of conduct, it was equally important for dancers to understand behaviour that was considered *unacceptable*. The fluidity of these tacit rules, however, made them complex and difficult to define. It was for this reason that new girls may at times have struggled to make sense of them. With this in mind, it was not unusual for mistakes to be made; this was common with regard to customer–dancer interaction. For example, private dances could become too intimate and the new girl in question could be accused of dirty dancing. During dancer–customer interaction it was also common for new girls to break the three-track rule.[12] However, by being corrected by other dancers, it was rare the same mistakes were made again, unless the dancer chose to deliberately challenge the rules and, in doing so, the other dancers.

On a fundamental level, what has been demonstrated is how through the careful observation of already established dancers and by being receptive to their guidance, the new girl would learn how to dance and interact with customers. However, beyond this she would become familiar with the club's tacit rules and the importance of social interaction with other dancers, which provided the new girl with the necessary skills, knowledge and outlook to progress to the transition stage. Although important fundamental knowledge would be imparted to the new girl, she would develop a more meaningful understanding of the club and its conduct during the next stage of transition, a period in which she would truly experience her job as a lap-dancer. While there was no definitive time limit to which a dancer would be classed as a new girl, there was inevitably time variation, with her hierarchical advancement being dependent upon how quickly she actually formed relationships with other dancers and developed the necessary basic knowledge discussed in this chapter. Sandy, an established dancer, once commented: 'One day you're this new girl and the next it's like your part of the furniture.' This indicates that, as 'invisible' stages, the dancers themselves were often unaware of the progression they were making through the hierarchy, suggesting the subtle ways in which changes occurred within the club. The following chapter will explore the transition stage dancers at Starlets experienced before reaching the ultimate old-school status.

Notes

1 Field diary extract.
2 Field diary extract.
3 Field diary extract.
4 Extract from an interview with a dancer named Ruby.
5 Extract taken from an interview with a dancer named Stacey.
6 Extract from interview with a dancer named Lisa.
7 Extract from an interview.
8 Field diary extract.
9 Field diary extract.
10 Field diary extract.
11 Persuade a customer to spend his money on private dances or sit-downs.
12 Dancers are permitted to sit with a customer for no longer than three songs without dancing for him or arranging a sit down.

Chapter 7

Experiencing lap-dancing

...It was really interesting to observe how Kat had changed since she began working at Starlets six months ago. Initially she was quiet and kept herself to herself. In fact I always thought it was difficult to make conversation with her. A few months ago she started hanging around with Davina and suddenly became very confident. Kat seems more comfortable with the other dancers and the customers. In the past I had never seen her sitting chatting to customers; however, recently Kat appears to have acquired a few regulars ...[1]

As suggested in the opening extract, Kat as a new girl lacked the confidence and skills to be successful with customers; however, as time progressed, changes in the way she conducted herself became evident, signalling a new phase as a lap-dancer. In relation to this, it was apparent that after completing a successful apprenticeship as a new girl, dancers at Starlets entered a 'transition' stage. In many ways this stage was about learning to become an established dancer. It was referred to as a transition stage as it was a period in which the dancer was considered neither new girl nor old school, and although seemingly less distinctive than the other status roles, it was particularly significant, being a period in which a dancer was subjected to the full and intense experience of being a lap-dancer. It was a time in which dancers would start to develop more advanced skills, both socially, within the context of lap-dancing club 'culture', and occupationally, evident in the development of dancing techniques, before reaching old-school status. More specifically, transition was an experimental stage in which a dancer would work on perfecting her skills as a performer and in further improving her interaction with customers. It was also a period when relationships with other dancers improved, becoming more stable as these women would engage intensely with 'social' and 'emotional rituals'. In addition, it was during this stage that dancers became more aware of the emotional strain of dancing, a common theme identified in the lap-dancing club (see, for example, Barton 2002; Frank 1998), but would learn to deal with these emotional and psychological pressures of working in this role. Finally, it was in this period of transition that the dancer would make more sense of the tacit rules of her working environment. By focusing on this crucial stage, this chapter therefore explores the core experiences of being a lap-dancer. More specifically it considers the ways in which dancers at Starlets developed their 'hustling' skills with customers through the adoption of a number of 'dance techniques'. Furthermore, the way in which dancers' strengthened their relationships with one another through engaging in various 'social' and 'emotional' rituals is also considered. This is along with the dancers' experience of both the stigma and work-related emotional and psychological pressures of lap-dancing.

The cynical performance

> ... Like you'll say to a guy, like you'll sit and chat to them and be 'You coming for a dance? Yes?' and you'll like nod your head, you know different sales [techniques] ... things like, the way you approach a guy, the way you walk over to a guy, the way you smile, it's just like different flirting things that you do ... it's just we have different personalities and whatever suits you works for you ...[2]

As discussed in the previous chapter, the new girl begins to learn how to flirt and interact with customers. However, it would not be until reaching the transition stage that she would begin to develop more advanced skills. During this stage the dancer would attempt to execute more sophisticated 'hustling' techniques in order to make money.[3] Using a dramaturgical analysis, in which 'actors play roles, giving interpretation of the script' and further 'engage in strategic behaviour as they manage their presentation of self' (Turner and Stets 2005: 26), it is possible to make sense of the 'performances' and 'techniques' dancers present to customers. Other authors have also used this analysis to emphasize the feigned relationships between dancers and customers (see, for example, Enck and Preston 1988;

Pasko 2002). Goffman (1959) first developed this framework through his work on 'impression management', conceptualizing the different performances offered by social actors. Using his notion of 'cynical performer', in which a performer has no belief in their performance and may deliberately act to delude their audience (p. 29), dancers at Starlets, in their use of various strategies to gain financially, can be described in this vain. Goffman (1959) describes what he calls 'front' as the 'expressive equipment' used in the performance, which includes 'setting', 'appearance' and 'manner', the 'setting' in this instance being the club, the stage, the different dance areas, seating, lighting, the decor, as discussed in Chapter 4. However, in this discussion, it is the 'appearance' and 'manner' that are particularly important in understanding the dancers' 'cynical performances'. While 'appearance' refers to the clothes a dancer wears and the general way she styles herself as well as her 'fixed' physical appearance, 'manner', on the other hand, refers to the way in which she acts and presents herself to the customer. The use of dancer techniques have in the past been accounted for by other researchers, such as Bell *et al.* (1998), Boles and Garbin (1974c), Enck and Preston (1988) and Wood (2000). As suggested by Ruby in the opening extract of this section, different dancers at Starlets were inevitably attracted to and would use different methods. Such variation in the techniques used was perhaps dependent on two main factors: firstly, the dancers they were at the time personally associated with and therefore influenced by; and secondly, the dancer's personal boundaries, in other words what she was willing to do in order to ensure a financial transaction. This contradicts Barton's (2006) claim that 'The more money clients offer a dancer, the more temptation it is to stretch her boundaries' (p. 95). Although some dancers in Starlets were more willing than others to make sexual contact with customers, there was no indication that dancers were crossing personal boundaries to do so.

Among the four techniques identified in Starlets, there is some overlap, despite the different processes apparent for each. Firstly, they often relied on the feigning of emotions (also see Barton 2006; Boles and Garbin 1974c; Enck and Preston 1988; Brewster 2003; Hochschild 1983), portraying dancers as sexually available as well as vulnerable. Secondly, these techniques manipulated the customer's emotions in order to extract money; the manipulation of customers by dancers in this way is also accounted for elsewhere (Bell *et al.* 1998; Boles and Garbin 1974c; Enck and Preston 1988). It is the feigning and insincerity of emotions as a method of manipulation that leads these performances to be described as 'cynical performances' (Goffman 1959).

The ego boost

This strategy involves the use of excessive flirting to maintain the customer's interest; the aim is to make the customer feel special and wanted, a general tactic of strippers also suggested by Rambo-Ronai and Ellis (1989). Verbally the dancer in question would attempt to flatter the customer; typical examples included: 'I can't believe you haven't got a girlfriend!'; 'You're the nicest guy in here'; 'You're not like all the other customers'. Cindy, one of the dancers at Starlets, used to joke about how she would make customers feel important by becoming 'involved' during conversations: 'I just always look like I'm fascinated by what they're saying. They're talking and I'm going: Oh really! Yeah that's really interesting! When really I'm not even listening to anything they're telling me.' Similarly other dancers would encourage customers to talk about themselves and give the impression of being interested in the topic of conversation. I witnessed this first hand, during my fieldwork, when I was sitting with another dancer, Princess, and two customers. Watching her method of interaction, it became clear how focused she was, her eyes fixed on her customer's every move, agreeing and sounding interested whenever it seemed appropriate. Her technique was successful as Princess danced for the customer several times during that particular shift.

The bimbo act

This was a popular strategy employed by many of the dancers, sometimes in combination with a technique called the 'empty promise' (see below). In a similar way to the 'ego boost', it aimed to make customers feel superior and portray the dancer as vulnerable, leading the customer to feel in control. This is of course untrue, and it was in fact the dancer who was in control during most of these enactments (Bell *et al.* 1998; Boles and Garbin 1974c; Enck and Preston 1988; Deshotels and Forsyth 2005).

The 'bimbo act' involved a 'manner' (Goffman 1959) of excessive flirting, including displays of playful and almost 'childlike' gestures. These might included hair flicking, enlarging eyes, pouting, making physical contact with the customer during conversations and giggling; as part of this technique dancers would 'dumb down' for customers. The act was enhanced by the dancer's appearance – bleached hair, hair extensions and sometimes breast enhancements. In relation to this Wesely (2003) argues that lap-dancers are encouraged to look like 'Barbie Dolls' by managers and club owners. Becks, one of the old-school dancers, claimed to put on a 'bimbo act' during her interactions with customers: 'I just look all wide eyed and giggle when they say anything. They think I'm thick as shit. But that's what they want.'

The empty promise

As previously mentioned, the 'manner' (Goffman 1959) displayed in this approach resembles that of those using the 'bimbo act' technique, although flirting would often be more intense. Examples include blowing or whispering in the customer's ear; however, more direct sexual contact was also observed during private dances. For example, some dancers would allow customers to make contact with their inner thighs, breasts, bottom and crotch. The 'empty promise' involved making the customer believe he was going to have sex or go on a date with the dancer in question. Adele described how she achieved this: 'I just tell him [the customer] I'll meet him back at the hotel and then never show up ... if he comes in again I just make some excuse up and the same trick works again.' The fact that he would often return to the club after Adele frequently 'stood him up' suggests not only the level of control she had over him through manipulating him sexually and emotionally, but also that this was a relationship he considered to be 'real' and not feigned. This type of behaviour is echoed by Egan (2003) who states: 'regulars engage in a fantasy wherein their relationship is perceived as real' (Egan 2003: 88). Further to sealing the 'deal', some dancers would even persuade customers to pay money up front for sex, arrange to meet them and then not turn up; Princess admitted to doing this and justified her behaviour by arguing: 'It's not like I'm ever going to see him again. He can afford it.' Although Princess rejects any issues about her safety in claiming she would never see the customer in this particular scenario again, by doing this the dancer is engaging in high-risk behaviour. Beyond this the managers at Starlets, although aware that this type of conduct occurs in the club, nonetheless regarded it as a punishable offence. Behaviour in Starlets deemed to be related to prostitution in any way could jeopardize the club's future and result in it being closed down.

The pity plea

This technique was often employed when the dancer was having an unsuccessful night. This strategy involved the dancer fabricating or relaying stories that would draw in the customer's sympathy, with the aim of making him/her purchase a dance out of pity. This strategy was not always successful as it could lead to customers complaining about the dancer's 'miserable' disposition – in these cases customers would avoid the dancer in question and even gossip about her to other dancers. It was something I observed on a number of occasions during my time in the field. Eric, for example, a regular Starlets customer who routinely enjoyed private dances and was happy to spend time talking to dancers, did not like those with an unhappy disposition, as reflected in the following field diary extract:

> *Eric: That lass over there with the pink dress on is a bit of a misery.*
> *RC: Why's that?*
> *Eric: Every time I speak to her it's the same old moaning: 'I'm having a really bad night! I can't afford to pay my rent! The commission's too high!'... It's the same story.*
> *RC: Do you ever have dances with her?*
> *Eric: No. Someone needs to tell her to smile!*

Despite Eric's negative reaction, some customers would successfully respond to this technique, although this would often be a regular who over a period of time had grown to know the dancers in the club. Simon, for example, one of the older customers who attended Starlets on a regular basis, would often spend time talking to the dancers and would purchase many private dances from different performers in the club. He was never rude or confrontational and happily parted with money. This was something many of the dancers used to their advantage:

> *... It was the end of the shift and there were only a handful of customers in the club, most of the dancers had given up and gone back to the changing room to get ready to go home. I spotted Simon sitting with Stella and I approached them both. Stella looked sad and was explaining to Simon how it had not been a financially rewarding night. As I sat down she put her arm around my shoulders, still looking sad: 'Why don't we give you a double dance? We've had a rubbish night' Stella's bottom lip protruding, her head hung low and eyes gazing at him like a wounded puppy. He took one look at her face and agreed ...[4]*

In this example Stella relied on a 'story' to convince Simon to engage in a financial transaction, this was given a sense of authenticity by her body language and an ally (me) to confirm her 'story'.

Social and emotional rituals

> *... All of the dancers were sitting around the main floor in their usual groups, chatting, laughing and drinking. It had been quiet all night and Gerard did not seem fazed by the dancers' lack of drive to get dances and make money. The atmosphere was even more social than usual; most of the dancers seemed to have given up trying to make money and instead seemed more intent on getting drunk ...*[5]

As well as learning to hustle through potentially adopting techniques and inevitably carrying out 'cynical performances', transition dancers would, more importantly, develop their relationships with one another. This was important as it enabled the dancer to continue to establish her status in the club. Further to this, developing strong bonds with other dancers, particularly with those of old-school status, inevitably enhanced their understanding of and influence over the tacit rules which, as it was suggested earlier, emerged from the dancers themselves. The bond between dancers was strengthened not simply by the shared experience of working in the lap-dancing club (Barton 2006; Forsyth and Deshotels 1998a), but through their actual engagement with various rituals. For instance, dancers would partake in a number of 'emotional rituals'; in this way dancers were able to build bonds with one another. This sets their relationship aside from the ones they shared with managers, other staff members and customers. Although 'emotional rituals' varied, they often involved dancers airing their personal concerns about issues relating to their work or home life, discussing mutual experiences of working and socializing in the club, and readily offering support to one another when needed, examples of which are apparent in many of the fieldnotes included in Chapters 4 to 9. 'Emotional rituals' would often take place in the changing room, away from the customers and other staff members. As dancers had a high degree of ownership over this space, it was the most appropriate place in the club for them to engage in an emotional exchange. For example, it was common for dancers to go to the changing room to discuss any personal issues they might have with managers, customers or another dancer. This type of process was suggested previously in Chapter 4, in the discussion about the changing room.

The second significant factor in strengthening bonds between dancers came from their mutual engagement in activities both inside and outside of the lap-dancing club environment. Sharing experiences, through lifestyle for example, was an important way in which dancers were able to connect. 'Social rituals' undertaken by dancers in the club, sometimes before, during and after working hours, demonstrate that there was a sense of commonality between dancers in Starlets. Such rituals included drinking alcohol and sometimes taking recreational drugs.

In relation to 'social rituals', at the beginning of a shift at Starlets, it was common for dancers to sit in groups on the main floor or dance reception area, talking and drinking alcohol. The use of alcohol in the lap-dancing club environment is well documented (see, for example, Boles and Garbin 1974b; Maticka-Tyndale *et al*. 2000; Montemurro 2001; Scott 1996). As was suggested in Chapter 6, dancers inevitably form small cliques with those with whom they naturally feel comfortable and familiar. Despite these associations not being as meaningful as the three status roles identified, they still form a significant part of the dancer's socialization within the club by presenting her with an opportunity to engage in various 'social rituals' which help her absorption into the wider lap-dancing club culture. In a dancer's connection with various social cliques, it is inevitable and necessary then that she adopt their particular social habits, evident through the group's engagement with specific 'social rituals'. Lisa demonstrated how this can lead to changes in a dancer's behaviour by using her own experiences as an example:

> ... *When I first started I never ever touched anything. And then just started taking it [cocaine] at work. Had a little bit of a dip where I'd like take it quite a lot at work ... It was a lot of things that started it. But mainly, I think coz I started hanging with Charley; she'd give us it for free. I think a lot of it starts coz they [dancer] want to be in this circle, in this gang. It's kinda like you smoke to be in the cool gang. That sort of thing ...*

This is not uncommon in Starlets; for instance, as she explained in the first part of her story which forms the prologue to Chapter 6, Karen never used cocaine before working at Starlets. It was after Karen increasingly became involved with what she refers to as the 'lifestyle' associated with lap-dancing that she started taking cocaine regularly. Again, like Lisa, it was after Karen began associating with a particular set of dancers who regularly used cocaine that she too began engaging in this particular 'social ritual'. As I have suggested elsewhere (see, for example, Colosi 2010a, 2010b forthcoming), the example of cocaine use as a 'social ritual' in Starlets became an increasingly popular activity within the club. The popularity of cocaine in the lap-dancing club environment may follow the steep rise in its general recreational use (Williams and Parker 2001). There was, as a result of the prolific use of cocaine in Starlets, an obvious desensitization to this 'social ritual' in the club:

> ... I was sitting in the changing room with a few other dancers, it was the middle of a shift, and some of the dancers had come in to have a break. Most of them were sitting together generally chatting when Charley, Phoenix and Eva walked in. They casually divided up 3 lines of cocaine on the dressing room counter, which they took in turns to snort away. The other girls in the changing room looked for a minute but then continued chatting. After Charley, Phoenix and Eva had left I asked Stacey who was sitting near me what she thought about it. She simply shrugged and smiled explaining to me 'It's not the first time I've seen that and it won't be the last'...[6]

Other popular recreationally used drugs in Starlets included ephedrine,[7] amphetamine and ecstasy. In a similar way to cocaine, these drugs were used within individual groups of dancers. Ephedrine was perhaps second to cocaine in popularity; some dancers did not consider it a serious or potentially dangerous drug, despite clinical evidence to suggest otherwise.[8] Nelly, for example, once casually offered me some ephedrine after I had commented that I was tired; when I declined she responded by saying: 'Why? It's just like Proplus.[9] It's not bad for you.' Again this perhaps reflects how desensitized dancers in Starlets are to drug-taking in general. Outside of the lap-dancing club environment, drug-taking within certain circles was still commonplace. It was not unusual, for example, for dancers to arrange a 'cocaine party' after their shift ended at Starlets. For example, Charley and Phoenix, in particular, often arranged them with other dancers. They were sometimes heard speaking openly in the changing room about these events. What was also significant about the use of alcohol and prolific drug-taking is the way in which dancers drew a sense of excitement and adventure by actively engaging in these activities as 'edgework' (Lyng 1990, 2005a). However, the implications of 'edgework' in these scenarios also move beyond thrill-seeking for the sensory pleasures it brings, but can also be argued to provide an escape from, and resistance to, work life (Lyng 2005a: 6). Although in its original context the 'weekend warriors', as Lyng (2005a) calls them, are used as an example, suggesting that 'edgework' is sought out of the workplace, in the context of the lap-dancing club, dancers engage with edgework within the workplace to escape the restraints of managers and to resist against their authority.

Furthermore, bonding over social rituals such as drug-taking helped dancers maintain their popularity in Starlets and simultaneously demonstrated their loyalty to other dancers in their immediate circle. This is compounded with the emotional rituals dancers engaged with. In relation to the tacit rules of the club, it was necessary for dancers to begin to establish themselves in the club before they could be part of the rule-making process. In many ways establishing status was about gaining the trust of other dancers, therefore the forming of allegiances and providing proof of loyalty quickly aided the process. Taking part in social rituals was very much part of this as it not only indicated that the dancer in question was of the same mindset as the circle with which she had chosen to associate, but that she could be trusted, particularly where drug-taking was concerned. As discussed in Chapter 8, cocaine represents more than a lifestyle choice and a form of social currency – in addition, it was also used as a bargaining tool with managers.

The experience of stigma

> The majority view of stripping holds that it is neither a vocation nor an art form: it is an aberration. Women who strip have forfeited their right to belong in the mainstream; they are outcasts. To be willing to pay such a price, one must be either insane or hopefully incorrigible. Either way, from the point of view of the moderate majority, the stripper is considered to be intrinsically tainted. (Scott 1996: 25)

According to Goffman (1963), stigma, as an 'undesired difference', is attributed to 'an individual who ... possessing a trait that can obtrude itself upon attention and turn those of us whom he meets away from him, breaking the claim that his other attributes have on us. He possesses a "stigma" ' (p. 15). Lap-dancing is seen as a 'deviant' occupation (in the context of Becker 1963), and as Goffman (1963) suggests, in the process of 'stigmatization', various words and phrases articulate this. In the case of lap-dancing, its 'deviancy' tends to exist on a dichotomy of 'victim–whore'. As has been suggested in previous chapters, the stigma of lap-dancing is something dancers are aware of. Karen, for example, asserted:

society says it's not right ... It's like a taboo isn't it ... They [employers] say they're not gonna judge [you] on whatever you put down on your CV, but I think a lot of people WILL ... say if you've got a person who is reading your CV, a woman, and they've lived a different life to you. They just won't understand it, they are gonna be like 'Oh God'.

Equally, other remarks dancers such as Adele made included: 'They [customers] think we're all slags ... they judge you'; another dancer, Lisa, reinforced this point: 'lasses [women] look down on you'. Indeed, as indicated from these examples, for the dancers at Starlets opposition seemed to come from a number of different sources, including the customers. Price (2008) suggests that the stigmatization of strippers is both an effect and symptom of the 'stripper stereotype', in which strippers are portrayed as 'heavy drinkers, spendthrifts, whiners, slobs, and unreliable workers' (p. 380). Ironically, this is something not only perpetuated by co-workers, customers and outsiders, but the dancers themselves who Price suggests describe each other in this way. The dancers at Starlets were also found to reinforce the 'stripper stereotype' visible through self-deprecation and directing these negative descriptions at their fellow dancers. This was particularly clear with the application of 'dirty dancing', discussed in Chapter 6, where, for example, Sally, a dancer at Starlets, once remarked about a co-worker's performance in order to malign her: 'She did work as a stripper[10] before so it's not surprising she's "dirty".' The 'stripper stereotype' which Price (2008) describes forms the opinions and attitudes of those close to dancers, including spouses and partners; in relation to this the impact on relationships is discussed further in Chapter 9. For example, some of the dancers working at Starlets experienced problems in romantic relationships, where their partners were unable to trust them on the basis that lap-dancers are sometimes stereotyped as 'promiscuous' (Scott 1996). Further to this, self-belief in this 'stripper stereotype' made some dancers refer to feeling 'dirty' and/or 'cheap'. Karen, for example, explained: 'People make you feel really bad ... like you're cheap and a bit of a tramp.' Adele, when talking about discussing her job with friends, family and strangers, remarked: 'They [people in general] just assume you are a prostitute ... they don't realize it's not like that.' As a result of such stigmatization, the dancers' self-esteem and confidence was inevitably affected, something which mirrors the experiences recounted by other sex workers (see, for example, Sanders 2005).

Various stigma management strategies adopted by dancers have already been accounted (Barton 2006; Bell *et al.* 1998; Deshotels and Forsyth 2005; Grandy 2008; Thompson and Harred 1992, 2003). These authors, to some extent, have adopted the work of Sykes and Matza (1957) to make sense of this stigma management as a process of neutralization. In Starlets it was found that lap-dancers adopted two main ways of managing the stigma, including concealing their occupation from family and friends or, more boldly, by challenging the deviant label associated with lap-dancing, in the same way that Sanders (2005) describes how sex workers lie about working as prostitutes. This is similar to Goffman's (1963) account of dividing up the social worlds so that those faced with a particular stigma control the information others receive about them. This simply means that these individuals will divide their 'social world' into one category that is aware of the attribute which contributes to the 'stigma' and the remainder who are not made aware of the attribute. This approach, along with the work of Sykes and Matza (1957), has also been utilized by Thompson and Harred (2003) in their assessment of the stigma management strategies of strippers. There are therefore similarities between Thompson and Harred (2003) and the findings discussed here in relation to stigma. In Starlets, for instance, it was found that dancers, while still maintaining their 'lap-dancer' lives and identities, would harbour a separate and very different existence on the 'outside' as a front for family and friends. For instance, Princess, a dancer, explained how she hid her job from her family: 'I don't tell people what I do. I say I work in a bar.' Adele also explained: 'I can't tell anyone, not even my sister!' In contrast other dancers attempt to challenge the stigma associated with lap-dancing and confront the negative perceptions of their job. A similar method of stigma management was identified by Thompson and Harred (1992, 2003), who suggest dancers deny and confront the negative associations made with the stripping industry. In Starlets, in relation to this strategy, Jan, for example, asserted: 'People can say what they want. I don't care. It's just a job.' Other dancers such as Linda explained: 'I'll always put it on my CV; I'm proud of it. If I was employing someone and they'd danced I would never hold it against them.' Although both techniques enabled the dancers at Starlets to cope, to some extent, with the stigma associated with their work, they did not help reduce the actual stigma. This is something that cannot be quickly alleviated as the stigma associated with sex work is deeply ingrained within the social psyche.

Feeling the strain of lap-dancing

> ... It takes confidence, it takes the ability to deal with people who are intoxicated, who are probably rude and definitely very different from yourself in most cases, also all kinds of different people ... I guarantee you, you meet people who make you feel about two inches tall and it takes a lot to be able to pull yourself round from that ...[11]

Hochschild (1983) describes 'emotional labour' as the management of emotions and the way in which emotions are then displayed to others; this is often applied to gendered forms of work. On this basis, lap-dancing, as other researchers have identified, involves 'emotional labour', as dancers must sometimes manage their emotions when interacting with customers in order to make money (also see, for example, Barton 2002, 2006, 2007; Holsopple 1999; Wesely 2002; Wood 2000). For this reason, sex work more generally is argued to involve emotional, as well as physical, labour (see, for example, Chapkis 1997; Kempadoo and Doezema 1998). In Starlets, although it was found that dancers, as cynical performers, engaged in techniques without emotional conviction, the acts themselves could still be draining, as Karen suggested: 'I really can't be bothered to go up to a guy and be all false and batter my eyelids, it does my head in.' Beyond this, dancing is an emotional experience in many other ways, and although it can be a rewarding experience, it can also cause emotional strain. For instance, after the 'honeymoon' period of dancing experienced as a new girl, in which, as Linda recalls, 'you're caught up with the glamorous side of it', the reality of working as a lap-dancer becomes apparent. This would be when dances not only encounter the pleasures associated with lap-dancing, but also the bad experiences. Barton (2006), in relation to this, argues that new dancers, or 'novice dancers' as she calls them, initially find their job rewarding, but the 'toll of stripping' inevitably leads these dancers to feel emotionally and physically strained. In Starlets it was not uncommon for the dancers to discuss the emotional strain their job could cause; this was more apparent with those from transition or old school stages, which reiterates, to some extent, Barton's (2006) argument. Even Karen described in her story how dancing can be emotionally draining, a factor which would affect how much money she earned in the club. In Starlets the derogatory comments made by customers was one of the contributory factors most commonly held responsible for the psychological and emotional strain, and was probably that most frequently observed and discussed by the dancers. This was echoed by other researchers concerned with the negative effects of dancing (Barton 2002, 2006, 2007; Holsopple 1999; Wesely 2002; Wood 2000) and reflective of some of the theoretical thinking around emotional labour (Hochschild 1983).

Linda, describing how customers would constantly criticize her weight, and call her 'fat', remarked: 'God, I've had moments when I've hated myself ... I've ended up getting into a lot of debates, a lot of arguments [with customers].' In relation to this, Jan explained: 'If they [customers] are in a huff they'll take it out on you, they'll try and make you feel like crap.' Another cause of emotional and psychological strain was a direct impact of the number of shifts worked, as Jan explained:

> ... We don't close 'til 4 am[12] now ... you come in at 10 and finish at 4. But really to be honest who wants to start getting ready for work at 10 o'clock at night. It feels like a night shift now, rather than a lap-dancing club; it feels totally different in the sense that how late it's continuing on. It really makes a difference on what time I'm getting home, on what time I go to sleep, coz you can't just go in and bang go to sleep straight away, you've got to wind down, from the music, from whatever gone on that night with the customers. If somebody's upset you a little bit in some sort of way, if something was said to you, you don't let it affect you really, but, when you go home and you lay down to sleep, you think 'My God I remember what he said to me', so your mind starts ticking over ...

Working long shifts during the evening into the early hours of the morning inevitably affect sleeping patterns, especially when shifts change from day to day and week to week. Limited sleep in addition to other pressures associated with lap-dancing can at times, as demonstrated by Jan, intensify the emotional strain. In addition, financial pressures are also offered as a source of stress; these include a dancer being unable to pay the set commission and not making enough money in general. Ruby, explained: 'It's like you get a bit emotional and I used to just let it get me down. I shouldn't 'av but, when you go in and you're sat there and ya like: Oh no I used to be like close to tears some nights when I wasn't making any money.' To further illustrate this, dancers were sometimes observed sitting in the changing room of Starlets tearful at the prospect of not making enough money to cover the commission. On more than one occasion dancers were observed asking others to supply their taxi fare home; something I also experienced, and clearly remember the embarrassment of having to ask other dancers for money to get home. As Jan explained: 'Lap-dancing can be a struggle, it's not always that easy to make money.'

As expected, management too was a source of discontent among a high proportion of the dancers, something echoed by Wesely (2003) and Price (2008). Wesely (2003), for example, suggests that through the generally negative and sexist treatment of strippers, dancers are reduced to feelings of insecurity. Similarly, many of the dancers at Starlets felt frustrated by the way in which the managers treated them. In a conversation with Sasha, she described to me how the managers were becoming increasingly greedy:

> **Sasha:** *It's just ridiculous. I was only 5 minutes late the other day and Gerard fined me £10!*
> **RC:** *Did you try and get out of it?*
> **Sasha:** *No. It's not worth arguing with him. It would just make the whole thing worse. Then I'd probably get another fine.*
> **RC:** *It is frustrating.*
> **Sasha:** *I'm sick of it. Gerard keeps putting the commission up just coz he's a greedy bastard and wants it to line his pockets.*

Some dancers also believed that the managers lacked empathy and refused to be supportive when the dancers needed it. As Becks explained to me: 'They've got no respect for us. Ken came in [the changing room] the other night and shouted: "You cunts better get your backsides out on to the main floor!".' Gerard too would verbally abuse dancers. For example, during one of the monthly meetings in which all dancers from Starlets were present, Gerard remarked: 'Remember who the boss is. As far as I'm concerned you're like dogs, if I say sit, you sit!' The managers' attempts to assert their authority in this way, as well as adding to the existing strains of lap-dancing, are also evidence of their conscious attempts to maintain the dancers' subordinate position in the club.

Finally, the excessive use of drugs and alcohol by some of the dancers was admitted as being a contributing factor to the psychological and emotional 'toll' (Barton 2006). For instance, Lisa explained: 'I'd like take it [cocaine] quite a lot at work. Went down to like seven stone ... I was like taking a gram and half at work and then go partying straight after and take another two or three grams ... my head was a mess, I felt and looked like shit basically.' This was not uncommon – some dancers claimed to have had (nervous) breakdowns because of excessive drinking and drug-taking. Cindy, for example, explained: 'I was taking coke every night, then in the day, and I'd just be watching TV and think "I want some coke!" It got to the point where I just couldn't function, I couldn't deal with life any more.' The level of self-destruction described is something emphasized by Maticka-Tyndale *et al.* (2000), who claim that strippers, in the research they conducted, were often negatively affected by alcohol, usually in the form of addiction.

The reactions and coping strategies employed by dancers at Starlets varied – some were more positive than others. Sanders (2005) too, in her exploration of the emotional management strategies of prostitutes, suggests that these women would engage in a number of different strategies in order to reduce the emotional toll of their work. In Starlets, dancers would initially prepare themselves *before* stepping out onto the main floor to work, in order to help build their sense of self-belief and confidence. As Karen explained in the second part of her story which formed the prologue to Chapter 6, it is important for a dancer to get into the correct frame of mind before working the main floor. For Karen this meant 'psyching' herself up. Altering the dancers' mood is done in several ways. Primarily dancers attempted to do this through their physical preparation for work on the floor; this preparation would go beyond the changing room, as many dancers would spend time and money on body maintenance, from hair extensions to cosmetic surgery, as suggested in Chapter 6. Wesely (2003) has made similar claims about dancers' level of body maintenance in American strip clubs, where she points out that cosmetic surgery has become commonplace. By investing in their physical appearance, besides making themselves more desirable to the customers and, as was suggested in Chapter 6, putting their appearance in line with management's standards, dancers were strengthening their own self-image, as Princess, who underwent breast enhancements while working at Starlets, indicates: 'I didn't do this for anybody but myself. After having Luke [her son] my boobs drooped. I wanted to feel good for myself.'

Another way in which dancers attempted to build their confidence was through the use of recreational drug-taking and/or alcohol consumption, which also acted as a pre-shift 'social ritual'. The following extract taken from my field notes demonstrates how commonplace drug-taking was as part of the dancers' preparation:

... Saturday night shifts are always chaos in the changing room, but on this particular night there were so many girls working it was difficult to find space to get changed. There was a queue of girls outside the changing room toilets; however, I was aware they weren't all waiting to use the toilet for the traditional reason. It was commonplace on a Saturday for many of the dancers to have a few lines of coke before starting their shift; when using the toilet after them you could sometimes see traces of white powder on the toilet lid ...

The use of drugs and alcohol, as already discussed, could ironically lead to emotional and psychological upset. Nonetheless, dancers described how it could also give them a temporary lift, something some of them felt they needed in order to work effectively. Paris, for example, admitted: 'It gives me that boost I need before I go on stage.' Similarly, Davina explained how getting drunk stopped her worrying about how badly she was doing financially during quiet shifts: 'I'd rather get pissed and enjoy myself than sit around feeling like crap coz there's no money to be made!' Maticka-Tyndale *et al.* (2000) have also suggested that dancers use alcohol and sometimes recreational drugs in order to boost their confidence. Scott (1996), in discussing the potentially traumatic experience of stripping, argues: 'Alcohol and drugs (usually marijuana and or cocaine) ... are often used as a means of anesthetizing ...' (p. 21). Karen, as well as using cocaine socially as she explains earlier in her story, admitted that it also provided her with an escape away from the stresses of lap-dancing and a confidence boost to work effectively.

Finally, part of the dancer's emotional preparation, through the use of 'emotional rituals', often involved developing a sense of superiority over the customers and managers. In relation to this, dancers would degrade some of the managers and customers. This is reflected in the following extract taken from my field diary:

... Kelly and I were sitting talking to Danny, a new regular [customer], who by all accounts fancied himself as one of the Gallagher brothers [from the rock band Oasis]. He sat back in his chair taking glugs from his bottle of 'Bud'[13] and said 'So what's the craic with you two tonight?' He suddenly sat upright as the DJ played a Massive Attack track; Danny looked at me and said, 'I bet you don't even know who this is?' referring to the song. Before I even had a chance to reply he said, 'Didn't think so. I know everything there is to know about music.' He was proving to be his usual 'cocky' self, so I thought I may as well have a bit of fun: 'You know who you remind me of

Danny?' He asked me who so I replied: 'Blues; he's just someone I live with'. Danny was twisting his face and started laughing at the name 'Blues', he kept shaking his head and chuckling for a few minutes. Although his curiosity soon got the better of him and Danny starting asking me about my 'friend' Blues. With my tongue firmly in my cheek I explained 'He's a bit of a bird catcher, quite hard, some say sexy, out all night on the prowl.' Danny seemed impressed and said: 'He sounds like my kind of guy. Maybe me and Blues should go out on the town sometime.' Kelly and I looked at each other and started laughing. Danny glared back at us both and asked why we were laughing; we told him it was nothing to be concerned about. But of course the reason we were laughing was because Blues was actually my cat! I never told Danny, but every time I saw him he always asked when he and Blues could 'hook up' ...

Part of the mockery aimed at customers is also related to the dancing techniques used, discussed earlier, in which trickery is used to seduce them into dancing. In relation to this, some of the dancers would often laugh about how gullible certain customers were, as illustrated in the following field diary extract:

...I was talking to some of the dancers in the changing room, as we were all getting ready to go home. Adele had been on a sit-down with Ricky, one of her regular customers, for most of the night. She told us he'd given her £600 for spending most of the night telling him how much she fancied him. 'He thinks I'm actually going to go on some date with him! I don't even like him, apart from being fat, he's the most boring man I've ever met!' Adele explained ...

Similarly, dancers mocked some of the managers, particularly Gerard, who was disliked for setting the high commission and the imposition of unreasonable fines. Dancers would mockingly impersonate his voice and ridicule his personal appearance: calling him 'ugly', 'slimy' and 'goofy'. Over time, confidence building and creating a feeling of superiority over customers and managers is an important way of combating, at least temporarily, the emotional and psychological pressures associated with lap-dancing. Jan was very practical in her understanding of these pressures:

... you've got to be secure in yourself. I think in this job that's something that can take time ... you're putting yourself in a situation where not everybody is going to like you, not everybody is going to

119

find you attractive, not everybody is going to find you sexy, and at the end of the day that's what you have to learn to accept ...

During the same interview Jan, in relation to the self-belief and confidence needed to cope with the emotional and psychological pressures of lap-dancing, described, for example, how she combats criticism from customers:

... So I sat down with them [customers] and had just general chit chat ... then one of the guys just came out and said to me 'Well how old are you then?' Why does he want to know how old I am? Does it matter? I was 31 at the time, so straight away I told him. 'I'm 31, why?' and his response, 'Are ya fuck?' and his other three pals just looked like [shocked] and I looked and I said: 'I don't lie about anything, I've got no reason to lie. I'm 31?' he went 'Erm ya older than me and I'm 40.' So I said 'Oh and how do ya know that?' and he went 'Well look at the lines there' pointing to my eyes, 'I said what do ya mean' and he said 'Well look at the lines there'. This was my response: 'Now look darling they're laughter lines coz I know how to smile, it's not your fault you're a miserable bastard is it' and I stood up and walked away ...

Although dancers employ a number of strategies to combat the emotional pressures of their work, as Jan suggests in the above extract, it was also necessary to learn to ignore some of the criticism experienced, or at least give the impression of having 'a thick skin'. Although to some extent this chapter has focused on the more negative experiences of dancing, it is nonetheless apparent through the 'emotional' and 'social' rituals, for example, and in the methods used to combat the strains and stresses of their job, that gratification can be found. In addition, the pleasures experienced by many of the dancers during performance, whether on the stage or for private dances, is also an equally important source of satisfaction. As Scott (1996) suggests, for some dancers, the intense sense of 'ego-gratification' sought from performance by some dancers can, for them, outweigh the negative experiences of their work. What is clear about lap-dancing is that it involves complex and contradictory sets of emotional experiences (Egan 2006a). This particular theme continues to be evident in Chapter 8, which focuses on the ultimate hierarchical old-school stage.

Notes

1 Field diary extract.
2 Extract from an interview with a dancer named Ruby.
3 Although these techniques are commonly practiced, they are only utilised when a dancer chooses to spend time engaging with a customer. During busy nights in particular it is not uncommon for dancers at Starlets to keep this type of interaction to a minimum; in these instances dancers will often move from customer to customer simply asking: 'Do you want a dance?'
4 Field diary extract.
5 Field diary extract.
6 Field diary extract.
7 A drug used clinically for asthma, however it is taken recreationally for its stimulant effects. Recreational use of ephedrine is currently illegal in the UK.
8 Adverse affects can include cardiovascular problems, brain damage and death in an over-dose situation.
9 Non-prescription fatigue relief caffeine tablets.
10 Refers to agency stripper.
11 Extract from an interview with a dancer named Linda.
12 Shortly before this interview was conducted the closing time of Starlets changed from 2.30am to 4am.
13 Refers to Budweiser, an American brand of lager.

Chapter 8

Being established

... I had been standing at the DJ booth talking to Deano [the DJ] for about 15 minutes. As usual he was complaining about the new girls. 'Some of these new girls are dogs. They can't dance, pick shit music.' Deano always seemed unimpressed with new dancers, although it was always short lived, as he often quickly befriended them. During his rant he continued 'It's not like the originals, the old-school dancers, like your Jans, your Davinas your Charleys.' Deano was always praising those he called 'old-school' dancers, I always got the impression he felt more secure with established dancers, in a sense he knew what to expect ...[1]

The previous two chapters introduced and discussed two of the three status roles which dancers at Starlets were found to take on. What has so far been suggested is that these dancers automatically entered an informal hierarchical career structure which was informed by their adoption of the lap-dancing 'code of ethics' supplied by the 'tacit rules' and, ultimately, their absorption of the 'culture'. The stages already discussed in Chapters 6 and 7 precede what can be seen as the ultimate hierarchical position in Starlets among dancers: that of 'old-school' status. As intimated in this opening extract, old-school dancers attain a level of respect that other dancers cannot equal. Deano's remarks suggest a gulf between those of old-school and new girl status. Attaining old-school status only occurred after the dancer had fully experienced her role, as was suggested in Chapter 7. Beyond being an accomplished dancer, both for private and stage shows, this means the dancer has developed coping strategies which equip her for the lap-dancing club environment; she would also be integrated within the social network of dancers through sustained engagement with both social and emotional rituals, and most importantly be in sync with the tacit rules of the club. As an established dancer in the old-school stage, the dancer has achieved full membership, giving her privileged status as a lap-dancer. Most significantly, this is a stage in which the dancer can help rewrite the tacit rules. As well as taking part in the subtle recreation of these rules, it is also the role of the old-school dancer to help maintain and reinforce them, as they are continuously challenged. This more central role which a dancer plays in the creation and maintenance of the club's tacit rules is therefore what most signals that a dancer has gained old-school status. Although not all of the dancers involved in this piece of research made a conscious effort to achieve old-school status, it was a role to which some dancers aspired because of the respect it commanded from other dancers. As with the other status roles, no time limit could be placed on the attainment of this particular position; nor was it inevitable that all dancers would reach this old-school status before they retired from dancing. This chapter discusses what it means to become an established dancer with old-school status by looking at the privileges along with the various strategies old-school dancers employed to maintain their role. Finally, the chapter considers the underlying meaning of the dancer hierarchy that has been identified, describing it as an 'occupational subculture', and by drawing on the work of Cressey (1932) in particular offers a framework for understanding lap-dancing in this way (also see Colosi, 2010a).

Old-school privileges

... In Starlets it was always the more established dancers who were recruited by management to take part in various media projects with which the club were involved. This privilege, however, could cause resentment. For example: last week it was announced that a local band were making a music video and were looking for a couple of girls to be in the video. Davina was put in charge of recruiting dancers; she chose Charley, Phoenix, Candy, Kitten and Lisa. Crystal, who had been at the club for only a couple of months, complained to me, 'They always get to do stuff. It's one rule for them and another for the rest of us!' However, she did not confront the dancers in question about this. Crystal knew that it was not worth the probable consequences ...[2]

The various privileges old-school dancers had were connected with the tacit rules of the club and sometimes impacted on the way in which other dancers of lower status conducted themselves. Despite old-school dancers having various privileges, not all of the high-status dancers necessarily used their position in this way. From the research conducted in Starlets here are some of the main areas in which the advantages of old-school status became apparent.

Territory

In Starlets, old-school dancers were often territorial about space, as Lisa suggests: 'Some people like to mark their territory.' This was particularly true in the changing room and main floor. As was suggested in Chapter 4, both areas were central to the lap-dancing club. To reiterate, the changing room, for example, was the 'home' quarters for the dancers: a place away from the customers and managers, the only place in the club reserved solely for dancers. In this space old-school dancers were able to maintain control over particular areas; they would, for example, allocate exclusive seating for themselves. Their position as governors of the tacit rules enabled old-school dancers to prevent others from using their seating, despite more formal rules set by the management leaving this space open to all. As was suggested earlier, the tacit rules of the club had more meaning among dancers than the house rules. It was thus the respect for these rules and ultimately the old-school dancers that lead to the cooperation of the other dancers:

> ... Paula was sitting in the changing room straightening her hair when Charley walked in. As soon as she saw her enter, Paula stood up and moved to another seat as she was sitting where Charley usually got ready. Unless she wanted to offend Charley, Paula was aware she was better to move ... Charley always sat in the same seat. There seemed to be an 'understanding' amongst the dancers which prevented others using her space ...[3]

In a similar way old-school dancers were sometimes territorial on the main floor; the tacit rules make it easy for old-school dancers to control the main floor which is where the dancers not only make money but, as suggested earlier, was also a social arena in which dancers congregated, sometimes drinking alcohol and relaxing with one another. As demonstrated in Chapter 6 and 7, although these social cliques of dancers were often mixed with dancers from all three stages of the hierarchy, it was often the old-school dancers who dominated their own group's site.

Customer ownership

On the main floor the dancers, according to the house rules set by the management, were equal and therefore did not have priority over customers entering the club. Old-school dancers, however, unlike lower-status dancers, by using the tacit rules were easily able to challenge this. Rambo-Ronai and Ellis have also suggested the role of strip club tacit rules in directing dancer–customer interaction: 'Making sure a customer was not spoken for by another dancer was important ... it was considered dangerous (one could get into an argument) and rude to sit with another dancer's customer' (1989: 453). In relation to this, in Starlets old-school dancers were given priority over both private dances and sit-downs with selected customers, as demonstrated in the following field diary extract:

> ... Jan had alerted Stacey that Melissa had been sitting with Gary for half an hour without dancing. I approached Stacey to ask what was wrong. 'Melissa has done it again! She knows he [Gary] comes in to see me. She can't be allowed to step on another girl's toes.' Stacey explained. Shortly afterwards, both Jan and Stacey confronted Melissa about sitting with Gary. I wasn't sure what was said but Melissa kept away from Gary after that and later on I noticed Stacey was the one sitting with him ...

In this example, two old-school dancers, Jan and Stacey, challenged Melissa, a new girl, which inevitably resulted in a positive outcome for Stacey because of her high status. It was not uncommon in Starlets for dancers to assert their ownership over certain customers in this way. However, not all old-school dancers took advantage of this privilege. For example, as Karen explained in her story which formed the prologue to Chapter 6, she did not feel compelled to challenge others for customers in order to make money, and likened this approach to 'selling her soul' in the name of money.

Dress code

The dress code at Starlets, as stated in the house rules set by management, stipulated that all dancers must wear evening style dresses[4] before 11 pm; after this time they were free to wear more revealing or themed[5] outfits. If these rules were not adhered to, dancers were often punished. Punishments varied, depending on the number of 'offences', from the managers issuing an informal warning to a dancer facing suspension. The latter was rare, but it was not unknown for dancers to be fined a fee for persistently breaking dress codes. The dress code was often challenged by many of the dancers from different stages of the dancer hierarchy. However, unlike dancers from other stages, those who had old-school status were less likely to be reprimanded for ignoring or challenging the dress code. Charley, for example, never abided by the formal rule stating that evening dresses must be worn before 11 pm; she would enter the main floor at the beginning of her shift wearing a bikini or similar attire, regardless of the time. Interestingly, Charley, like some of the other late stage dancers, seemed exempt from punishment. Although not changing from an evening dress into a more revealing or themed costume did not breach the club's house rules, management nonetheless frowned upon it. Despite this, some of the old-school dancers who wore the same outfit throughout the entire shift went unnoticed. Davina, for example, went through stages in which she would not only wear the same outfit throughout one shift but also from day to day. Although the managers never reprimanded her for not varying her dance costumes, other less established dancers would be reprimanded for the same offence.

Shift patterns

As discussed in Chapter 3, during my fieldwork in Starlets rules were put in place by management stating that dancers must work at least two Saturday night shifts and two shifts between Monday and Wednesday, other than that they were free to work when they wanted. Every month shift rotas were completed and submitted by the dancers for the following month. Any irregularities would often be dealt with during the submission of rotas and followed either a telephone call from Gerard or, if the dancer in question was present, her being questioned in the manager's office.

Although many dancers, including old-school dancers, followed this rule, some, however, challenged it. This involved refusing to work any of the shifts stipulated by management, going on the sick or not showing for a shift. For example, Phoenix, an old-school dancer, avoided working early week shifts on a number of occasions and was known to sometimes call in sick or not turn up for work. However, despite persistent rule-breaking, managers never punished her and she was only ever asked to explain her actions:

... Gerard and Phoenix were arguing in the office. We could all hear them through the changing room wall. I wasn't sure what it was about until I heard Charley laughing and explaining that: 'She [Phoenix] was supposed to be in last night but she was at mine'. Charley didn't seem concerned that her friend was getting told off. Everyone in the changing room knew that it was not unusual for Phoenix and Gerard to argue over this ...[6]

Customer-dancer interaction

As was explained in Chapter 6, in Starlets, the house rules prohibit any sexual contact between customers and dancers at any point during interaction: this rule is a direct result of various licensing conditions. The punishment for making sexual contact with a customer would involve a fine or dismissal from the club. Despite management being keen to punish dancers for breaking this rule, the harsher forms of punishment such as suspension or dismissal were seldom imposed on old-school dancers. In fact it was not uncommon for contact between an old-school dancer and customer to be overlooked. Although not every old-school dancer attempted to make sexual contact with customers, this was not the case for all:

... It is obvious ... some dancers frequently exploit rules around contact, particularly some of the more established ones. Charley, for example, will use her knee to rub a customer's penis whilst dancing. I have also witnessed her licking customers' ears and allowing them to suck her breasts. Other dancers are aware of this and yet no complaint has been made to management ...[7]

Dirty dancing was condemned by most of the dancers. Dancers who were aware of Charley's behaviour would sometimes gossip about her conduct in the changing room but would have never considered reporting her to the managers. However, the same dancers would not think twice about reporting a less established dancer for the same offence, as suggested in the following field diary extract:

... This was Kate's third shift and unbeknown to her, her last. Phoenix, Davina, Charley and some of the other dancers had taken a dislike to her as soon as she'd started. Kate was dating Trev [Saturday/Friday night DJ]; some of the dancers were claiming this meant she was getting away with too much ... She [Kate] had been sitting with a customer for most of the evening getting progressively more drunk.

> *Davina, Phoenix and Charley had been watching her all night and told Gerard she'd been dirty dancing. This resulted in him watching her from the main floor, after which he swiftly had her removed ...*

This demonstrates the way in which house rules were manipulated and used to the advantage of the old-school dancer. It also, as with the other old-school privileges discussed, demonstrates how the tacit rules of the club were enforced and shaped in favour of old-school dancers.

Maintenance of the tacit rules

To ensure the tacit rules were given priority and maintained in a way that benefited the dancers, those of high status employed a number of different strategies in order to help with this process. Although old-school dancers were the main contributors to these tacit rules, it was nonetheless still necessary for lower-status dancers to cooperate in order for them to be effective. As was suggested in Chapter 6, by maintaining these tacit rules, the various career stages (or status roles) which are part of the dancer hierarchy were clearly defined and preserved. More specifically, this special code of ethics and conduct enabled old-school dancers to secure their position as high-status figures in the club and both control and regulate the other dancers. As will be discussed, there are three main ways in which the tacit rules are maintained and prioritized.

Monitoring dancers

The behaviour and conduct of all the dancers were under varying degrees of scrutiny, the most vigilant applying to new girls, as indicated in Chapter 6. The monitoring process tended to be more intensive for new workers than more experienced transition dancers, but was still something the latter would be subjected to. Monitoring the conduct of dancers was an effective way of making sure all dancers were in tune with and adhered to the tacit rules of the club. This was not a process exclusively carried out by old-school dancers, but sometimes transition dancers would often work in the interests of these rules and be mindful of rule-breakers, particular attention being paid to customer–dancer interaction, social conduct, use of space in the club, predominantly on the main floor and changing room, appearance and dancer–dancer interactions. It was often those behaviours that were at odds with, or relate to the old-school privileges discussed earlier in this chapter, which are of particular interest. For instance, it was ensured that dancers stuck to their own territory in the changing room and on the main floor. In addition, misuse of social rituals, such as 'overt' drug use by new girls in particular, would be watched for. Dirty dancing, as has already been suggested, was one of the primary concerns for dancers as they monitored each other. Breaking this 'rule' in particular was perhaps the most likely 'offence' which would cause dancers to involve management. Generally those who challenged the tacit rules were often corrected by other dancers – rule-breaking did not always result in the involvement of management. If the dancer amended her behaviour and acted in accordance with the tacit rules thereon, the consequences were often not serious. However, persistent rule-breaking, as already demonstrated, could lead to segregation or removal of the dancer in question.

Bargaining tools

There were two main ways in which old-school dancers would attempt to bargain with management for control in the club. These 'bargaining tools' include drugs and sex, as I have suggested elsewhere (see Colosi, 2010b forthcoming). Although the use of these bargaining tools was beneficial for the wider dancer community within the club, it inevitably led to a direct advantage for the old-school dancer who was the most likely to apply this strategy successfully. Lower-status dancers, particularly new girls, would rarely attempt to bargain for control in the club, as such a strategy in these cases would be rejected by managers as well as be frowned upon by other dancers. The principle reason for this rejection was on the basis that new dancers in particular were often quite unfamiliar to managers and it was therefore likely that their actions would not be trusted and accepted without suspicion. Personal success, which is more probable for old-school dancers, worked to benefit them, first and foremost, as it reinforced their privileged status. Ultimately it follows that managers and other staff were likely to tolerate the dancers' engagement with conduct that was often prohibited, such as dirty dancing for example.

Where recreational drugs, usually cocaine, were offered to managers, this was in exchange for control in the club. Sometimes, old-school dancers would use cocaine, for instance, as a form of payment, something that for some proved to be a useful way of avoiding commission payments, as the following field diary extract indicates:

Candy: You know that Cindy doesn't always pay commission?
RC: Why's that?
Candy: You watch next time when we're all paying Gerard [manager].
  She sometimes slips him a wrap of coke.
RC: I've never noticed.
Candy: Only because they're careful. You watch next time she's in
  there at the end of the night.

In a similar way it was suggested by some of the dancers that Charley, as an old-school dancer, would supply Gerard with cocaine and in exchange she was able to conduct herself liberally in the club. As the conduct of old-school dancers such as Charley, for example, was overlooked they were therefore able to implement their own rules without much interference from management. In a similar way dancers sometimes used sex as a 'bargaining tool'. As suggested by Leanne in the following field diary extract, some old-school dancers provided sexual favours in exchange for more freedom and control in Starlets:

> *...I sat at the bar and talked to Leanne as the day shift came to a close; the club was quite empty with only three or four customers remaining. We got into a conversation about Gerard and his relationships with other dancers. He'd dated a few dancers, including Princess and a couple of European dancers who no longer worked at Starlets. Leanne suggested that some dancers were quite happy to sleep with Gerard despite the widespread dislike of him. 'I've walked in on a couple of lasses shagging him in the office. I'm not mentioning any names, but all I'm saying is that they get away with stuff'...[8]*

The dancers at Starlets, across the three career stages, were aware that some dancers used sex and drugs as bargaining tools; interestingly it was the managers who dancers vilified for the exchanges made. Although some of the old-school dancers who employed these strategies occasionally faced criticism from their fellow dancers, ultimately it was felt that the managers, by engaging in this behaviour, were acting unprofessionally and should therefore be neither trusted nor respected as a source of authority. Dancers were more likely to respect old-school dancers who were seen as an alternative source of authority (see Colosi 2010b forthcoming).

The role of respect

The respected role of old-school dancers was evidenced by the various privileges they have access to which were unavailable or limited among those with lower status. Although old-school dancers were able to maintain the tacit rules and therefore their autonomy in the club through a process of monitoring and correcting other dancers along with various bargaining strategies, it was also their revered position that allowed old-school dancers to proceed unchallenged in their role as rule-makers. The role old-school dancers played in the production and maintenance of the tacit rules was what ultimately gained the respect of other dancers, who appeared to admire (and perhaps sometimes fear) the established dancer's sense of authority, as Eva demonstrates: 'Have you noticed how nobody will mess with Charley? She'd get away with murder.' As in the case of Eva, as new girls entered the club, they were able to observe the respect that was directed at the old-school dancers by other less established dancers and inevitably followed this pattern of behaviour. The respect of other dancers enabled old-school dancers to continue to manipulate and ultimately maintain the tacit rules of the club without being regularly challenged. Beyond this, old-school dancers were also able to use their respectful role to the benefit of other lower-status dancers, as demonstrated in this field diary extract:

> ... Jan had been working in Starlets since the club opened; she was one of the few original dancers left. She was highly respected, particularly by some of the newer dancers, who I had often seen her comforting in the changing room, if they had for whatever reason been upset. In many ways Jan was like a mother figure for many of the dancers, even to some of the other more established dancers. The managers too have acknowledged this and offered Jan the unofficial role of housemother, although they are refusing to pay her for this. Nevertheless it just demonstrates her value in the club ...

As this extract suggests, in her respected role Jan was seen as a protector and 'mother' figure to the dancers; she was someone dancers trusted and felt they could rely on. In addition, in their cognizance of the respect old-school dancers received, the management were not only rewarding Jan by giving her the unofficial role of housemother, but were also able to use the trust and respect she had gained among the dancers to their advantage.

Re-establishing status

It was not uncommon for women to temporarily retire before returning to Starlets to work again as lap-dancers. Women's re-entry into a career in lap-dancing after 'retirement' has only been addressed briefly in academic literature (see, for example, Forsyth and Deshotels 1998a), with no accounts made of these patterns in a UK context. After spending time away from Starlets, even old-school dancers, depending on the length of time they retired for, on their return had to re-establish themselves within the club setting. Although this process was not as lengthy or as intense as the initiation experienced by a new girl, it is nonetheless a process that involved rebuilding and strengthening existing bonds. Further to this, it sometimes involved a relearning of club conduct and for dancers to be reacquainted with the current version of the club's tacit rules, which, as has already been suggested, were subject to shift and change. Sam, for example, returned to Starlets after almost two years away. On her return she had to relearn how to perform private dances within the context of the tacit rules, to which there had been several changes made during her absence:

> ... Sam was surprised initially about how much more contact was allowed with customers during private dances 'I remember when I first started there was a three foot rule, now you can grind on their laps,' she explained ...[9]

Further to this, although Sam inevitably knew some of the established dancers, it was still necessary for her to rebuild those bonds. It was interesting to observe how some of the dancers who had not originally worked with Sam responded to her shortly after her return. Leanne, for example, who was now an old-school dancer, commented: 'She's stuck up, I think she's full of herself.' Other dancers who, like Leanne, had never worked with Sam before made similar remarks; it was as though Sam were now a new girl once more, and would have to overcome some of the hurdles which confront a dancer when first starting out in a lap-dancing career. In a conversation with Lucy who returned after a year away, she remarked on the way some of the dancers treated her: 'They've got no fucking respect. I was here before they even started ... there's one girl who doesn't even answer if you ask her a question ...' Similarly Janine commented on the negative reception she felt she received from some of the 'newer' dancers:

... I asked her [Janine] what she thought of the dancers. Janine laughed and explained: 'There's only a few of us originals left! I feel like a stranger ... some of the dancers seem very rude and ignorant, there's not that class that used to be about' ...[10]

Janine reacted to this isolation by focusing on making money, and did not, as she had before her retirement, socialize with dancers. As was conveyed in Chapter 6, this detachment was something new girls initially experienced until they were fully integrated into the dancing community at Starlets.

In contrast, when Mandy returned to Starlets, it was not re-establishing herself with the dancers she found difficult, but gaining the approval of the managers – Ken in particular. It was apparent that he was concerned that Mandy had returned to work prematurely following the birth of her child; this caused tension between the two of them:

... Mandy was shaking with anger, she'd been arguing with Ken in the manager's office: 'If he wants to be a prick I'll send my husband down to sort him out! Fucking arsehole wants me to take some time off 'til I've lost a bit more weight!'... This had been building for some time since Mandy had returned to work. Ken had never been keen on Mandy for some reason and I was given the impression that he was using her recent birth to make things difficult for her to return permanently ...[11]

Although Mandy eventually 'cooperated' by temporarily leaving Starlets to 'get back in shape', her and Ken's relationship continued to deteriorate. However, unlike Sam and Janine, the other dancers quickly accepted Mandy and her original old-school status was re-established. A practical explanation is that Mandy was not absent from the club for as long as Sam and Janine; more specifically, in the time Mandy was absent from Starlets, the tacit rules did not dramatically change, thereby making it easier for her to relearn them, nor had the initial respect she had gained had time to dissipate.

The meaning of status

What is apparent from the hierarchical nature of the way in which dancers in Starlets were organized is the extent to which they were able to self-regulate and govern themselves as workers (Colosi 2010b forthcoming). In this way dancers were able to achieve some level of autonomy and control within an occupation which is essentially patriarchal (Wesely 2002). The self-regulation evident in Starlets suggests how the dancers attempted to resist against the control club owners and managers had over these workers. For instance, investing in the tacit rules and putting emphasis on the pursuit of fun and excitement, evidenced through their avid engagement with the social rituals acted to challenge the existing house rules and therefore, on some level, is indicative of the dancers' rejection of the management's authority. The placing of emphasis by the dancers on the social rituals to some extent was in conflict with the club's central aim: to make money. Dancers finding a space in which they were able to resist patriarchal domination and derive some level of power is in line with some of the arguments put forward by Egan (2006a, 2006b) and Frank (2003). Others, however, have been more cynical about dancers' sense of empowerment and suggested that it cannot truly be achieved (see Barton, 2002, 2006; Wesely 2002). However, what is evident is that through the tacit rules, which were to some extent negotiated with managers, the dancers at Starlets were able, at least momentarily, to transcend any occupational and, more widely, any cultural, social, economic and political patriarchal subordination they were subjected to. Further to this, what is also suggested by the discussions over the last three chapters is how the power relationships between the actual dancers were not only central to the way in which they were organized as workers, but how these relationships impacted on dancer conduct and also how this power was both unbalanced and always in flux. Previously discussions about the power relationships within strip clubs have been focused around those between customers and dancers (Egan 2006a; Frank, 2003) and dancers and managers/club owners (Wesely 2003). Understanding how dancers' actions and interactions are influenced by the power relations between the dancers themselves, which are transmitted through the tacit rules, perhaps helps us think more broadly about how they might influence the relationships dancers also have with customers and managers. Rather than making sense of these sets of relationships in isolation, it is perhaps necessary to take into account how the different power relations evident between the various social actors of the lap-dancing club are to some extent intertwined and further suggest the complexity and multifaceted nature of 'power' per se (Foucault 1977, 1980). This is something which other writers have alluded to (see, for example, Frank 2007).

What is also apparent from the discussions over the last three chapters is how the dancers at Starlets were part of a unique hierarchical occupational subculture, of which new-girl, transition and old-school dancers comprise. Others have also suggested that stripping is subcultural (see, for example, Bernard *et al.* 2003; Forsyth and Deshotels 1998a) but without being explicit. The subculture identified in Starlets is not strictly defined by the traditional theoretical parameters one might associate with youth cultures, such as the Centre for Contemporary Studies (CCCS), or with the American 'delinquent subcultures' outlined by Cohen (1955) or Cloward and Ohlin (1960), or even the post-subcultures approach often associated with 'club cultures' (see, for example, Thornton 1997; Malbon 1999).[12] Although it might be argued that the subculture identified is resistant like those theorized by the CCCS and also part of the solution to the challenges dancers face in the workplace, as suggested in the American model, however, the internal world of the lap-dancer is more nuanced than this. Instead then, analysis can be derived from the early Chicago examples of 'subculture', evident in the work of Cressey (1932) and Whyte (1943), in which 'subculture' is suggestive of the 'distinctive social worlds' of groups. More specifically, each 'distinctive social world' expresses a unique 'scheme of life' (Park 1925). Those studied by both Cressey (1932) and Whyte (1943) were identified by their own distinct sets of rules, values and rituals. Cressey (1932), for example, explored the distinctive social world of taxi-hall dancers in the 1920/30s, which he suggested was characterized by the dance-hall setting, the unique language and the special 'code of conduct'. Parallels in this way, can be seen between the occupational subculture of lap-dancing and that of taxi-dancers; the use of this term, along with a discussion of Cressey's (1932) taxi-dancers in relation to the contemporary lap-dancer, is addressed further in Colosi (2010a). The occupational subculture identified in this ethnography is characterized by the setting of Starlets, the tacit rules which shape club conduct as well as cultivate and maintain the dancer hierarchy, and finally the social and emotional rituals. For instance, through the engagement of social and emotional rituals, lap-dancers experienced a sense of subcultural membership, a theme which is also reflected in Cressey's work (see Colosi 2010a, for a full discussion). In relation to this, Chapter 7, in particular, explores the way in which bonds between dancers were developed in Starlets, through engaging with various emotional and social rituals. It was also argued that these bonds were important in securing the dancer's role in the lap-dancing club, aiding her in her advancement through the dancer hierarchy and building and maintaining her popularity with other dancers. The strong bonds developed between dancers are indicative of the *experience* of subcultural membership between dancers. This can also be seen in Chapter 9 in the dancers' reactions to their retirement from Starlets. For instance, after leaving the club, dancers would often comment on missing certain elements of their time at work; this usually revolved around socialization and friendship. It was not unusual for dancers who left Starlets to revisit as customers and thus continue to socialize with the other, working dancers. For example, as is discussed in Chapter 9, both Becks and Phoenix, having left the club due to pregnancy, regularly visited Starlets and spent time socializing with the dancers on the main floor during this period. Further to this, several dancers both in their retirement and re-entry into dancing, stress the emotional bonds they developed with their colleagues. As well as emphasizing the importance of the dancers' re-engagement with this occupational subculture, it also highlights the emotional nature of their subcultural bonds, something which has remained unexplored in both mainstream 'subculture' and 'post-subculture' literature (see Colosi 2010a). The sense of membership experienced between dancers is a theme that is also threaded through the discussions in Chapter 9. This penultimate chapter looks at the exit routes of dancers, reflecting some of the key reasons provided by women at Starlets for their retirement.

Notes

1 Field diary extract.
2 Field diary extract.
3 Field diary extract.
4 It is stipulated in the house rules that evening dresses must be no shorter than below the knee.
5 Nurse, school girl and dominatrix themes were popular amongst the dancers at Starlets.
6 Field diary extract.
7 Field diary extract.
8 Field diary extract.
9 Field diary extract.
10 Field diary extract.
11 Field diary extract.
12 For a detailed discussion of these positions see Colosi (2010a) and Blackman (2005).

Part 3

Karen's story – Part 3: leaving Starlets

... I got sacked ... I'd had no sleep so I couldn't possibly face coming in [to Starlets]. But I thought: I can't ring up? Should I ring Gerard or should I just ring the office? So I thought: right, withhold the number and ring. So I rang [Gerard] and was like: Hi Gerard you all right? It's Karen. I won't be in today coz I really don't feel well ... Tony [Karen's partner] always used to be saying things like: 'you not going to work?' I'd be like: no I don't feel well. He's like: 'Karen they're gonna like sack you if you keep doing this'. I was like: I know. I'll do what I want. Get off my case. I started being a bitch to him over it ... this one day I was actually really ill. I think I had like two grams [of cocaine] and I think it was like really strong ... it must have been like poisoning, you know like the same sort of thing as alcohol poisoning. So anyway, I had two grams. One of them was supposed to be for Dana [dancer friend] ... and I was like: yeah I'll keep it for you ... the next morning I was supposed to be in Starlets, for like 12 or something. God I felt like shit, I was like for fuck sake man! Why did you do that, why? Why couldn't you just keep it for Dana? I was like oh shit I'm skint I've got no money, I thought: is it even gonna help if I had some more [cocaine]? Can I even be bothered to pick up the phone and like ring someone to get some? No I can't ... I walked to the bus stop to get the bus to work. Oh my God I felt like shit. I had to wait for the bus. I rang Gerard and said I was too ill to come in. Well he was going off it! He totally went off it! He

had a disgusting attitude on the phone. I wanted to kill him! I put the phone down straightaway! I was like: Oh my God he is a nutter! He's a knob ... had to get a taxi to work in the end coz I was really late ... I was still feeling really ill ... my stomach was jittery and stuff ... I felt like I was [moving] in like slow motion ... I got to work, I walked up them stairs. I was like: fucking hell. I don't want to be here ... I had to go to the toilet and I sat down. I knew I had to work but couldn't, so I go into the office to see Ken. I was like: look I'm gonna have to go home, I really don't feel well ... Ken was like: 'if you leave you lose your job'. I was like: look I feel really bad. But I just left anyway before he could say anything. There was no way I could have actually worked ... I rang Dana ... went to Dana's and I just like lay on the couch just shivering and stuff, like really shivering ... Ended up phoning Gerard, and he started being a twat on the phone ... but it was out my hands, he just sacked me. I thought: fucking hell! That was it. Sacked ... Dana was working that night and Gerard was being a right cock to her so she ended up just walking out. She just left ... I rang Gerard back and tried to get my job back ... I was like: just give us my job back and I'll change. But Gerard was like: No! But they did us a favour, it doesn't matter, it was doing my head in anyway ... Like after getting sacked from Starlets everything came to a head ... ended up getting evicted coz I owed like £2000 in rent ... I was actually becoming quite sick of my life at the time. Really sick of it. [I] hardlies [sic] had any friends. I was just like friends with like dancers and stuff. Like just going to work and taking coke, socializing and stuff. And then, I think this is what actually saved us, the U-turn, was when I got evicted ... I had to like get all my stuff and put it in storage. I was so, so sad that night ... the night before I was like crying. Packed all my stuff and waved goodbye to it ... I told Tricia [dancer friend] and I explained the situation and I was like: can I stay at yours tonight. She was cool with it. So I ended up staying with her for a bit until I got myself sorted ... I was good, I didn't have any coke ... I knew in the back of my mind what I had to do [pause] and that coke was what got me into this situation in the first place. I was like: I'm not getting it [cocaine] because if I get some coke when I go back to Tricia's I don't want to act like a tit and talk her head off. D'y know what I mean? Coz people would be like: 'oh she's a fucking coke head' ... so I was like not having any for that reason ... I got into a routine. On Sunday I'd go out with her [Tricia] and have a few drinks and then on Monday I'd go to Edinburgh. Work there ... but then I started working at Blues [lap-dancing club]. Still didn't have coke ... the whole time I lived with Tricia, when I used to work at Blues, for the whole three months, I didn't ever go to work and buy coke. I thought: right get yourself on the straight and narrow and sort it out. I just stopped buying coke all together and that was it ... but then I started taking it again, but not as much, just enough to keep me working ... worked at Blues on Thursdays and eventually I'd buy a gram [of cocaine] when I got there, make £70, and have £30 for the following Friday to buy some more [cocaine] ... it wasn't a problem, not like before ... everything changed when I fell pregnant with Dylan so I stopped dancing ... when I had Dylan I wasn't going to go back, full stop, that's it I thought. But I actually did go back for money in the end. Coz now I've got to think about him [Dylan]. So started working at Jazz [lap-dancing club]. It's OK there, the money's good coz the club's still new ... you can make £300 in a night, £400 if you work your arse off ... I know I can't do it forever, I want to go to college and make a future for me and Dylan. But I'll maybe dance to support myself through that ... it's weird though coz Dana was saying: 'I was just walking past this lap-dancing club today, and I just thought to myself, God imagine when you're say 40 and you can't do it anymore!' I was like: I know the feeling. I felt like I was 40 or something. I got this sudden feeling where your heart starts racing, like an addiction thing ... at the end of the day I think the addiction thing must be right ... I think it's the fact that you are sort of morphing into a different life and ... living on the dangerous side and you're doing things that the majority of people wouldn't do ... it's like Mercedes [retired dancer], she has got a comfortable life but I know she'll probably go back (to dancing) somewhere down the line ...

Chapter 9

Leaving Starlets

... Returning to Starlets as a customer, there primarily to observe, was a strange experience for me. I had been away from the club for a few months and on my return noticed several new dancers. Many of the dancers who had worked at Starlets when I first started my fieldwork were no longer there. I learned from Leanne that some of these dancers had moved to other clubs or simply left without explanation ... It was good to talk to Nelly, Davina and Jan again; all of these dancers had been here when Starlets opened, and they were some of the most established dancers in the club ...[1]

It has been suggested that lap-dancing rarely translates into a long-term career for the women (Forsyth and Deshotels 1998a; Reed 1997), something reflected in the patterns of behaviour observed in Starlets. There are a number of influencing factors leading to a dancer's exit from lap-dancing which will be discussed in this chapter. One factor which inevitably prohibits women working in this profession throughout their lives is age. As suggested in Chapters 6 and 7, physical appearance is a significant aspect of being a lap-dancer. In relation to this point dancers themselves at Starlets were aware of the implications of getting older for their lap-dancing careers, something Tilly, a dancer in her mid-thirties confirmed: 'I've got a few more years left, but you've got to be practical about it, they're not going to want me here when I'm in my 40s.' Although no age limits were set in place at Starlets looking 'youthful' is something managers were keen to promote, indicated by the high numbers of dancers in their late teens and early twenties, with the most populous age bracket being

18 to 25. Tilly was, unusually, older than the majority of lap-dancers at Starlets, but was, despite this, a consistently high earner, with her age in fact being advantageous in her ability to make money. Many of the customers, particularly those in the 30s or above, appeared to find Tilly more confident with seemingly more in common.

Most of the dancers who exited Starlets during the time I conducted my fieldwork did so for reasons other than age; the length of the lap-dancer's career varied and was dependent on a number of factors both inside and outside of her control. This penultimate chapter follows the theme of retirement and explores some of the exit routes taken by the dancers at Starlets. It not only addresses the voluntary exit of dancers but also the dismissal of dancers from the club, reflecting on some of the reasons for this. Surprisingly the exit of dancers is an area that has only been briefly touched on by other researchers (Barton 2006; Bradley 2007). Finally, this chapter will consider why some dancers returned to Starlets after temporarily retiring.

Saying goodbye

Whatever a dancer's reason might have been for leaving Starlets, it was often an emotional experience, suggestive of the 'emotional' nature of the work dancers engage in. As discussed in Chapter 7, there has been acknowledgement of sex work involving emotional as well as physical labour (Barton 2006; Chapkis 1997; Kempadoo and Doezema 1998; Sanders 2005), although little has been indicated about the emotional *attachment* lap-dancers form with one another, with the exception of Barton (2006) and Forsyth and Deshotels (1998a). Sociology rarely discusses the role of emotions, despite the fact that 'emotions are the "glue" binding people together and generating commitments to large-scale social and cultural structures' (Turner and Stets 2005: 1). This is a principle clearly indicated by the sense of membership experienced between the dancers at Starlets. Of course, as previous examples and discussions have indicated, lap-dancing, for the dancers at Starlets, was the proverbial emotional roller coaster. Different dancers left Starlets with powerful, but often mixed feelings about their exit, as the following examples indicate.

Janine decided to exit her job as a dancer at Starlets after facing disapproval from her partner; similar behaviour has been observed by Bradley (2007). It was perhaps, in part, due to the circumstances of her retirement that Janine was very emotional and saddened by the prospect of leaving the club, as is demonstrated in the following field diary extract:

... It was Janine's last day at Starlets and at the end of the shift everyone was crowded round her. She was hugging some of the dancers who were all telling her to stay; they all seemed to disapprove of her reason for leaving ... Janine became increasingly emotional about leaving; it wasn't long before her eyes were puffy from crying. She continued to cry and kept telling people that she didn't want to leave: 'I'm going to miss you girls so much, I wish I could stay' ...

In contrast Adele was far more satisfied about her decision to leave:

... I remained in contact with Adele after she left Starlets; I met up with her a few months after she retired from dancing ... I wanted to know how she felt now that she had left Starlets ... Adele explained: 'No I would never go back to dancing ... So glad to get out of it ... to be honest I don't like the thought that I ever did it!' However, I wasn't surprised by her lack of sentimentality; before leaving Adele had faced several conflicts with some of the dancers ...

Adele's reaction to leaving Starlets was common among those who did not appear to feel part of the apparent lap-dancing 'subculture'. Sandy, for example, expressed similar contempt for lap-dancing after retiring from Starlets: 'I can't tell you how much better things are ... it's like a weight has been lifted.' This sense of dissatisfaction with lap-dancing also included dancers who were dismissed (sacked) rather than leaving of their own accord. For example, Linda, after being dismissed from Starlets, was disparaging about the club and the people who worked there:

... Starlets overall was an absolutely horrible experience for me because even now, if you said go back and work at Starlets, which is quite sort of glamorous and desirable, or go back to the Dog and Crown and strip, I would choose the Dog and Crown[2] any day because there isn't that sort of snobbiness that you get at Starlets. And you know what I detest. I hate those girls at Starlets who call themselves dancers, we're not dancers we're strippers! We're strippers and I have no problem with going 'I am a stripper' ...

In this extract Linda attacks the dancers at Starlets by calling them 'snobs', something she emphasizes by drawing attention to their preferred choice of working title 'dancer' as opposed to 'stripper'. Interestingly, there is some truth in what Linda contends: many of the dancers at Starlets *did* refuse to be called strippers, particularly those who had *not* previously worked for stripping agencies or indeed as freelance strippers in pubs and clubs. For these dancers the name 'stripper' had negative connotations, further suggestive of the stigma, along with the dancer cognizance of this, which is attached to erotic dancing and more widely the sex industry, as discussed in Chapter 7. This rejection of the 'stripper' label is something emphasized in Sally's reaction after a customer referred to her as a 'stripper': 'I'm not a stripper, I'm a dancer! Strippers are dirty ... Lap-dancing is far more tasteful.'

Unlike Janine, Adele, Sandy and Linda, other dancers seemed less certain and had mixed feelings about leaving. Tilly, for example, who although had not originally planned to leave until age so dictated, nonetheless left prematurely to concentrate on the fitness training business she had built with her husband. For Tilly the prospect of ending her career at Starlets was something she felt positive about. However, she also admitted feeling sad about leaving the other dancers: 'I know it's time to leave ... but it's difficult saying goodbye.' Similarly, Becks, who, when she became pregnant, left Starlets to focus on the role of being a 'full-time mother', conveyed a mixture of sadness and happiness about leaving the club. Talking to Becks a few months after she left the club, she said that although she was pleased with her decision to stop dancing she nonetheless missed the closeness she had experienced with other dancers: 'I don't miss the dancing so much, but my friends ... It would be nice to be back for them.' Even Karen, who explained in the final part of her story that the managers did her a favour by dismissing her, goes on to admit that she found the thought of completely giving up dancing very difficult to accept. Although the dancers' responses to leaving are different, what is apparent is the emotional impact that working at Starlets had on these workers. More specifically, these emotional reactions are somewhat indicative of the close bonds formed between the dancers. In some ways the manner in which leaving Starlets was addressed by dancers is rather reminiscent of the emotional reactions produced after the breakdown of a close personal relationship.

Exit routes

... I hadn't seen Davina since I was last in Starlets ... I was surprised to hear she was planning to leave the club in the next couple of months; Davina explained: 'I've had enough of dancing ... my boyfriend's in the RAF and I'm planning on going with him when he's posted

away ...' Davina went on to tell me how happy she was in this new relationship ... although he was supportive of her choice of occupation, she explained that he was one of the main reasons she wanted to retire from dancing ...[3]

In the above extract it is apparent that Davina attributed her eventual exit from Starlets to her relationship with her partner. This was not unusual, as it was evident from this research that relationships were sometimes a catalyst for dancers retiring from Starlets. Although not all of the dancers left Starlets of their own free will, this section focuses on those who did; the dismissal of dancers is discussed later in this chapter. Following the same pattern as the entry routes documented in Chapter 5, two similar types of exit routes have been identified: those which are practically driven and those which are emotionally driven. Like those entry routes discussed in relation to entering a career in lap-dancing, within these exit routes there are several different patterns of choice. Practical exit routes include those that relate to change of career, childbirth and relocation, whereas more emotionally driven exit routes include the stresses and demands associated with relationships and the general psychological strain associated with the job. It is important to point out that these exit routes do not necessarily lead to permanent retirement; as was indicated in Chapter 8, it was not uncommon for dancers to re-enter this occupation. Returning to dancing after retirement is something that is discussed in more detail later on in this chapter.

In relation to the exit routes, it is important to make the following points. Firstly, with regard to the relocation of dancers as an exit route, although it refers to the retirement of dancers from Starlets, it does not mean that the dancers associated with this route necessarily excluded themselves from working at other lap-dancing clubs. Secondly, it is also important to emphasize the connection between the two emotionally driven exit routes, relationships and psychological strain. Both, as will become clear in the following discussion, are inevitably linked. Finally, in a similar fashion to the entry routes discussed in Chapter 5, the exit routes do not necessarily work in isolation, as more than one route might be associated with a dancer's retirement.

Change of career

This refers to dancers who ended their lap-dancing career in pursuit of another occupation. The nature of the career change varied, as reflected in the choices made by some of the dancers who left Starlets to pursue new jobs, for example, Sandy, an old-school dancer, who, after working in the club for two years, retired from dancing to work with a local group which supported disadvantaged children. This change in career was something she had planned and trained for while working at Starlets. Sandy explained to me that she wanted a career that would provide her with security in the future: 'It's time to get out ... I want a real job, a proper career.' For Sandy, lap-dancing was not something she ever considered as permanent or as a job with credibility, hence why she did not consider it a *real job*.

Jenna, another old-school dancer, worked at Starlets for a couple of years before leaving to pursue a new occupation:

> ... *I was talking to Davina about Jenna leaving Starlets ... Jenna left the club to manage a new bar that had opened in the city centre, something that she had previous experience of before lap-dancing. Davina, who was still friends with her, explained that she was really happy in her new occupational role and was pleased to have left Starlets ...*[4]

Returning to bar management was a convenient change of career for Jenna as she already had the required skills. Although immediately prior to dancing Jenna had waitressed at Starlets, it was never made clear why she had left bar management in the first place, though some dancers did speculate that she had been dismissed from this role rather than her taking voluntary leave.

Following the departure of these old-school dancers, Adele also exited Starlets in pursuit of a new occupation. Lap-dancing had provided Adele with financial support throughout the degree course she studied at university, having started dancing while she was a student. However, after completing her degree Adele had applied for various jobs and been successful in gaining a temporary yet promising post working for a newspaper:

> ... *It seems Adele has settled into her new position at the newspaper, after initially being taken on for a short contract, they have now offered her a longer one. She sounded so excited and happy about how things had worked out for her: 'Work's going so well ... the place is fantastic' ...*[5]

Finally, Sam, an old-school dancer ended her career at Starlets in order to pursue a career in modelling. This change of career was initiated after meeting a photographer in Starlets who helped create

145

her portfolio. Like other dancers, Sam talked openly about leaving the club and some dancers in fact commented that she was 'bragging' about her career move. As one of the dancer's commented: 'She thinks she's going to be a big star.'

What appears to be evident from the examples provided in this section is that those who used a change of career to exit lap-dancing did so for jobs they considered more meaningful or more stable or permanent. For example, Adele and Sandy in particular pursued occupations they had both worked towards and about which they felt strongly; not only does this suggest that their new roles carry more meaning for them, but that lap-dancing was something they considered as a means to an end and therefore more temporary. Women using stripping in this way, as a means to an end, has also been suggested by Lewis (1998). In a similar way, Sam in her pursuit of a career in modelling was choosing a job that offered her more meaning; again this would suggest that lap-dancing, for Sam, was a means to an end. Tilly and Jenna, on the other hand, both left dancing to focus on occupations of which they had previous knowledge and for which they had acquired the relevant skills. Not only does this suggest a move of convenience, but also that both Tilly and Jenna, due to the nature of their preferred occupations, were opting for ones that, in different ways, offered more stability. Tilly, for example, as a dancer in her 30s was aware that her age would soon prevent her from continuing to work at Starlets. With this in mind, by focusing on her fitness training business, she was opting to pursue something that did not have the same restrictions. Finally, Jenna, by returning to a managerial role, was choosing an occupation that offered her a more fixed income and therefore more stability.

Pregnancy and childbirth

Some dancers who ended their careers either permanently or temporarily did so to give birth. For all of the dancers in this position during my fieldwork, almost half saw retirement as temporary and some of those dancers did indeed return to work as lap-dancers. Re-entering a career in lap-dancing is something that is explored later in this chapter. Although dancers inevitably did not have a choice about exiting dancing when they were pregnant, their jobs as lap-dancers usually remained open. With this in mind dancers could use childbirth as an opportunity to take a temporary or more permanent retirement from dancing. Therefore in the long run, this exit route should still be considered voluntary.

Mandy was the first dancer to leave Starlets due to pregnancy during the time I spent in the field. She did not talk openly about the circumstances of her pregnancy but neither did it appear to be something she regretted. Mandy was keen to return to dancing after the birth of her child:

> ... Mandy was sitting with Candy, Becks and myself on the main floor near the DJ booth. She had just told us she was pregnant and seemed so happy about it. We all congratulated her. Mandy explained that she planned to leave when her pregnancy started to show: 'I'm going to dance for as long as I can ... I've had a word with Ken and Gerard and I'm going to stop doing the stage shows soon' ...

Due to financial reasons, other pregnant dancers planned to continue working until it was physically evident they were pregnant. However, in Starlets, it could be sensed that the managers were ever watchful for pregnant dancers – a dancer who showed her condition was not good for business as it could be calamitous for the club's reputation. After all, the visible signs of pregnancy are not in keeping with the desired dancer physique or the sexual availability lap-dancing managers want their dancers to advertise (Barton 2006; Wesely 2003). In relation to this, Ken's attitude towards Mandy seemed to change when she announced she was pregnant, and although she planned to stay for as long as possible, it was shortly after her announcement that she retired from Starlets. Approximately a year later Phoenix also became pregnant:

> ... I was talking to Davina in the changing room and was told that Phoenix was pregnant. This was not unexpected; Phoenix had apparently been trying for a baby for some time. As Candy later explained: 'God yeah. I wasn't surprised. She's been trying for ages. Not sure if her boyfriend was expecting it though!' ...

Like Mandy, Phoenix continued to dance for a short time after discovering she was pregnant. However, when Becks became pregnant she stayed at Starlets for as long as possible in order to save money in preparation for motherhood, but still left before her pregnancy was obvious. Despite having a good relationship with management, Becks was still subjected to the same disapproval other pregnant dancers faced. When the time came to leave the club, she was happy to go and focus on becoming a mother. Becks explained to me that although she intended to return to dancing, motherhood would be her primary consideration: 'I will probably go back and work part time, maybe on a Saturday afternoon.' However, despite Becks' plans to return to work on a part-time basis, she decided not to lap-dance again soon after the birth of her son: 'I'm just happy being a mum ... after having Scott, I feel differently about it.' Becks explained to me that she did not think it was appropriate for her to work in the sex industry any longer. Although she had not made any moral judgement about lap-dancing prior to becoming a mother, Becks now saw a conflict between being a good role model for her child and taking her clothes off for money.

Relocation

This refers to dancers who left Starlets to work in other lap-dancing clubs or simply relocate geographically for various non-work-related reasons. It was not uncommon for dancers to relocate to other lap-dancing clubs either nationally or internationally. Relocating in this way is still significant as an exit route: firstly, the dancers in question left behind the culture associated with working at Starlets and, secondly, it raises questions about their reasons for leaving Starlets in favour of other clubs. Exiting Starlets in this way was not necessarily a permanent relocation; some dancers worked in other clubs for short periods of time and then returned to Starlets. Ruby for example, on more than one occasion worked in other lap-dancing clubs nationally and abroad, often spending two or three months working away in various clubs: 'I worked there [Red Diva lap-dancing club] for a good few months until the summer and then I went to Ibiza and I had a few months off, then I got back into it [working at Starlets] when I got back from Ibiza.' Some of the dancers who relocated to other clubs intended the move to be permanent. Stella, for example, had started a relationship with another dancer who did not live locally and on that basis relocated to another club outside of the city where Starlets was based to be nearer to her partner. Other dancers, including Dina and Lucy, planned to relocate abroad to work in various lap-dancing clubs. Neither dancer had any fixed plans; however, Lucy in particular indicated that she did not intend to return to Starlets:

> RC: *Are you coming back?*
> Lucy: *No. I want to dance over there and then try and get back into professional dancing. I've had enough of working here.*
> RC: *What about Dina?*
> Lucy: *Fuck knows. She's away with the fairies but she doesn't reckon she'll be back.*[6]

Before working as a lap-dancer at Starlets Lucy had been a professionally trained dancer, and her original entry into lap-dancing was intended to be temporary while she waited between jobs; using stripping as a career break has also been accounted for by Skipper and McCaghy (1970). In contrast, Bella left Starlets to relocate geographically with her partner. Her intention was also to stop lap-dancing and go back into nursing, something for which she had originally been trained. It was not, however, clear exactly why she had left nursing to become a lap-dancer in the first place. Bella only worked at Starlets for six months and her departure was sudden, with only a few dancers informed of her reasons for leaving:

> ... Sandy and I were sitting together on the main floor; I had noticed Bella hadn't been in Starlets for a few days, which was unusual as she worked most nights. Sandy and she were friendly so I asked her why she hadn't been working; to my surprise I was informed that Bella had in fact left Starlets and moved away with her boyfriend ...

Relocation, as an exit route, is not isolated as it is often associated with other routes. For example, Stella relocated to work at another lap-dancing club to be closer to her partner, suggesting that her relationship was the driving force for her relocation. What is also apparent from this section on relocation is the flexible nature of lap-dancing as a form of employment. For example, as has been demonstrated, dancers were able to relocate to other clubs with ease, both nationally and internationally. Further to this dancers were able to return to Starlets after a period of working in other lap-dancing clubs.

Relationships

This refers to dancers who ended their career at Starlets due to the disapproval of partners and/or the tension caused in those relationships by the very nature of the job. Although not all of the dancers who found it difficult to maintain their relationships left Starlets as a result, it was still a common problem and one that is reflected in this ethnography. It is clearly suggested that dancers struggle in many instances to maintain healthy personal relationships outside the club; this is something echoed in the work of Barton (2006) and Bradley (2007), who both also reported tensions between dancers and their partners over the nature of the industry in which they were involved. Further to this, Bradley (2007) describes how nearly all of the former dancers she interviewed reported that relationship difficulties were influential in their decisions to end their careers. Of those dancers at Starlets who did confront romantic difficulties, some talked openly about their problems:

> ... Paris was still in a relationship with Dan despite his dislike of her working as a dancer. As a result of his jealousy she had become very cynical about men and their ability to cope with her dancing: '... Why can't I meet someone who doesn't care what I do' ...[7]

Barton (2006) in a similar way found that heterosexual relationships are not the only ones in which jealousy of customers arose; as she suggests, lesbian relationships are also affected. This was something also reported by some of the dancers at Starlets. For example, prior to dating Andrea, Stella had been in a relationship with someone outside the industry. Her partner had not prevented her from working, but neither had she approved of Stella lap-dancing; she explained: 'She's jealous! She doesn't like me dancing for men, like I'm going to go off with one when I'm gay!' This jealousy was not specific to dancers who had relationships with individuals outside of the industry; in some cases dancers who were in relationships with staff members were also confronted by difficulties. Vienna, for example, who was in a relationship with Bobby, one of the bouncers, found it increasingly difficult to work as a dancer due to Bobby's resentment of the customers. Other dancers knew of their difficulties and would sometimes talk about it:

> **Hally:** He's really possessive ... He doesn't like her dancing here.
> **Jan:** She'll end up leaving.
> **Hally:** I know that they argue about it all the time.
> **Jan:** That's typical. He knew what she did when he started seeing her![8]

Contrary to expectations, Vienna did not leave Starlets because of her relationship, but other dancers, including Sally and Janine, did exit the club as a result of personal relationships. For example, Sally, soon after meeting her partner, ended her career at Starlets. Her exit was abrupt and although she did not confirm her relationship as the reason for her departure, other dancers suggested this was so. Candy explained: 'Think it was her bloke ... he didn't want her dancing. Fucking hypocrite, he met her here!' Significantly McCaghy and Skipper (1970) suggest that it is not uncommon for men to attempt

missal

...Kate ran into the changing room crying, Gordon [head bouncer] was waiting for her by the door to escort her out of the club after she had gathered her clothes together. Some of the dancers stared at her with contempt and she collapsed on the floor and wept. Sally turned to her and screamed: 'What do you expect, you fucking weirdo! Don't expect to get any sympathy from us.' I felt sorry for Kate, even though she'd broken the rules and had been sacked as a result, and felt Sally's remarks were unnecessarily hurtful. Looking around some of the dancers seemed equally concerned for her but decided to keep quiet; in the long run they were aware it would only cause more conflict ...[12]

Although some of the dancers left Starlets of their own accord, others were dismissed by management. Although there were a number of different reasons for the dismissal of dancers, mostly it was due to rule-breaking. However, the breaking of rules did not necessarily relate directly to the official house rules set by the club, but were often related to the tacit rules of the club. To reiterate, as well as guiding the general conduct of the dancers, they also set the boundaries for what was considered acceptable behaviour in accordance with the stage in the hierarchy the dancer was at. Therefore each stage had different rules to follow and was also subject to various restrictions and/or privileges. Along with rules around dirty dancing, another example, to reiterate, included the consumption of recreational drugs; although this was somewhat normalised in Starlets across the hierarchy, overt drug-taking was still more acceptable among old-school and transition dancers than it was with new girls, who did not have the same privileges. This is conveyed in the prologue to this section, which revisits the story of Kate, originally explored in Chapter 6, who was dismissed from Starlets after other dancers witnessed her dirty dancing and suspected her of 'openly' consuming recreational drugs. Her new-girl status prohibited these overt actions and as a consequence she was dismissed from the club. In this case, as with others in which the breaking of the tacit rules was at the root of a dancer being sacked, it was the other dancers who were actually complicit in the dancer's dismissal. As illustrated earlier in Chapters 6 and 8, dancers were scrutinized by their colleagues, and if they continually failed to comply with the rules would be reported to the managers. To reiterate, this inevitably meant in such cases involving the tacit rules the majority of old-school dancers were exempt from being dismissed. However, regardless of a dancer's

---

to persuade the dancers with whom they are in a relationship to abandon their dancing career.

Like Sally, Janine met her partner while working at Starlets; he was a customer at the time. As their relationship intensified, she admitted that he was becoming increasingly possessive and raised objections to her working as a lap-dancer. Before she left Starlets, from the various conversations I had with her, it became apparent that the nature of her job was causing their relationship to fragment:

... I felt sorry for Janine, she'd been with Andrew for a little while but her relationship was not happy. Janine explained to me that he would argue with her about leaving Starlets: 'He hates it. I don't want to leave but I don't want to lose him'. She went on to explain that she felt helpless about the situation she was in. Those dancers to whom she was close did not approve of his attitude towards Janine and would often try and persuade her to leave him ...[9]

Ironically, before meeting Andrew, Janine had always appeared to take pleasure from her job and as a result had been one of the highest earners in the club. The pressure she experienced emotionally from Andrew's disapproval became increasingly apparent in her lack of willingness to dance for customers:

... Janine was sitting alone on the floor at the back of the changing room, she looked depressed. Every night she was the same. I sat next to her and asked her what was wrong. She smiled and looked at me as though I should know: Andrew of course. Janine explained: 'I can't go on like this ... I just don't want to come to work. He hates it so much' ...[10]

As Bradley (2007) argues, for dancers in this situation, 'they face particular challenges as dancers attempt to balance the expectations of their partners with the demands of their profession' (p. 379). For Janine striking this balance became impossible. It was therefore inevitable that she made the decision to end her career and leave Starlets. In contrast, although Angelica did not have relationship difficulties, she made the decision to leave Starlets because of the effect she believed lap-dancing would inevitably have on her relationship. In a conversation I had with Angelica, she explained how she did not believe her job was compatible with relationships: 'I don't think it's right. If I was a bloke I'd hate it if my lass was a lap-dancer.' Interestingly, both Angelica and Janine returned to Starlets while in the same relationships; this will be revisited and discussed further later in this chapter.

Psychological strain

This is an area of the lap-dancing experience that has been acknowledged by a number of authors (Barton 2002, 2006, 2007; Deshotels and Forsyth 2005; Holsopple 1999; Maticka-Tyndale *et al.* 2000; Wesley 2002; Wood 2000). In the wider context of gender and work, the idea discussed is often understood in relation to Hochschild's (1983) work on emotional labour. The emotional pressures and learning to cope with the psychological strain of lap-dancing was discussed in Chapter 7. For example, emphasis was placed, by dancers, on the importance of being able to adapt emotionally and psychologically in order to continue working in this role. Although, as has been suggested, these women learned, in various ways, to cope by employing different strategies, there were inevitably those who were never able to 'grow a thick skin' or who had periods in which the pressure of dancing became psychologically overwhelming, as suggested by Paris' experience:

> ... Paris admitted to suffering from depression, and because of this she drank quite heavily, particularly when she was at Starlets. I was sitting talking to her on the main floor; she was quite drunk but very coherent. We were talking about the emotional pressures of lap-dancing, something Paris often talked about. She wasn't happy, it was obvious, and she seemed to be very negative about lap-dancing in general: 'So many dancers are on anti-depressants you know. It's this job, it gets to you in the end'. I was aware of a few other dancers, Lucy and Cindy, who also claimed to be taking anti-depressants, but to what extent this was due to lap-dancing alone I was uncertain ...[11]

Not all of the dancers who were affected in this way would necessarily leave Starlets; some would cope by using drugs and alcohol to blot out the feelings of anxiety (Forsyth and Deshotels 1998b; Maticka-Tyndale *et al.* 2000; Wesely 2003), as suggested in Chapter 7. This emotionally driven exit route was rarely offered as a prime reason for leaving. For example, dancers would often cite other reasons such as relocation, career change and relationships, but sometimes simultaneously indicate their struggle to cope with the psychological demands of the job. In terms of relationships, where partners disapproved of a dancer's occupation, lap-dancing inevitably became

a psychological strain; this is why the two wer linked. This does not, however, indicate that d dancing a psychological strain were necessarily ha their relationships, but it was not unexpected or was the case. Returning to dancers Paris and Janin that both were affected emotionally by their par of lap-dancing, which in turn impacted upon the their occupation and caused them to feel the psych dancing. In relation to this, Janine, for example, bega career as a lap-dancer, believing that dancing, and no itself, was the catalyst for her troubles. This again c the work of Bradley (2007), in which it is argued: report constant feelings of guilt associated with their feelings appear to be triggered by their partner's actic discussed earlier, these conflicts inevitably led to Jan from Starlets.

Other dancers were also affected emotionally by the job, but not directly as a result of a relationship. Sandy although excited in the pursuit of a new career as sugge this chapter, also admitted that she was finding dancing difficult:

> ... Sandy and I sat talking about leaving the club; she was ... I knew from subsequent conversations that there was m leaving than pursuing a new job. For a few months now talked about how dancing would eat away at her, that it ha to knock all her confidence. I reminded her of how she'd bee and she explained: 'I hate coming in now. It's like a black cl my head' ...

Similarly, in my final conversation before she left Starlets, Je usually presented a happy disposition, talked about deve dislike of lap-dancing: 'I'm sick of it ... sick of the manage everything. Just need a fresh start'. In these cases it seems psychological pressure induced by lap-dancing became a pro dancers to find ways out of the industry, through, in the case o and Jenna, a change of career. In general, the social stigma ass with lap-dancing which the dancers at Starlets often experienc them to re-evaluate their occupation. As Karen explained: 'Yo to question what you're doing!'

status in Starlets the managers ultimately had the power to override any dancer privileges, and although they often choose not to, did so on occasion in order to dismiss a dancer. For example, as highlighted in the final part of Karen's story at the end of Chapter 8, Gerard dismissed Karen for bad time keeping and poor attendance which was a result of her heavy cocaine consumption. It was often the use of the various 'bargaining tools' discussed in Chapter 8 and elsewhere (see Colosi 2010b forthcoming) which ultimately prevented old-school dancers from being dismissed for drug-taking. Interestingly this was something Karen did not involve herself in. Other dancers, including Vienna and Amy, were also both eventually dismissed for drug-taking. In Vienna's case, she was caught smoking marijuana at the club and instantly sacked. However, Amy's dismissal was a result of her alleged involvement in the dealing of cocaine in Starlets. It had been rumoured that Amy had been selling drugs to other dancers on the premises, and the managers, according to some of the other dancers, had apparently been aware of this for some time. Ruby described the build-up to this particular incident:

> ... I was in Ibiza in the summer, there was, like, 2 bag searches ... I think what happened was, there was a few different people selling it [cocaine] then, at work, this certain person [Amy] used to get all the new starters on it and they would like, kinda buy it off this person and I dunno there was other people who would, like, bring it in ...

Ironically, both Vienna and Amy's drug-taking continued for some time and, although previously overlooked, it was subsequently used as a reason to dismiss them both. This might suggest that there were other reasons for which the managers no longer wanted them to work at Starlets, reasons that were only known to the managers and dancers in question. It was suggested by some dancers that managers would sometimes dismiss dancers for illegitimate reasons. In relation to this, Linda explained to me during an interview I conducted with her how Gerard had sacked her from Starlets: 'I got sacked in the end. They said, what was it, what was their excuse? I can't remember. I can't remember what the excuse was. But it was something silly.' Linda goes on to blame her awareness of the managers' own drug-taking for her dismissal. Despite her claim, other old-school dancers, who had worked with Linda since the club opened, made other suggestions. For example, during one of my subsequent visits to Starlets Davina remarked during a conversation: 'They were horrible to her [Linda], Gerard said she was too fat, but she wasn't ... Loads of guys loved her; she had the same sort of body as Marilyn Monroe.' Interestingly the hypocrisy Linda talked about in relation to the managers was something Ruby also describes when she refers back to the incident in which Amy was dismissed from Starlets. She argued:

> ... *They're all hypocrites anyways, the managers. Coz they're all on it [cocaine]. Even if they don't do it in work. I don't know how they can preach to people when they're not like the best to judge; do you know what I mean ... It's all lap-dancer politics ...*[13]

Ruby blames it on lap-dancing 'politics', without being explicit about what she actually means. However, as Linda suggests, dancers were sometimes targeted if they were seen to be a threat to the managerial setup or to an individual manager. This perhaps explains why managers would suddenly turn against an old-school dancer, dismissing her for activities that had previously gone unpunished. What is further indicated by this is that, although the tacit rules provided dancers with some autonomy, ultimately their resistance could be turned on its head (Price 2008). Some of the dancers who were dismissed from Starlets were removed following their sexual involvement with a manager. Although this was not always the case, managers were perhaps not always keen to work alongside dancers with whom they had been intimately involved and who, as a result, might possess sensitive personal information that could be used against them. Tricia, for example, after becoming pregnant following a casual relationship with one of the managers, was quickly dismissed. This was discussed by other dancers on more than one occasion:

> **Karen:** *You know why he sacked her, don't you?*
> **RC:** *I've heard a rumour.*
> **Karen:** *That she was pregnant. That's why.*

Similarly Eliza, after having a sexual relationship with a manager at Starlets, was targeted by the manager in question, who, following the breakdown of their relationship, seemed to closely police her behaviour in the club. Eventually, following a 'routine' bag search, Eliza, having been found with alcohol among her personal belongings, was dismissed. This was on the basis that alcohol consumed inside the club and purchased from elsewhere was forbidden. In relation to this point, the sale of alcohol was not only aimed at the customers but also the dancers. Ironically, Eliza was not caught consuming the alcohol in question. Beth, soon after it happened, commented: 'He knows we all drink stuff [alcohol purchased outside the club] but he just wanted rid of her ... They've got history.' Common to all these stories of dismissal is a sense of drama and intensity. This, it is argued, is a characteristic of the lap-dancing club: 'The melodrama that goes down on a daily basis in clubs is often so predictable it seems rehearsed' (Dragu and Harrison 1988: 87). Furthermore, it is the lack of professionalism of the managers and the unfair treatment they were prone to inflicting on the dancers at Starlets that is also highlighted. This is discussed further in Chapter 10.

Returning to Starlets

... After speaking to Davina, I spent about half an hour talking to Nelly. I hadn't seen her for almost two years. She'd left Starlets and had been working in various other jobs, it was rumoured that she was working for Veronica's agency [stripping agency]. In some ways I was surprised to see her back at Starlets, mainly due to the fact that Nelly had made enemies in the club among both dancers and managers. Despite this she seemed nonchalant about the situation: 'Nah, that's water under the bridge' ... We talked about the club and how she felt to be back: 'It's like I haven't been away ... It's like having a school reunion being back ... It's good ...'[14]

It is important to point out that many of the dancers who retired from Starlets voluntarily, eventually returned there to work or were known to have sought similar employment in other clubs. Significantly, this was despite the many claims made by retiring dancers that they did not intend to return to Starlets or work in any other lap-dancing clubs. Similar patterns of behaviour are indicated by other researchers (Boles and Garbin 1974b; Forsyth and Deshotels 1998a). According to Forsyth and Deshotels (1998a): 'Many dancers attempt to leave the occupation only to return after a short hiatus' (p. 90). As demonstrated in the opening extract Nelly returned unexpectedly. She was not hesitant about admitting that she loved dancing and had missed the dancers at Starlets. As our conversation continued that evening she explained: 'Nothing's changed [here], it's just the same as it was when I left [Starlets], it'll never change.' Further to this, Nelly likens returning to Starlets to a school reunion; although this reflects her sense of nostalgia it is also indicative of how her relationships with the other dancers made lasting impressions. As is discussed later in this chapter, the emotional attachment dancers had to one another was particularly significant in their being drawn back into dancing. Some dancers, however, returned causing surprise; this, for instance, is evident in the return of Janine.

> ... I couldn't believe my eyes when I saw Janine getting ready in the changing room. I went over and gave her a hug and asked her what brought her back. She explained: 'I know I said I'd never come back but I need the money, I'm only working Saturdays anyway'. Later that evening I spoke to Gerard [manager] about Janine's return and he simply said: 'I knew she'd come back, they always do.' ...

Returning to dancing was justified by dancers primarily as a way of regaining economic security and/or appeared to coincide with the breakdown of a romantic relationship between a dancer and her partner. In relation to regaining economic security, Mandy, for example, who had planned to return to dancing after the birth of her child, explained that now more than ever the financial rewards of dancing were paramount, as she had a child to support: '... aside from other things, I really do need the money now.' In a conversation with Ken (manager) in which we discussed the dancers who return to dancing after retirement, he provided his theory: 'They all say they're not coming back. But they get too greedy and as soon as they can't make the same money elsewhere, they're back.' Aside from this remark being suggestive of the managers' disdain for the dancers, it is also indicative of their cynicism about dancers exiting lap-dancing; many were unconvinced by those who claimed they were leaving permanently. The belief that dancers were primarily money driven was shared among managers, bouncers and some customers, as well as being a common perception held by those who are outsiders to the stripping industry. Customers, on a regular basis, would accuse dancers of being 'greedy' or 'money obsessed'. Some of the bouncers would gossip about dancers being unjustified in their complaints about the money they earned. Gordon [head bouncer], for example, once commented: 'You girls spend all your time moaning about how little money you make ... It's all bullshit, you just like to complain.' As suggested in Chapter 5, although economic factors were regularly cited as a central motivation, contradictory behaviour indicated by dancers' engagement in social activities in the club was very apparent, bringing this explanation into question.

The breakdown of relationships often appeared to coincide with a dancer's re-entry into lap-dancing. Boles and Garbin (1974a) made similar findings with regard to initial entry into dancing; they argue that becoming a dancer usually overlaps with a sudden change in the status of personal relationships between dancers and their partners. Along with Janine's assertion that her re-entry into dancing was financially motivated, her return followed the breakdown of her relationship with Andrew. This revelation was made following a conversation I had with Janine, in which the status of her relationship with her partner, Andrew, was discussed. Janine explained: 'We're still together but it's on the rocks ... I got sick of him telling me what to do.' Boles and Garbin (1974a) suggest that entering lap-dancing following the breakdown of a relationship was used to '... punish a former husband' (p. 115). In relation to this, Janine's return could be understood as a method of punishment directed at Andrew as a reaction to his negative treatment of her. In this way, lap-dancing, something he despised her doing, was being used as a weapon, wielded with the intention of defeating him emotionally. Similarly, when Stella ended her relationship with Andrea, she soon returned to work at Starlets; to reiterate, her purpose for leaving the club was to relocate and in doing so be closer to her partner. It was therefore perhaps inevitable that Stella would return to her family and friends if and when her relationship ended. Although there was an obvious sense of unhappiness conveyed in Stella's mood about the breakdown of her relationship, from her behaviour it seemed apparent that she was nonetheless happy to be working alongside the friends she had initially left behind at Starlets:

> ... Sandy and Stella were as close as ever ... Sandy had been quite angry about Stella's decision to leave Starlets in the first place, but seemed to have forgiven her. I noticed both dancers were walking around the club arm in arm, working together as a team. It was good to see them laughing and joking with each other, especially after the way in which Stella's departure had disrupted their relationship ...[15]

Stella's reaction to returning and the support offered by Sandy over the breakdown of Stella's relationship with Andrea are yet further indications of the close relationships present between dancers within Starlets.

Beneath the surface of these two motivational factors for the return of dancers, including the regaining of economic security and the breakdown of a relationship, dancers are fuelled by the need for self-empowerment and excitement and to regain dancer camaraderie (regaining subcultural membership). For example, (re)gaining a sense of self-empowerment by dancing at Starlets could be achieved financially and socially through re-engaging with the lifestyle associated with lap-dancing. The drive of self-empowerment, whether deemed achievable or not, is a motivational factor previously identified (see, for example, Pasko 2002; Price 2000; Wesely 2002). Self-empowerment, for some of the dancers at Starlets, involved retaining independence by avoiding romantic relationships – the avoidance of relationships by sex workers has previously been acknowledged (Barton 2006; Sanders 2005). A typical example was Janey, a dancer at Starlets, who was suspicious of men and reluctant to enter a serious relationships: 'I'm happy being single and just having fun; it's too much aggro.' Similarly Sandy also remained single and in this way tried to retain her independence, as she reflected in a conversation about relationships: 'I don't want to get too deep into things ... I start getting jittery when things start getting too serious.' Sandy had recently, at the time, ended a relationship: 'It was too intense, he'd want to know where I was all the time ... I don't want to be controlled.' In a similar way Princess explained that she had set boundaries within her relationships: 'I've been in abusive relationships before, if they step out of line I won't take it any more ... I am selfish but you have to be.'

Beyond this, and in relation to the adventure sought through the social engagement of dancer-associated behaviour in the club, some suggested that they returned to Starlets as they craved the excitement back in their lives. This was a route discussed in Chapter 5 for the initial entry of dancers, in which the work of Lyng (1990) was used to make sense of the dancers' 'thrill-seeking'. Lyng (1990, 2005a) argues that social actors are drawn back to 'edgework' because of its addictive qualities; this relates to the dancers' re-engaging with risk. In relation to this, in the third part of Karen's story presented at the end of Chapter 8, she talked about how engaging with the lap-dancing lifestyle is not only about living dangerously, something most would want to avoid, but that this, for her, is addictive. In Starlets, thrill-seeking was specifically achieved through re-engaging with social rituals such as drinking alcohol and drug-taking. For example, Lucy, on her return to Starlets after spending some time working abroad, quickly re-engaged with the excessive behaviour she was famous for at the club when she initially worked there:

> ... Lucy had been working abroad and then spent some time in another local lap-dancing club. During our last conversation, before she left, Lucy claimed she was going to leave lap-dancing permanently ... She was very drunk, and seemed to have fallen into the same habits she

talked about leaving behind, one of which was the amount of alcohol she consumed ...[16]

Lyng (1990, 2005b) defines the 'edge', which suggests the boundaries transgressed by thrill-seekers, as 'the line between life and death, between sanity and insanity, between an ordered and disordered social reality' (2005b: 28). For Lucy, getting drunk presents a different 'edge', one which situates her in a state between consciousness and unconsciousness. For some, the very action of re-entering a career in lap-dancing was a risk in itself. This is particularly applicable for those in relationships, in which a dancer's partner objects to their occupation. Janine, for example, returned to Starlets knowing that her partner Andrew disapproved and that this was potentially catastrophic for their relationship. Janine's return under these circumstances suggests not only the level of importance she places on working at Starlets, but beyond this that she was willing to engage in this as a risk-taking action. Interestingly, it was not unusual for dancers at Starlets to become involved in high-risk relationships. The majority of the dancers during the time in which my fieldwork was conducted were either in or had been involved in abusive or 'complicated' relationships.[17] In relation to this, Paris claimed: 'Ask any girl in here and they'll all tell you the same, that they're with some arsehole.' I too as a dancer was not exempt from this pattern of behaviour. Despite being in a balanced relationship at the time this ethnography was conducted, prior to this, while working as an agency stripper and Starlets I had been in a difficult relationship. Not all of the high-risk relationships observed were necessarily abusive; some were, for example, taboo or forbidden for other reasons. These relationships might, for example, include customers, married men and/or criminal entrepreneurs[18]. Paris and Hally, for example, were in long-term relationships with married men. Both dancers claimed that these relationships were difficult to manage and were fraught with turmoil:

> ... *Paris had been crying in the changing room most of the night. After our conversation it became clear she was having problems with her boyfriend. A very upset Paris explained: 'It's OK for him, he's married, but he wants me to himself ... He's so possessive. He keeps thinking I'm fucking other blokes when I'm not!' ...*[19]

Ironically, despite her apparent unhappiness, Paris remained in this relationship and inflamed the situation by simultaneously having short-term relationships with other men. Instead of improving her personal situation, it was as though she wanted to maintain a high level of risk. It was perhaps this which attracted her to the relationship initially and which continued to make it thrive. In the spirit of Paris' high-risk behaviour, she would often engage in other risk-taking activities inside the club, including excessive alcohol and drug consumption. In relation to this, Jenna once remarked: 'She [Paris] can't just have a quiet drink and get merry she has to get so pissed she can't walk.'

Interestingly, of those who were involved in low-risk relationships, many, though not all of course, were quickly ended in favour of something more 'exciting'. For example, Karen, who considered her relationship with Tony to be low-risk and balanced, began to find it unexciting: 'I think I got to a point in my relationship with my boyfriend where I was just like BORED ... if you feel bored you need to do things to stop yourself from being bored.' It was following Karen's entry into lap-dancing that she finally ended their relationship. In a similar way, Hally, who had previously been in a stable relationship, ended it in favour of a high-risk one. Unfortunately it was not one she was in a position to easily control:

> ... Hally had been talking about Bert [her partner] to the other dancers ... he [Bert] was abusive and most of the girls were aware of this, but many felt it was better not to interfere. After Hally had left the changing room Charley commented: 'She's stupid for getting involved with him in the first place, I did warn her. If she wants to leave him she'll have to leave the country. Seriously' ...[20]

Furthermore, emotional attachment along with thrill-seeking were further factors found to be associated with the return of dancers to Starlets. Like Stella discussed earlier, most of the dancers expressed an emotional attachment to the other dancers; this is reminiscent of the sense of camaraderie and subcultural membership of dancers indicated in Chapters 6, 7 and 8. It is also necessary to revisit some of the examples provided earlier in the opening discussion about the feelings dancers expressed about dancing as they reflect on their relationships with dancers at Starlets, claiming to miss them after retirement. When Stella returned to the club it was apparent in the way in which she appeared to physically cling to Sandy that the close bonds she had developed with some of the dancers were important to her. In general the data generated from the fieldwork indicates that the dancers are more concerned with leaving their fellow dancers than the club and indeed the job itself. To reiterate, Becks explained: 'I don't miss the dancing so much, but my friends … It would be nice to be back for them.' Significantly, in a brief discussion about the return of dancers following retirement, Forsyth and Deshotels (1998a) emphasize this point by arguing: 'They [dancers] reported that they missed the membership groups and participating in the subculture of dancers' (p. 90). This again emphasizes the meaningful bonds present between dancers as members of a lap-dancing subculture.

Notes

1 Field diary extract.
2 A pub on the stripping circuit, in which agency strippers regularly worked.
3 Field diary extract.
4 Field diary extract.
5 Field diary extract.
6 Field diary extract.
7 Field diary extract.
8 Field diary extract.
9 Field diary extract.
10 Field diary extract.
11 Field diary extract.
12 Field diary extract.
13 Field diary extract.
14 Field diary extract.
15 Field diary extract.
16 Field diary extract.
17 It was common for dancers to refer to their relationships as 'complicated' and by doing so they were inferring that they were unstable.
18 This term is specific to those involved with organised crime.
19 Field diary extract.
20 Field diary extract.

Chapter 10

Lap-dancing: complex and contradictory

This ethnography has presented the occupational cultural experiences of lap-dancers working in this industry within the UK, following their progression from entry into lap-dancing to their eventual exit. Furthermore, it has focused on the relationships between dancers and the (sub)cultural significance suggested in their engagement with their work. This chapter draws this ethnography to a close by discussing some of the important themes which have emerged from the study, but also by addressing the future of lap-dancers and the industry as the recent licensing regime under the Policing and Crime Act 2009 is put into practice.

Power and resistance

Along with the location of Starlets, the distinct 'Cressian' (see Cressey 1932) subculture of lap-dancers (Colosi 2010a) is characterized by its own code of conduct, through the tacit rules, and the various social and emotional rituals engaged with by the lap-dancers at Starlets. The dancers' engagement with various social rituals is not only indicative of their subcultural behaviour but of their attempts to resist against management control and authority. Aware of the constraints on them as workers, dancers therefore opted for more unconventional and nuanced methods of resistance. Prioritizing fun by putting emphasis on the practice of social rituals simultaneously demonstrates the dancers' belittlement of the 'work' they were expected to engage in. In this instance, dancers momentarily transcended the constraints placed upon them by managers and club owners. However, this worker resistance was limited and disrupted by the dancers themselves who, unwittingly, through the very subcultural hierarchy that brought about their power and autonomy, simultaneously benefited the managers and the wider industry. What is suggested here is the complex and fluid nature of power between different social actors in the lap-dancing club, which can only be made sense of through a Foucauldian (1977, 1980) perspective as discussed in Chapters 6 and 8. This is a frame of understanding which helps us to acknowledge that dancers are both 'powerful' and 'powerless', 'liberated' and 'repressed', an interpretation reiterated by other contemporary writers in this field (Barton 2002, 2006; Egan 2004, 2006a; Frank 2003, 2007; Lerum 1999; Liepe-Levinson 2002; Murphy 2003; Wesely 2003). The hierarchical subculture, identified by three distinct status roles (or career stages) of 'new girl', 'transition' and 'old school' were acknowledged implicitly by the lap-dancers and other workers, who were aware of the evident different and changing power dynamics between dancers. Each stage had a distinct set of conduct and level of (subcultural) membership (Colosi 2010a). With the advancement of status through the hierarchy came the power to shape the lap-dancer code of conduct. Through exploring the hierarchical relationships between dancers it is possible to recognize exactly how these (power) relationships were both complex and contradictory. The imbalance of power between groups of dancers suggests a rank of inequality, with high-status dancers holding privileges which often made them exempt from the rules and punishments new girls were subjected to. Furthermore, although the managers inflicted fines and suspensions and instructed the dismissal of dancers, it was the higher-status dancers, through their own system of policing, who alerted their bosses to the irregular behaviour of new girls. Despite this and somewhat contrarily, the relationships between dancers were equally a site of trust and subcultural solidarity, brought about by their engagement with social and emotional rituals.

Like Paul Willis' (1977) 'counter-culture' of working-class lads, what is also evident from the dancer (subcultural) hierarchy is the way in which these sets of relationships between dancers further benefited club owners and managers. For instance, instead of the managers guiding new workers as their senior employment role suggests they should, it was actually the established dancers, as unofficial mentors, who instructed early status dancers how to perform, interact with customers and conduct acceptable behaviour.

In addition, old-school workers, through policing dancer conduct and acting as the managers' 'informants', were effectively doing the managers' job for them. The managers' lack of professionalism, suggested by the very fact that dancers were able to bargain with and manipulate the workers through the use of sex and/or drugs, ultimately removed the dancers' respect for managers as a source of 'authority'. This resulted in dancers redirecting their respect inwards and seeking authority from high-status dancers such as the old schoolers; it was this which was crucial in helping maintain the self-regulation of dancers (Colosi 2010b forthcoming) but simultaneously and conflictingly continued to benefit managers who directed their power (and control) through old-school authority. Therefore what led to the dancers' sense of autonomy and power through their elevated status and was also evidence of their attempts at resistance could simultaneously reinforce their inequality.

Worker exploitation

Although the exploitation of dancers as workers was not the focus of this book, it is nonetheless an important theme suggested throughout and something also discussed in the American literature (see, for example, Barton 2006, and Wesely 2003). In the UK, both public and political discussions about the lap-dancing industry have focused on the extent to which lap-dancers are exploited by the customers and the wider gendered oppression this suggests as opposed to the poor working conditions of these women. Although the physical conditions in which the dancers at Starlets worked were not particularly unpleasant or problematic, with the environment in many ways being very safe and clean, these women were still subjected to poor working conditions through their general ill treatment inflicted by the managers and wider industry. The use of security and CCTV cameras helped limit dangers posed by customers but did not help kerb the greater exploitation lap-dancers faced as workers. This exploitation is perhaps more widely symptomatic of the inequality women tend to face across the job market. For example, according to recent figures produced by the European Commission (2008), in the EU, women's pay is 15 per cent lower on average than men's. It is perhaps equally unsurprising that women are more likely to work part-time, with 75 per cent of these workers being female and less than 10 per cent men. Women also are also more likely to be on temporary contracts and the victims of long-term unemployment than their male counterparts. It is suggested more widely that women are more likely than men to be subjected to poverty and that this is an indicative of the feminization of poverty (Lister 2004).

One of initial areas of worker exploitation relevant to the discussion of the working conditions of lap-dancers relates to the contractual process. For instance, despite working at the club on a self-employed basis, the lap-dancers at Starlets were still expected to sign contracts (codes of conduct) which limited their rights but unsurprisingly benefitted the managers and wider industry. The 'dancer' contracts obligated these workers to pay a club commission to work on the club premises and be subject to fines and possible suspension if house rules were breached. The house fees, which were unfixed, changed frequently with no prior warning or notice, without taking into consideration dancers' earnings during a shift. Further to this, fines and suspensions were forced upon dancers, often without good reason, perhaps as a way of managers attempting to assert their authority. For example, it was not uncommon for dancers to be fined for turning up to a work shift late; this could be by as little as 5 or 10 minutes. As well as the injustice of these actions, it is also ironic that a dancer who is of 'self-employed' status and even pays a fee to work, should be fined for being 'late'. The dancers at Starlets did not see themselves as 'self-employed'; rather they viewed the managers as their 'employers', and many suggested they felt an obligation to their 'bosses' as they would in any regular job. The self-employed status of dancers is beneficial to the managers and wider industry as it means there is no employer obligation to contribute to their workers' National Insurance. Further to this, the contract signed by dancers, as well as binding dancers to unfair obligations and fooling them into a sense of employee loyalty, also causes confusion among these workers who were often unsure of their employment rights. In addition to this, the managers were verbally disrespectful to dancers, shouting orders at them and calling them insulting names. Although many of the dancers at Starlets learned to cope with the poor treatment inflicted upon them by their 'employers', it was nonetheless a factor which contributed to the psychological and emotional strain of doing this job, as suggested in Chapter 7. The pressures placed upon dancers by managers and the wider industry to maintain a particular standard of appearance is another factor indicative of their unfair treatment and exploitation. As Wesely (2003) argues, lap-dancers are encouraged to look like Barbie dolls, leading these women to undergo various cosmetic procedures and maintain the perfect weight. Although in Starlets not all dancers adhered to the industry's expectations, there was still a sense that these women were often preoccupied with their appearance. Managers regularly commented on and criticized the dancers' physical appearance, whether it related to the stage clothing worn or their physical features. As indicated earlier in this book, at times dancers were punished for not meeting the standards of appearance expected by managers. Despite the formation of the International Union of Sex Workers (IUSW), affiliated with the GMB (Britain's general workers' union), potentially offering support to lap-dancers by attempting to strengthen and legitimize their employment status as 'sex workers', dancers at Starlets, aware of their precarious position in the club, were reluctant to join this union for fear of being dismissed. The employment rights of lap-dancers need to be addressed politically through appropriate policy. It is important that lap-dancers are given the same rights as other 'mainstream' workers who are employed outside of the sex industry. Furthermore, it is important that dancers are contracted in a manner which provides them with protection from the exploitation by the employer and clearly outlines their rights.

Dancer morality

Despite the proliferation and commercialization of the lap-dancing industry, it is still evident that lap-dancing is a stigmatized occupation considered deviant both publicly and politically. What has been suggested in this ethnography and elsewhere (Lewis 1998; Thompson and Harred 1992, 2003) is that the dancers themselves are aware of the stigma associated with their job. Although in Starlets lap-dancers attempted to counteract and challenge this stigma in various ways, ultimately it impacted negatively on their relationships outside the club and with their self-image. Along with the emotional and physical demands of working as a dancer, these workers had to contend with the judgement of others who framed their understanding of sex work ultimately through a moral discourse, which reinforces the stigma. Lap-dancers were put in a position where they start to question their own morality and credibility as a lap-dancer, which despite being a viable form of employment is still not recognized publicly as a legitimate form of work. What has been observed is how the impact of the stigma tuned in to the dancers' own motivational explanations, whereby they felt the need to legitimize their involvement in this occupation through offering acceptable and anticipated reasons. For example, it is apparent that although the popular financial motivation of lap-dancers in Starlets was significant, as I have claimed elsewhere (see Colosi 2010b forthcoming) there were other equally significant factors. Offering a financial explanation became a way in which these lap-dancers were able to validate and justify their career choice without facing judgement. This helps the lap-dancer appear somehow divorced from what many see as an 'abhorrent' occupation (see the discussion in Scott 1996) and therefore removes the possibility that the women themselves are 'abhorrent', as they are financially obligated to work in the industry. Explanations such as 'the money is good' and 'I did it because I needed the money' guard the dancer against being seen by others as 'immoral'. Of the motivational strategies identified, what became evident was how women's attraction to and continued participation in lap-dancing was complex, and tied in with practical and emotionally driven reasons. As I have suggested elsewhere (Colosi 2010b forthcoming) the pursuit of pleasure through engaging with the social experience of dancing was particularly significant as a motivational strategy for their continued participation as lap-dancers. In Starlets pleasure could be derived from the dancers' performance – through stage shows and private dances these women were transformed into sensual beings and experienced the desire and admiration of the club's customers. Further and more significantly, it was through lap-dancers' engagement with social and emotional rituals that these women found a strong sense of satisfaction, which not only provided an escape and temporary solution from the stresses and strains associated with this occupation, but reinforced their sense of subcultural membership (Colosi 2010a).

The future? What future?

As was discussed in Chapter 2, lap-dancing clubs were recently subjected to a new licensing regime as 'sexual entertainment establishments' under the Policing and Crime Act 2009. It is necessary to revisit this discussion as this new legislation has wider implications for the dancers, but it is also necessary to draw attention to the fact that government ministers are unaware of or perhaps unwilling to address the real problems within the lap-dancing industry. One of the immediate problems associated with both the initial political focus on the licensing of lap-dancing establishments is that this shifts the political focus away from the practices of the employers within this industry. As has been suggested throughout the book and in this concluding chapter, dancers are subjected to many inequalities in the workplace. It is therefore necessary for government ministers to address this, and direct attention away (at least temporarily) from the assumed issues of community safety, an area in relation to lap-dancing clubs that has not been properly researched in the UK.

The relicensing of lap-dancing clubs as 'sexual entertainment venues' potentially threatens the future of the industry. As these are annual licences, the expense and administration involved may prevent potential club proprietors from opening new lap-dancing clubs. The expense alone may also prevent established club owners from being able to renew licences for existing venues, leading to their closure. There are of course other potential financial costs. For instance, for those who do not apply for a 'sexual entertainment licence' where the local authority still deems it necessary, the proprietor may face various penalties from between £1,000 and £20,000. The expected reduction in lap-dancing establishments as a result of relicensing is argued to help alleviate the exploitation and general subordination of women (Object 2008). It is further suggested that limiting these venues will reduce anti-social behaviour, despite little evidence to suggest such crime and disorder is brought about by the existence of lap-dancing clubs.

In the long term the closure of lap-dancing clubs means that some women will simply lose their jobs. In addition to increased unemployment, fewer lap-dancing clubs could mean that erotic dancers will seek alternative employment through unregulated stripping agencies and/or work freelance. This therefore risks pushing the industry underground into a world of unsafe and unregulated sex work. As was suggested in Chapters 1 and 2, lap-dancing clubs, particularly chain-operated venues, are often safe and well-organized environments, in which dancers are offered the protection of security staff and CCTV surveillance. As was suggested in Chapter 1, both freelance and agency stripping can be particularly physically dangerous with women often working in unpredictable environments. Stella, a dancer in Starlets, confirmed this: 'When you're stripping you've got men touching you, the customers are all horrible, at least here you're safe coz [sic] the bouncers look after you.'

Although the intended licence title of 'sex encounter' was replaced with 'sexual entertainment' in order to provide what was seen in the House of Lords as a more appropriate and less deviant title, 'sexual entertainment' is nonetheless still suggestive of the act of 'sex'. Entertainment that is 'sexual' may not simply imply semi or fully nude 'sensual' performances but that the entertainment on offer is explicitly 'sexual'. As well as deepening the stigma of this form of work, this licence, by implying that some kind of 'sex' is on sale, may lead to higher (sexual) expectations being forced on the dancers in these clubs. Although it was suggested that the dancers at Starlets rarely performed outside of their comfort zones and were therefore unlikely to stretch their personal boundaries during performances, the added financial and client pressures could potentially overturn this. It would have perhaps been more fitting for the prefix of 'sexual entertainment' to be renamed as 'adult' or 'erotic' entertainment.

The Policing and Crime Act 2009 reflects the current government's intolerance of 'sex work' per se evident through its abolitionist approach to prostitution under section 14 and its recent criminalization of lap-dancing under section 27. As Phoenix (2009) observes, what is further suggested is that these policy reforms contradict the 'evidence-based policy' approach outlined in the *Modernising Government* White Paper (Cabinet Office 1999). Instead, the premise, for example, for relicensing lap-dancing clubs as 'sexual entertainment establishments' is based on anecdotal evidence from abolitionist groups who have framed their understanding in a moral discourse. This does not suggest that the licensing of lap-dancing should not be debated or revised; instead it is necessary for government ministers to take an 'evidence-based' approach in the policy process, something which New Labour so adamantly claimed to do at the start of their period in power in the late 1990s.

Although it is valuable to consult existing research produced in the US and Canada, there is still a need for further understanding of this industry in a UK context in order to make a more evidence-based judgement. Despite the focus of this ethnography being on the relationships between dancers and the occupational (sub)culture with which they engage, it has still provided a more accurate picture of the wider industry than the ad hoc accounts which have so far been offered in Britain's public and political arena (see, for example, Bindel 2004). What is suggested by this ethnographic exploration of lap-dancing is the contradictory and complex nature of the work and culture dancers engage with. As other authors have demonstrated this is an occupation that is at times empowering and can also be exploitative; it is a source of pleasure and discontentment, of excitement and yet frustration (Barton 2006; Egan 2006a; Frank 2003). These sex workers are both autonomous and yet must bargain for their freedom. Lap-dancing is a site of transgression in which dancers working at the centre of this patriarchal industry are able, if only temporarily, to resist the constraints of their job and wider socially subordinate position. However, simultaneously, the industry still directs these workers by using the dancers' own source of resistance to gain back control. This ethnography has opened up a number of additional questions which beg further empirical enquiry, specifically within a UK context, regarding the working conditions of dancers, the dancer–'employer' relationships, the perceived and actual risks associated with lap-dancing and of course the customers who frequent these venues. Exploring these areas may help develop a more accurate understanding of the key issues associated with this area of the sex industry in the UK that may provide the necessary 'evidence' in the policy process.

Epilogue: the last dance ...

'I lost my heart ... under the bridge ... to that little girl ... so much to me ... and now I'm old ... and now I holler ... she'll never know ... just what I found ...'

The gravelly tone of PJ Harvey's voice singing 'Down by the Water' washed through the club as I walked on to the stage for the last time, for my final performance. I felt exhilarated and had to catch my breath as the heavy bass line of the song vibrated through my body. I felt alive and almost empowered experiencing the gaze of the silhouetted figures scattered across the main floor of Starlets. My head was filled with snapshots of the time I had spent working at Starlets; I was overwhelmed and I did not want my time here to end. As I danced on the stage I continued to think about the different stories I had both observed and been at the centre of. It was like watching back several episodes of an engaging, yet somewhat bizarre, soap opera. It dawned on me how frantic, how exciting, how painful, how confusing, how pleasurable and unique my time at Starlets had been; I would never experience this again, but could never forget it. Working at Starlets, being a stripper, was something I would always carry around with me, not as a burden, but somethat that is now fixed as an essential part of my identity. So lost in thought, I suddenly realize my performance on stage is reaching its end. I slip off my dress for the final 30 seconds and spend my last moments taking in the experience of the stage, the music, the bright lights reflecting off my skin and the crowd. As my performance finishes, I pick up my dress which is bundled in a heap on the stage floor, then clutching it against my naked chest as I walk back stage. I sit for a moment before getting dressed, take a large gulp of wine and just absorb the surrounding of the worn backstage area. I look fondly at the heel marks and holes from the dancers' shoes on the opposite wall and at the lipstick marks on the full length mirror. I think back to the first time I ever sat backstage and how different it looked and smelled; I closed my eyes for a moment and could smell the freshly painted brilliant white walls. As I opened my eyes a feeling of sadness washed over me as I remembered it had all come to an end. I slipped on my dress and quietly left the backstage area ...

Bibliography

Adler, P. and Adler, P. (1991) 'Stability and flexibility: maintaining relations within organized and unorganized groups', in W. Shaffir and R. Stebbins (eds), *Experiencing Fieldwork: An Inside View of Qualitative Research*. London: Sage.

Adult Entertainment Working Group (2006) *Adult Entertainment Working Group Report and Recommendations to Ministers on the Adult Entertainment Industry in Scotland*. Edinburgh: Scottish Executive. Online at: http://www.scotland.gov.uk/Resource/Doc/112705/0027365.pdf (accessed 1 December 2008).

Aitkenhead, D. and Sheffield, E. (2001) 'G-strings join the A-list', *Evening Standard*, 7 November. Online at: http://www.thisislondon.co.uk/news/article-927718-details/G-strings+join+the+A-list/article.do (accessed 12 July 2005).

Appleton, D. (2006) 'Parishioners join the fight against lap dancing club', *Oldham Advertiser*, 23 August. Online at: http://www.oldhamadvertiser.co.uk/news/s/516746_parishioners_join_the_fight_against_lap_dancing_club.

Armitage, J. and Prynn, J. (2004) 'Is Spearmint Rhino an endangered species? Lap-dancing club loses its City clientele', 4 November. Online at: http://www.thefreelibrary.com/Is+the+Spearmint+Rhino+an+endangered+species%3F+Lapdancing+club+loses...-a0122785440 (accessed 12 August 2008).

Armstrong, G. (1993) 'Like that Desmond Morris?', in D. Hobbs and T. May (eds), *Interpreting the Field*. Oxford: Oxford University Press.

Attwood, F. (2009) 'Introduction: the sexualisation of culture', in F. Attwood (ed.), *Mainstreaming Sex: The Sexualisation of Western Culture*. London: I. B. Tauris.

175

Barley, S. (1989) 'Careers, identities, and institutions: the legacy of the Chicago School of Sociology', in M. Arthur, D. Hall and B. Lawrence (eds), *Handbook of Career Theory*. Cambridge: Cambridge University Press.

Barton, B. (2002) 'Dancing on the Mobius strip: challenging the sex war paradigm', *Gender and Society*, 16 (5): 585–602.

Barton, B. (2006) *Stripped: Inside the Lives of Exotic Dancers*. London: New York University Press.

Barton, B. (2007) 'Managing the toll of stripping: boundary setting among exotic dancers', *Journal of Contemporary Ethnography*, 36 (5): 571–96.

BBC Bradford and West Yorkshire (2002a) 'Students campaign against lap-dancing club', 4 October. Online at: http://www.bbc.co.uk/bradford/news/2002/10/04/lap_dancing.shtml (accessed 12August 2004).

BBC News (2002b) 'Lad culture alive and well', 16 July. Online at: http://news.bbc.co.uk/1/hi/scotland/2131575.stm (accessed 12 August 2004).

BBC News (2002c) 'Protest over lap-dancing club', 6 July. Online at: http://news.bbc.co.uk/1/hi/northern_ireland/2097761.stm (accessed 12 August 2004).

Becker, H. ([1963] 1991) *Outsiders: Studies in the Sociology of Deviance*. New York: Free Press.

Becker, H. and Faulkner, R. (2008) 'Studying something you are part of: the view from the bandstand', *Ethnologie Française*, 38: 15–21.

Bell, H., Sloan, L. and Strickling, C. (1998) 'Exploiter or exploited: topless dancers reflect on their experiences', *Journal of Women and Social Work*, 13 (3): 352–68.

Bell, R. (2008) 'I was seen as an object not a person', *Guardian Unlimited*, 19 March. Online at: http://lifeandhealth.guardian.co.uk/women/story/0,,2266504,00.html (accessed 10 April 2008).

Beninger, M. (2004) 'The almost naked revolution', in *An Eye Opener Online*. Online at: http://www.theeyeopener.com/storydetail.cfm?storyid=939 (accessed 15 August 2004).

Bennett, A. (1999) 'Subcultures or neotribes? Rethinking the relationship between youth style and musical taste', Sociology, 33 (3): 599–617.

Bennett, A. (2005) 'In defence of neo-tribes: a response to Blackman and Hesmondhalgh', *Journal of Youth Studies*, 8 (2): 255–9.

Bernard, C., DeGabrielle, C., Cartier, L., Monk-Turner, E., Phill, C., Sherwood, J. and Tyree, T. (2003) 'Exotic dancers: gender differences in societal reaction, subcultural ties and conventional support', *Journal of Criminal Justice and Popular Culture*, 10 (1): 1–11.

Bernstein, E. (2001) 'The meaning of the purchase: desire, demand and the commerce of sex', *Ethnography*, 2 (3): 389–420.

Bhopal, K. (2000) 'Gender, "race" and power in the research process. South Asian Women in East London', in C. Truman, D.M. Mertens and B. Humphries (eds), *Research and Inequality*. London: UCL Press.

Bindel, J. (2004) *Possible Exploits: Lap Dancing in the UK*. Glasgow: Glasgow City Council.

Bindel, J. (2008) 'It's more like a strip club than a restaurant', *Guardian Unlimited*, 11 April. Online at: http://lifeandhealth.guardian.co.uk/food/story/0,,2272815,00.html (accessed 15 April 2008).

Blackman, S. (2005) 'Youth subcultural theory: a critical engagement with the concept, its origins and politics, from the Chicago School to postmodernism', *Journal of Youth Studies*, 8 (1): 1–20.

Blackman, S. (2007) 'Hidden ethnography: crossing emotional borders in qualitative accounts of young people's lives', *Sociology*, 41 (4): 699–716.

Boles, J. and Garbin, A. (1974a) 'The choice of stripping for a living: an empirical and theoretical explanation', *Sociology of Work and Occupations*, 1 (1): 110–23.

Boles, J. and Garbin, A. (1974b) 'The choice of stripping for a living: an occupational study of the night club stripper', *Sociology of Work and Occupations*, 1 (1): 4–17.

Boles, J. and Garbin, A. (1974c) 'Strip club and stripper–customer patterns of interaction', *Sociology and Social Research*, 18: 136–44.

Bott, E. (2006) 'Pole position: migrant British women producing "selves" through lap-dancing work', *Feminist Review*, 83: 23–41.

Bradley, H., Erickson, M., Stephenson, C. and Williams, S. (2000) *Myths at Work*. Cambridge: Polity Press.

Bradley, M. (2007) 'Girlfriends, wives and strippers: managing stigma in exotic dancer romantic relationships', *Deviant Behaviour*, 28: 399–406.

Bradley, M. (2008) 'Selling sex in the new millenium: thinking about changes in adult entertainment and dancers' lives', *Sociology Compass*, 2 (2): 503–18.

Bradley-Engen, M. (2009) 'Social worlds of stripping: the processual orders of exotic dance', *Sociological Quarterly*, 50: 29–60.

Brannan, M. and Pearson, G. (2007) 'Ethnographies of work and the work of ethnography', *Ethnography*, 8 (4): 395–402.

Brewer, J. (2000) *Understanding Social Research: Ethnography*. Buckingham: Open University Press.

Brewster, Z. W. (2003) 'Behavioural and interactional patrons: tipping techniques and club attendance', *Deviant Behaviour: An Interdisciplinary Journal*, 24 (3): 221–43.

Bronfenbrenner, U. (1952) 'Principles of professional ethics: Cornell studies in social growth', *American Psychologist*, 7: 452–5.

Bruckert, C. (2002) *Taking It Off, Putting It On: Women in the Strip Trade*. Toronto: Women's Press.

Bulmer, M. (1986) *The Chicago School of Sociology*. London: University of Chicago Press.

Burgess, E. (1929) *The Hobo*. Chicago: Chicago University Press.

Burgess, R. (1984) *In the Field: An Introduction to Field Research*. London: Unwin Hyman.

Burgess, R. (1991) 'Sponsors, gatekeepers, members, and friends: access in educational settings', in W. Shaffir and R. Stebbins (eds), *Experiencing Fieldwork: An Inside View of Qualitative Research*. London: Sage.

Cabinet Office (1999) *Modernising Government*, Cm 4310. London: The Stationery Office.

Cabinet Office (2009) Policing and Crime Act 2009. Online at: http://www. opsi.gov.uk/acts/acts2009/ukpga_20090026_en_1 (accessed 15 January 2010).

Carey, S. H., Peterson, R. A. and Sharpe, L. K. (1974) 'A study of recruitment and socialization in two deviant female occupations', *Sociological Symposium*, 11: 11–24.

Cartledge, J. (2004) 'Lap-dancing crackdown', *Evening Mail*, 3 February. Online at: http://www.withreference2.org/trafficking/ab.2004/abstract.2004.02. htm (accessed 14 January 2010).

Chapkis, W. (1997) *Live Sex Acts: Women Performing Erotic Labor*. New York: Routledge.

Chatterton, P. and Hollands, R. (2000) *Changing Our 'Toon'*. Newcastle upon Tyne: University of Newcastle upon Tyne.

Chatterton, P. and Hollands, R. (2002) 'Theorising urban playscapes: producing, regulating and consuming youthful nightlife city spaces', *Urban Studies*, 39 (1): 95–116.

Chatterton, P. and Hollands, R. (2003) *Urban Nightscapes: Youth Cultures, Pleasure Spaces and Corporate Power*. London: Routledge.

Cixous, H. and Clement, C. (1986) *The Newly Born Woman*. Minneapolis, MN: University of Minnesota Press.

Clarke, J. (1976) 'The skinheads and the magical recovery of community', in S. Hall and T. Jefferson (eds), *Resistance Through Rituals: Youth Subcultures in Post-War Britain*. London: Hutchinson.

Clifton, L. (2002) *Baby Oil and Ice: Striptease in East London*. London: Do-Not Press.

Cloward, R. and Ohlin, L. (1960) *Delinquency and Opportunity*. New York: Free Press.

Coffey, A. (2002) 'Ethnography and self: reflections and representations', in T. May (ed.), *Qualitative Research in Action*. London: Sage.

Cohen, A. (1955) *Delinquent Boys: The Culture of the Gang*. New York: Free Press.

Colosi, R. (2010a) 'A return to the Chicago school? From the subculture of taxi-dancers to the contemporary lap-dancer', *Journal of Youth Studies*, 13 (1): 1–16.

Colosi, R. (2010b forthcoming) '"Just get pissed and enjoy yourself": understanding lap-dancing as "anti-work"', in K. Hardy, S. Kingston and T. Sanders (eds), *New Dimensions in Sex Work Research*. Farnham: Ashgate.

Corrigan, N. (2008) 'Protest over lap-dance bid', *Gazette Live.co.uk*, 24 February. Online at: http://www.gazettelive.co.uk/news/teesside-news/2008/01/24/protest-over-lap-dance-bid-84229-20389242/ (accessed 2 April 2008).

Cressey, P. ([1932] 1968) *The Taxi-Dance Hall*. Chicago: Chicago University Press.

Cressey, P. ([1932] 1997) 'The life-cycle of the taxi dancer', in K. Gelder and S. Thornton (eds), *The Subcultures Reader*. Routledge: London.

Crown, S. (2004) 'Tale of two cities divided by day and night', *Guardian*, 2 February. Online at: http://www.guardian.co.uk/uk_news/story/0,3604,1136913,00.html (accessed 14 June 2004).

DeMichele, M. T. and Tewksbury, R. (2005) 'Sociological explorations in site-specific social control: the role of the strip club bouncer', *Deviant Behaviour*, 26 (5): 537–58.

Deshotels, T. and Forsyth, C. (2005) 'Strategic flirting and the emotional tab of exotic dancing', *Deviant Behaviour*, 27: 223–41.

Doward, J. (2001) 'Putting it on the table', *The Observer*, 11 February. Online at: http://observer.guardian.co.uk/business/story/0,6903,436238,00.html (accessed 14 June 2004).

Dragu, M. and Harrison, A. S. A. (1988) *Revelations: Essays on Striptease and Sexuality*. London: Nightwood Editions.

Dressel, P. and Peterson, J. (1982) 'Becoming a male stripper: recruitment, socialization and ideological development', *Work and Occupations*, 9: 387–406.

Dudash, T. (1998) 'Peepshow feminism', in J. Nagle (eds), *Whores and Other Feminists*. London: Routledge.

Duncan, S. and Edwards, R. (1999) *Lone Mothers, Paid Work and Gendered Moral Rationalities*. London: Macmillan.

Dunn, A. (2010) 'The "dole or drudgery" dilemma: education, the work ethic and unemployment', *Social Policy and Administration*, 44 (1): 1–19.

Eaves, E. (2002) *Bare: On Women, Dancing, Sex and Power*. New York: Alfred A. Knopf.

Egan, D. (2003) 'I'll be your fantasy girl, if you'll be my money man: mapping desire, fantasy and power in two exotic dance clubs', *Journal of Psychoanalysis, Culture and Society*, 8 (1): 109–20.

Egan, D. (2004) 'Eyeing the scene: the uses and (re)uses of surveillance cameras in an exotic dance club', *Critical Sociology*, 30 (2): 299–319.

Egan, D. (2005) 'Emotional consumption: mapping love and masochism in an exotic dance club', *Body and Society*, 11 (4): 87–108.

Egan, D. (2006a) *Dancing for Dollars and Paying for Love: The Relationships Between Exotic Dancers and Their Regulars*. Basingstoke: Palgrave Macmillan.

Egan, D. (2006b) 'Resistance under the black light: exploring the use of music in two exotic dance clubs', *Journal of Contemporary Ethnography*, 35 (2): 201–19.

Enck, G. E. and Preston, J. (1988) 'Counterfeit intimacy: dramaturgical analysis of an erotic performance', *Deviant Behaviour*, 9: 369–81.

Ephedrine Legal Advice (2004) 'What Is Ephedrine?' Online at: http://www.ephedrine-ephedra.com/pages/what_is_ephedrine_1234.html (accessed 20 August 2004).

Erickson, J. and Tewksbury (2000) 'The "gentlemen" in the club: a typology of strip club patrons', *Deviant Behaviour: An Interdisciplinary Journal*, 21: 271–93.

European Commission (2008) Report on Equality Between Men and Women. Luxembourg: European Commission, Directorate-General for Employment, Social Affairs and Equal Opportunities.

Fawcett Society (2009) 'Reform lap dancing club licensing', Fawcett on-line. Online at: http://www.fawcettsociety.org.uk/index.asp?PageID=631 (accessed 12 December 2009).

Ferdinand, J., Pearson, G., Rowe, M. and Worthington, F. (2007) 'A different kind of ethics', Ethnography, 8 (4): 519–43.

Festinger, L., Riecken, H. and Schachter, S. (1956) *When Prophecy Fails*. New York: Harper & Row.

Fetterman, D. A. (1991) 'Walk through the wilderness: learning to find your way', in W. Shaffir and R. Stebbins (eds), *Experiencing Fieldwork: An Inside View of Qualitative Research*. London: Sage.

Fielding, N. (1993) 'Ethnography', in N. Gilbert (ed.), *Researching Social Life*. London: Sage.

Flanagan, B. (2002) 'Table dancers', *The Observer*, 5 February. Online at: http://www.guardian.co.uk/money/2002/may/05/wageslaves.careers (accessed 20 August 2004).

Foote, N. (1954) 'Sex as play', *Social Problems*, 1: 159–63.

Ford, R. (2010) 'Peter Stringfellow prepares for battle before new lap-dancing rules', *Times on-line*, 12 February. Online at: http://www.timesonline.co.uk/tol/news/uk/article7024181.ece (accessed 15 March 2010).

Forsyth, C. J. and Deshotels, T. (1998a) 'A deviant process: the sojourn of the stripper', *Sociological Spectrum*, 18, Part 1: 77–92.

Forsyth, C. J. and Deshotels, T. (1998b) 'The occupational milieu of the nude dancer', *Deviant Behaviour*, 18: 125–42.

Foucault, M. (1977) *Discipline and Punish: The Birth of the Prison*. London: Penguin.

Foucault, M. (1980) *Power/Knowledge: Selected Interviews and Other Writings, 1972–1977*. London: Harvester.

Frank, K. (1998) 'The production of identity and the negotiation of intimacy in a gentleman's club', *Sexualities*, 2: 175–201.

Frank, K. (2002a) *G-Strings and Sympathy: Strip Club Regulars and Male Desire*. London: Duke University Press.

Frank, K. (2002b) 'Stripping, starving, and the politics of ambitious pleasure', in M. L. Johnson (ed.), *True Confessions of Feminist Desire: Jane Sexes It Up*. London: Four Walls Eight Windows.

Frank, K. (2003) 'Just trying to relax: masculinity, masculinizing practices and strip club regulars', *Journal of Sex Research*, 40: 61–76.

Frank, K. (2007) 'Thinking critically about strip club research', *Sexualities*, 10 (4): 501–17.

Futterman, M. (1992) *Dancing Naked in the Material World*. New York: Prometheus Books.

Gelder, K. and Thornton, S. (eds) (1997) *The Subcultural Reader*. London: Routledge.

Gerson, K. and Horowitz, R. (2002) 'Observation and interviewing: options and choices in qualitative research', in T. May (ed.), *Qualitative Research in Action*. London: Sage.

Glass, R. (1964) *London: Aspects of Change*. London: MacGibbon and Kee.

Glasscock, J. (2003) *Striptease – From Gaslight to Spotlight*. New York: Harry N. Abrams.

Goffman, E. ([1959] 1971) *The Presentation of Self in Everyday Life*. Middlesex: Pelican Books.

Goffman, E. (1963) *Stigma: Notes on the Management of Spoiled Identity*. Middlesex: Pelican Books.

Grandy, G. (2005) 'Case. For your eyes only', in A. J. Mills, T. Simmons and J. Helms Mills (eds), *Reading Organizational Theory. A Critical Approach to the Study of Organizational Behaviour and Structure*, 3rd edn. Aurora, ON: Garamond Press.

Grandy, G. (2008) 'Managing spoiled identities: dirty workers' struggles for a favourable sense of self', *Qualitative Research in Organizations and Management: An International Journal*, 3 (3): 176–98.

Greener, T. and Hollands, R. (2006) 'Beyond subculture and post-subculture? The case of virtual psytrance', *Journal of Youth Studies*, 9 (4): 393–418.

Griffin, R. (2001) 'SFI to sell table dancing venues', *Guardian on-line*, 24 January. Online at: http://www.guardian.co.uk/business/2001/jan/24/6 (accessed 15 August 2008).

Gubrium, J. (2007) 'Urban ethnography of the 1920s working girl', *Gender, Work and Organization*, 14 (3): 232–58.

Hall, S. and Jefferson, T. (eds) (1976) *Resistance Through Rituals*. London: Hutchinson.

Hammersley, M. ([1991] 2004) 'Some reflections on ethnography and validity', in C. Seale (eds), *Social Research Methods*. London: Routledge.

Hammersley, M. and Atkinson, P. (2004) *Ethnography*. London: Routledge.

Hanmer, J., Radford, J. and Stanko, A. E. (1989) *Women, Policing, and Male Violence: International Perspectives*. London: Routledge.

Hannigan, J. (1998) *Fantasy City: Pleasure and Profit in the Postmodern Metropolis*. London: Routledge.

Hargreaves, D. (2008) 'Lap dance ethos at heart of city sexism, say campaigners', *Guardian Unlimited*, 31 March. Online at: http://www.guardian.co.uk/business/2008/mar/31/gender?gusrc=rss&feed=global (accessed 2April 2008).

Hargreaves, D. H. (1980) 'The occupational culture of teachers', in P. Woods (eds), *Teacher Strategies: Explorations in the Sociology of the School*. London: Croom Helm, pp. 125–48.

Harvey, D. (2000) *Spaces of Hope*. Edinburgh: Edinburgh University Press.

Hausbeck, K. and Brents, B. (2002) 'McDonaldization of the sex industries: the business of sex', in G. Ritzer (ed.), *McDonaldization: The Reader*. London: Sage.

Hearn, J. (1994) 'The organization(s) of violence: men, gender relations, organizations, and violences', *Human Relations*, 47: 731–54.

Hesmondhalgh, D. (2005) 'Subcultures, scenes or tribes? None of the above', *Journal of Youth Studies*, 8 (1): 21–40.

Hickman, B. (2008) 'Lap dancing hours row', *Chronicle Live*, 16 February. Online at: http://www.chroniclelive.co.uk/north-east-news/todays-evening-chronicle/2008/01/16/lap-dancing-hours-row-72703-20356286/ (accessed 17 February 2008).

Hobbs, D. (1993) 'Peers, careers, and academic fears: writing as fieldwork', in D. Hobbs and T. May (eds), *Interpreting the Field*. Oxford: Oxford University Press.

Hobbs, D., Lister, S., Hadfield, P. and Hall, S. (2000) 'Receiving shadows: governance and liminality in the night-time economy', *British Journal of Sociology*, 51 (4): 701–17.

Hobbs, D., Hadfield, P., Lister, S. and Winslow, S. (2003) *Bouncers, Violence and Governance in the Night-time Economy*. Oxford: Oxford University Press.

Hochschild, A. (1979) 'Emotion work, feeling rules and social structure', *American Journal of Sociology*, 85: 551–75.

Hochschild, A. ([1983] 2003) *The Managed Heart: Commercialization of Human Feeling*. London: University of California Press.

Hogan, P. (2004) 'Laddism lives on', *The Observer*, 8 February. Online at: http://www.guardian.co.uk/Columnists/Column/0,5673,1142834,00.html (accessed 25 August 2004).

Holdaway, S. (1983) *Inside the British Police*. Oxford: Blackwell.

Holland, S. and Attwood, F. (2009) 'Keeping fit in six-inch heels: the mainstreaming of pole dancing', in F. Attwood (ed.), *Mainstreaming Sex: The Sexualisation of Western Culture*. London: I. B. Tauris.

Hollands, R. (2002) 'Divisions in the dark: youth cultures, transitions and segmented consumption spaces in the night-time economy', *Journal of Youth Studies*, 5 (2): 153–71.

Hollands, R. and Chatterton, P. (2003) 'Producing nightlife in the new urban entertainment economy: corporatization, branding and market segmentation', *International Journal of Urban and Regional Research*, 26: 361–85.

Holsopple, K. (1999) 'Stripclubs according to strippers: exposing workplace sexual violence', in D. Hughes and C. Roche (eds), *Making the Harm Visible: Global Sexual Exploitation of Women and Girls, Speaking Out and Providing Services*. Kingston: Coalition Against Trafficking in Women, pp. 252–76.

Home Office (2000) 'Liquor Licensing Statistics for England and Wales', 27/98.

Home Office (2008) *Policing and Crime Bill: Putting People First*, Home Office Press Office. Online at: http://press.homeoffice.gov.uk/press-releases/policing-crime-bill.html (accessed 12 December 2009).

Horton, J. (2006) 'New lap dancing rules are steps in wrong direction', *News.Scotsman.com*, 10 May. Online at: http://news.scotsman.com/edinburghssexindustry/New-lap-dancing-rules-are.2774155.jp (accessed 20 April 2007).

Hubbard, P., Matthews, R., Scouler, J. and Agustín, L. (2008) 'Away from prying eyes? The urban geographies of "adult entertainment" ', *Progress in Human Geography*, 32 (3): 363–81.

Humphreys, L. ([1971] 1997) 'The sociologist as voyeur', in K. Gelder and S. Thornton (eds), *The Subcultural Reader*. London: Routledge.

Humphries, P. (2003) 'Morals maze', *Guardian Unlimited*, 29 February. Online at: http://society.guardian.co.uk/societyguardian/story/0,7843,883949,00.html (accessed 9 June 2004).

Irigaray, L. (1985a) *The Sex Which Is Not One*. New York: Cornell University Press.

Irigaray, L. (1985b) *Speculum of the Other Woman*. New York: Cornell University Press.

Jarrett, L. (1997) *Stripping in Time: A History of Erotic Dancing*. London: Pandora.

Jarvinen, M. (1993) *Of Vice and Women: Shades of Prostitution* (Scandinavian Studies in Criminology), Norway: Scandinavian University Press.

Jeffreys, S. (2008) 'Keeping women down and out: the strip club boom and the reinforcement of male dominance', *Journal of Women in Culture and Society*, 34 (1): 151–73.

Johnson, F. (2006) 'Why Prince Harry must fight hard against his inner chav', *The Telegraph.co.uk*, 13 April. Online at: http://www.telegraph.co.uk/opinion/main.jhtml?xml=/opinion/2006/04/13/do1301.xml&sSheet=/portal/2006/04/13/ixportal.html (accessed 20 June 2006).

Johnson, M. L. (1998) 'Pole work: auto ethnography of a strip club', *Sexuality and Culture*, 2: 149–57.

Jones, P., Shears, P. and Hillier, D. (2003) 'Retailing and the regulatory state: a case study of lapdancing clubs in the UK', *International Journal of Retail and Distribution Management*, 31 (4): 214–19.

Judd, T. (2008) 'MP calls for greater control of lap-dancing clubs', *The Independent*, 26 April. Online at: http://www.independent.co.uk/news/uk/politics/mps-back-call-for-greater-control-of-lapdancing-clubs-815853.html (accessed 27 April 2008).

Junker, B. H. ([1960] 2004) 'The field work situation: social roles for observation', in C. Seale (eds), *Social Research Methods: A Reader*. London: Routledge.

Jupp, V. (eds) (2006) *The Sage Dictionary of Social Research Methods*. London: Sage.

Kaplan, I. M. (1991) 'Gone fishing, be back later: ending and resuming research among fisherman', in W. Shaffir and R. Stebbins (eds), *Experiencing Fieldwork: An Inside View of Qualitative Research*. London: Sage.

Kehily, J. (2007) *Understanding Youth: Perspectives, Identities and Practices*. Buckingham: Open University Press.

Kelly, L. (1987) 'The continuum of sexual violence', in J. Hanmer and M. Maynard (eds), *Women, Violence, and Social Control*. Atlantic Highlands, NJ: Humanities Press International.

Kempadoo, K. (1998) 'The Exotic Dancers Alliance: an interview with Dawn Passar and Johanna Breyer', in K. Kempadoo and J. Doezema (eds), *Global Sex Workers Rights, Resistance and Redefinition*. London: Routledge.

Kempadoo, K. and Doezma, J. (eds), *Global Sex Workers Rights, Resistance and Redefinition*. London: Routledge.

Klein, N. (2000) *No Logo: No Space. No Choice. No Jobs*. London: Flamingo Publishers.

Kleinman, S. (1991) 'Field-workers' feelings: what we feel, who we are, how we analyze', in W. Shaffir and R. Stebbins (eds), *Experiencing Fieldwork: An Inside View of Qualitative Research*. London: Sage.

Lagan, B. (2007) 'Labor leader caught in lap-dance club scandal – but does Australia care?', in *The Times on-line*, 20 August. Online at: http://www.timesonline.co.uk/tol/news/world/article2288014.ece (accessed 20 April 2008).

Lap Dancing Association (LDA) (2008) *The Real Body of Evidence: Exploding the Myths Around the Lap-dancing Industry*. Memorandum submitted to the House of Lords. Online at: http://www.publications.parliament.uk/pa/cm200809/cmselect/cmcumeds/492/8112507.htm (accessed 15 July 2009).

Lauder, M. (2003) 'Covert participant observation of a deviant community: justifying the use of deception', *Journal of Contemporary Religion*, 18 (2): 185–96.

Lerum, K. (1999) 'Twelve step feminism makes sex workers sick: how the state and recovery movement turn radical women into useless citizens', in B. Dank and R. Refinetti (eds), *Sex Work and Sex Workers: Sexuality and Culture*, 2: 7–36.

Lewis, J. (1998) 'Learning to strip: the socialization experiences of exotic dancers', *Canadian Journal of Human Sexuality*, 7 (1): 51–66.

Lewis, J., Maticka-Tyndale, E., Shaver, F. and Schramm, H. (2005) 'Managing risk and safety on the job: the experiences of Canadian sex workers', *Journal of Psychology and Human Sex Work*, 17 (1/2): 147–67.

Liepe-Levinson, K. (2002) *Strip Show: Performances of Gender and Desire*. London: Routledge.

Linz, D., Blumenthal, E., Donnerstein, E., Kunkel, D., Shafer, B. J. and Lichtenstein, A. (2000) 'Testing legal assumptions regarding the effects of dancer nudity and proximity', *Human Behavior*, 24: 507–33.

Lister, R. (2004) *Poverty*. Cambridge: Polity Press.

Lofland, J. ([1971] 2004) 'Field notes', in C. Seale (ed.), *Social Research Methods: A Reader*. London: Routledge.

Lyng, S. (1990) 'Edgework: a social psychological analysis of voluntary risk taking', *American Journal of Sociology*, 95 (4): 851–86.

Lyng, S. (2005a) 'Edgework and the risk-taking experience', in S. Lyng (eds), *Edgework*. London: Routledge.

Lyng, S. (2005b) 'Sociology at the edge: social theory and voluntary risk-taking', in S. Lyng (eds), *Edgework*. London: Routledge.

MacDonald, R. and Shildrick, T. (2006) 'In defense of subculture: young people, leisure and social divisions', *Journal of Youth Studies*, 9 (2): 125–40.

McCaghy, C. and Skipper, J. (1974) 'Lesbian behaviour as an adaptation to the occupation of stripping', in C. D. Bryant (ed.), *Deviant Behaviour: Occupational and Organisational Bases*. Chicago: Rand McNally College Publishing.

McKay, G. (1996) *Senseless Act of Beauty: Cultures of Resistance Since the Sixties*. London: Verso.

McNair, B. (2002) *Striptease Culture*. London: Routledge.

McRobbie, A. and Garber, J. (1976) 'Girls and subcultures: an exploration', in S. Hall and T. Jefferson (eds), *Resistance Through Rituals: Youth Subcultures in Post War Britain*. London: Hutchinson.

McVeigh, T. (2002) 'Wives hit back as husbands feed growing addiction to lapdancing', *Guardian Unlimited*, 24 November. Online at: http://www.guardian.co.uk/uk/2002/nov/24/tracymcveigh.theobserver (accessed 15 August 2004).

Malbon, B. (1999) *Clubbing: Dancing, Ecstasy and Vitality*. London: Routledge.

Manaster, S. (2006) 'Treading water: an autoethnographic account(ing) of the lap dance', in D. Egan, K. Frank and M. L. Johnson (eds), *Flesh for Fantasy: Producing and Consuming Exotic Dance*. New York: Thunder's Mouth Press.

Mason, J. (2002) 'Qualitative interviewing: asking, listening and interpreting', in T. May (ed.), *Qualitative Research in Action*. London: Sage.

Massey, D. (1995) 'The conceptualization of place', in D. Massey and P. Jess (eds), *Exploring Human Geography*. London: Arnold.

Massey, D. (1998) 'The spatial construction of youth culture', in T. Skelton and G. Valentine (eds), *Cool Places: Geographies of Youth Cultures*. London: Routledge.

Maticka-Tyndale, E., Lewis, J. and Clark, J. (2000) 'Exotic dancing and health', *Women and Health*, 31 (1): 87–108.

Maticka-Tyndale, E., Lewis, J. and Clark, J. *et al.* (1999) 'Social and cultural vulnerability to sexually transmitted infection: the work of exotic dancers', *Canadian Journal of Public Health*, January–February, pp. 19–22.

Measham, F. (2004) 'The decline of ecstasy, the rise of "binge" drinking and the persistence of pleasure', *Journal of Community and Criminal Justice*, 51 (4): 309–26.

Melbin, M. (1978) 'Night as frontier', *American Sociological Review*, 43 (1): 3–22.

Mestemache, R. and Roberti, J. (2004) 'Qualitative analysis of vocational choice: a collective case study of strippers', *Deviant Behaviour*, 25: 43–65.

Miles, S. (1998) *Consumerism: As a Way of Life*. London: Sage.

Mintel Report (2003) *Stag and Hen Holidays*. Online at: http://reports.mintel.com/sinatra/reports/search_results/show&&type=RCItem&page=0&noaccess_page=0/display/id=1380 (accessed 12 December 2008).

Mintel Report (2008) *Changing Face of Leisure*. Online at: http://reports.mintel.com/sinatra/reports/index/letter=1/display/id=280363&anchor=a280363/list/id=280363&type=RCItem (accessed 12 December 2008).

Montemurro, B. (2001) 'Strippers and screamers: the emergence of social control in a noninstitutionalized setting', *Journal of Contemporary Ethnography*, 2 (3): 275–304.

Montemurro, B., Bloom, C. and Madell, K. (2003) 'Ladies night out: a typology of women patrons of a strip club', *Deviant Behaviour: An Interdisciplinary Journal*, 24: 333–52.

Morris, S. (2002) 'Los Angeles to Harrogate', Guardian.co.uk. Online at: http://www.guardian.co.uk/uk/2002/mar/16/stevenmorris1 (accessed 20 November 2008).

Muggleton, D. (1998) 'The post-subculturalist', in S. Redhead, D. Wynne and J. O'Connor (eds), *The Clubcultures Reader: Readings in Popular Cultural Studies*. Oxford: Blackwell.

Muggleton, D. (2000) *Inside Subculture*. London: Berg.

Murphy, A. (2003) 'The dialectical gaze: exploring the subject–object tension in performances of women who strip', *Journal of Contemporary Ethnography*, 32 (3): 305–35.

Nagle, J. (eds) (1997) *Whores and Other Feminists*. London: Routledge.

Nayak, A. (2003) *Race, Place and Globalization: Youth Cultures in a Changing World*. Oxford: Berg.

Nayak, A. (2007) 'Displaced masculinities: chavs, youth and class in the post-industrial city', *Sociology*, 40 (5): 813–31.

Norris, C. (1993) 'Some ethical considerations on field-work with the police', in D. Hobbs and T. May (eds), *Interpreting the Field*. Oxford: Oxford University Press.

Oakley, A. ([1981] 2004) 'Interviewing women', in C. Seale (eds), *Social Research Methods*. London: Routledge.

Object (2009) *Campaign to Reform Lap-dancing Clubs*. Online at: http://www.

object.org.uk/files/Object%20Fawcett%20campaign%20briefing%20Feb%2 009(1).pdf (accessed 1 March 2009).

Park, R. (1925) 'The city: suggestions for the investigation of human behaviour in the city environment', in R. Park and E. Burgess (eds), *The City*. Chicago: University of Chicago Press.

Pasko, L. (2002) 'Naked power: the practice of stripping as a confidence game', *Sexualities*, 5 (1): 49–66.

Pearce, D. (2007) 'Wessex sells 28 pubs to Ladhar Group', *The Publican on-line*, 27 March. Online at: http://www.thepublican.com/story.asp?storyCode=54776 (accessed 21 August 2008).

Pearson, G. (1993) 'Forward-talking a good fight: authenticity and distance in the ethnographer's craft', in D. Hobbs and T. May (eds) *Interpreting the Field-Accounts of Ethnography*, Oxford: Oxford University Press.

Philaretou, A. (2006) 'Female exotic dancers: intrapersonal and interpersonal perspectives', in *Sexual Addiction and Compulsivity*, 13 (1): 41–52.

Phoenix, J. (eds) (2009) *Regulating Sex For Sale: Prostitution Policy Reform in the UK*. London: Polity Press.

Prewitt, T. J. (1989) 'Like a virgin: the semiotics of illusion in erotic performance', *American Journal of Semiotics*, 6: 137–52.

Price, K. (2000) 'Stripping women: workers control in strip clubs', *Current Research on Occupation and Research*, 11: 3–33.

Price, K. (2008) 'Keeping the dancers in check: the gendered organization of stripping work in the lion's den', *Gender and Society*, 22: 367–89.

Punch, M. (1986) *The Politics and Ethics of Fieldwork*, Qualitative Research Methods Vol. 3. London: Sage.

Rabinow, P. (ed.) (1985) *The Foucault Reader*. New York: Pantheon.

Rambo-Ronai, C. (1992) 'The reflexive self through narrative: a night in the life of an erotic dancer/researcher', in C. Ellis and G. Flaherty (eds), *Investigating Subjectivity: Research on Lived Experience*. London: Sage.

Rambo-Ronai, C. and Ellis, C. (1989) 'Turn-ons for money: interactional strategies of the table dancer', *Journal of Contemporary Ethnography*, 18: 271–98.

Redhead, S. (ed.) (1993) *Rave Off: Politics and Deviance in Contemporary Youth Culture*. Aldershot: Ashgate.

Redhead, S. (1998) *Subculture to Clubcultures*. Oxford: Blackwell.

Reed, S. (1997) 'All stripped off', in J. Nagel (ed.), *Whores and Other Feminists*. London: Routledge.

Reid, S., Epstein, J. and Benson, D. E. (1994) 'Role identity in a devalued occupation: the case of female exotic dancers', *Sociological Focus*, 1: 1–15.

Richardson, J. (1991) 'Experiencing research on new religions and cults: practical and ethical considerations', in W. Shaffir and R. Stebbins (eds), *Experiencing Fieldwork: An Inside View of Qualitative Research*. London: Sage.

Roberts, R., Bergstrom, S. and La Rooy, D. (2007) 'Sex work and students: an exploratory study', *Journal of Higher Education*, 31 (4): 323–34.

Ryan, C. and Martin, A. (2001) 'Tourists and strippers – liminal theatre', *Tourism Research*, 28 (1): 140–63.

Ryder, A. (2004) 'The changing nature of adult entertainment: between the hard rock of going from strength to strength', *Urban Studies*, 41: 1659–86.

Salutin, M. (1971) 'Stripper morality', *Transaction*, 8: 12–22.

Sánchez-Jankowski, M. (2002) 'Representation, responsibility and reliability in participant-observation', in T. May (ed.), *Qualitative Research in Action*. London: Sage.

Sanders, K. (1999) 'Prospects for a post-modern ethnography', *Journal of Contemporary Ethnography*, 28 (6): 669–75.

Sanders, T. (2005) *Sex Work: A Risky Business*. Cullompton: Willan.

Schweitzer, D. (2000) 'Striptease: the art of spectacle and transgression', *Journal of Popular Culture*, 34: 65–75.

Scott, D. (1996) *Behind the G-Strings*. Jefferson, NC: McFarland.

Sharp, C., Baker, P., Goulden, C. *et al.* (2001) *Drug Misuse Declared in 2000: Key Results from the British Crime Survey*. London: Home Office.

Skelton, T. and Valentine, G. (eds) (1998) *Cool Places: Geographies of Youth Cultures*. London: Routledge.

Skipper, J. and McCaghy, C. (1970) 'Stripteasers: the anatomy and career contingencies of a deviant occupation', *Social Problems*, 1: 391–405.

Spivey, S. E. (2005) 'Distancing and solidarity as resistance to sexual objectification in a nude dancing bar', *Deviant Behaviour*, 26: 76–91.

Stebbins, R. (1991) 'Do we ever leave the field? Notes on secondary fieldwork involvements', in W. Shaffir and R. Stebbins (eds), *Experiencing Fieldwork: An Inside View of Qualitative Research*. London: Sage.

Summers, M. (2007) 'Appeal to join lap-dance silent protest', *Northern Echo*, 1 December. Online at: http://www.thenorthernecho.co.uk/search/display. var.1874067.0.appeal_to_join_lap_dance_silent_protest.php (accessed 20 March 2008).

Sweet, N. and Tewksbury, R. (2000) 'What's a nice girl like you doing in a place like this? Pathways to a career in stripping', *Sociological Spectrum*, 20: 325–43.

Sykes, G. M. and Matza, D. (1957) 'Techniques of neutralization: a theory of delinquency', *American Sociological Review*, 22 (6): 664–70.

Taylor, S. (1991) 'Leaving the field: research, relationships, and responsibilities', in W. Shaffir and R. Stebbins (eds), *Experiencing Fieldwork: An Inside View of Qualitative Research*. London: Sage.

Taylor, S. and Tyler, M. (2000) 'Emotional labour and sexual difference in the airline industry', *Work, Employment and Society*, 14 (1): 77–95.

Tewksbury, R. (1993) 'Male strippers: objectifying men', in C. L. Williams (ed.), *Doing 'Women's Work' Men in Non-traditional Occupations*. London: Sage.

Thompson, W. and Harred, L. J. (1992) 'Topless dancers: managing stigma in a deviant occupation', *Deviant Behaviour*, 13: 291–311.

Thompson, W. and Harred, L. J. (2003) 'Managing the stigma of topless dancing: a decade later', *Deviant Behaviour*, 24 (6): 551–70.

Thornton, S. (1995) *Club Cultures: Music, Media and Subcultural Capital*. Cambridge: Polity Press.

Thornton, S. (1997) 'General introduction', in K. Gelder and S. Thornton (eds), *The Subcultural Reader*. London: Routledge.

Thrasher, F. (1927) *The Gang*. Chicago: University of Chicago Press.

Travis, A. (2008) 'Loophole has allowed spread of lapdancing clubs, say campaigners', in *Guardian Unlimited*, 22 April. Online at: http://www.guardian.co.uk/politics/2008/apr/22/planning.communities.

Turner, J. and Stets, J. (2005) *The Sociology of Emotions*. Cambridge: Cambridge University Press.

Tyke (2002) 'The London striptease scene', in *Exotic Dancer*. Online at: http://www.mypole.co.uk/thelondonstripteasescene.htm (accessed 15 August 2004).

Tyke (2008) 'A bizarre alliance and repeated lies set to create bad legislation for UK clubs', in *Strip Magazine On-line*. Online at: http://www.strip-magazine.com/mmagazine/new_welcome.php?subaction=showfull&id=1224187727&archive=&start_from=&ucat=2&category=2.

Van Den Hoonaard, W. C. (2003) 'Is anonymity an artifact in ethnographic research', *Journal of Academic Ethics*, 1: 141–51.

Van Maanen, J. (1995) 'An end to innocence', in J. Van Maanen (ed.), *Representation in Ethnography*. London: Sage.

Weppner, R. (1977) 'Street ethnography: selected studies of crime and drug use', *Natural Settings: Street Ethnography*, Vol. 1. London: Sage.

Wesely, J. (2002) 'Growing up sexualised: issues of power and violence in the lives of female exotic dancers', *Violence Against Women*, 8 (10): 1182–207.

Wesely, J. (2003) 'Exotic dancing and the negotiation of identity – the multiple uses of body technologies', *Journal of Contemporary Ethnography*, 32 (6): 643–69.

Wesely, J. (2006) 'Negotiating myself: the impact of studying female exotic dancers on a feminist researcher', *Qualitative Inquiry*, 12 (1): 146–62.

Whyte, W. F. ([1943] 1981) *Street Corner Society*. Chicago: University of Chicago Press.

Whyte, W. F. (1984) *Learning from the Field*. London: Sage.

Williams, L. and Parker, H. (2001) 'Alcohol, cannabis, ecstasy and cocaine: drugs of reasoned choice amongst young adult recreational drug users in England', *International Journal of Drug Policy*, 12 (56): 397–413.

Willis, P. (1977) *Learning to Labour*. Farnborough: Saxon House.

Wood, E. A. (2000) 'Working in the fantasy factory', *Journal of Contemporary Ethnography*, 29: 1–31.

Worpole, K. (1992) *Towns for People: Transforming Urban Life*. Buckingham: Open University Press.

Index